THE
1,000
FABULOUS
SANDWICHES
COOKBOOK

THE
1,000
FABULOUS
SANDWICHES
COOKBOOK

by Doris McFerran Townsend

A Ridge Press Book
Thomas Nelson & Sons
Edinburgh • New York • Toronto

THE
1,000
FABULOUS
SANDWICHES
COOKBOOK

Contents

Acknowledgments:

*We wish to thank the following organizations for
their assistance in the preparation of this book:
American Dairy Association; American Institute of Baking;
American Meat Institute; Armour and Company;
Austrian Information Service; Best Foods, Division Corn Products
Company; Borden Company; Bureau of Commercial Fisheries,
Fish and Wildlife Service, U.S. Department of the Interior;
Danish Information Office; General Foods Kitchens;
Holland Cheese Exporters Association;
Hunt Foods and Industries, Inc.; Maine Sardine Council;
The Netherlands Information Service; The Netherlands
National Tourist Office; Norwegian Embassy Information Service;
Ocean Spray Cranberries, Inc.; Oscar Mayer & Co.;
Pepperidge Farm, Inc.; Principality of Monaco Information Center;
Standard Brands, Inc.; Switzerland Cheese Association;
Ward Baking Company; and Wilson & Company, Inc.*

A Way of Life

I am a very good cook. I say this with no modesty. In fact, I am a good enough cook to be forgiven the way I keep the rest of my house. When my husband asks me why his favorite shirt is buttonless, I counter with a preview of the dinner menu. Drooling gently, he puts the shirt back and chooses another, without a word of reproach.

My culinary way around the kitchen was taught me by my elderly great-aunt Hazel, beginning with the day when—so the story goes—she plumped a bowl of cake batter down on the tray of my high chair and commanded, "Now, beat!" I beat.

That was fortunate, because my mother had somewhere picked up the notion that cooking wasn't ladylike. She worked on a simple premise: if something well-cooked is good, it will be infinitely improved by being unmercifully overcooked.

When Aunt Hazel died, full of years and soufflés, I took over the kitchen, Mother went on being a lady, and all hands were completely satisfied.

Aunt Hazel's kitchen philosophy has remained with me, and I happily pass it along.

Take your time. Plan. Don't try to make a first-class dish out of second-grade ingredients. Be an honest cook. For example, roast pork does *not* make the best chicken salad . . . quite naturally, chicken does. But pork makes a perfectly wonderful pork salad, and you'll be complimented on your inventiveness.

Don't try new recipes on company unless your guests are dear old friends inured to your foibles. Invest in good kitchen tools, and know all their uses.

Don't try a complicated new dish unless you've first read the recipe carefully—not five minutes before starting, but the day before, so that you'll be certain to have all the necessary ingredients on hand. A frustrated cook is a peril to any digestive system.

Be inventive—but sensibly and sensitively. An herb will perk up a sauce, but six different ones dumped at random into the same saucepot can make the diners cry havoc. Taste as you go—always, all along!

Think taste, but also think color and texture. An all-brown all-soft dinner, no matter how tasty the individual dishes, can wear out its welcome long before the dessert—Chocolate Bavarian, to carry out the soft brown motif—comes to the table.

For each area of cooking, a good cook must work out her basic philosophy by trial and error. She finds, for example, that if she cannot afford prime steak, she saves broiled steak as a treat for very special occasions and learns how to cook the less-expensive cuts of meat so that they are the best-tasting inexpensive cuts that ever graced a family board.

In working out a philosophy for sandwich-making, certain primary points leap to the mind. For instance, the filling should be dominated by the basic ingredient if your sandwiches are going to be worth eating. Don't try to make a chicken-salad filling out of half a cup of diced chicken and a cup of diced celery.

There are two kinds of sandwiches—bad and good. The bad ones consist of two slices of bread with a slab cut from the heel of Sunday's roast or a spoonful of some weary leftover slapped between them. The good ones are the product of time and effort. All good cooking is. No cooking, other than the preparation of certain very delicate sauces and cakes and pastries, is truly difficult, provided one can read and follow instructions. But all good cooking is time- and effort-consuming.

On the other hand, there are some time and/or effort savers that are even better than the good-enough-for-grandma way, and those I do recommend. Onion juice and garlic juice in bottles, for instance—one brand, with cheerful pixie-hat caps, is of excellent consistency and a fine, clear, fresh flavor. Use these juices when it's only the flavor you need. If you want the consistency, too, as in chopped onion for some salad-type sandwich fillings, start from scratch. Frozen or freezer-dried chives take the place of fresh and do an admirable job, especially in seasons when fresh chives are hard to come by. Use your good cooking sense when making a substitution. If it's a shortcut for timesaving's sake, skip it; if it's honestly just as good, or even better, by all means go ahead.

Bread is the sandwich starting point—good bread, not the foam-rubber variety. And, please, not always white! (There's a list of good breads, in all their infinite variety, on page 15 to guide you.) In general, the bread should be thin-sliced, unless you're catering for an after-the-poker-party stag affair. Butter should be spread thinly and evenly, so take it out of the refrigerator in plenty of time to allow it to soften. In some cases, mayonnaise or another dressing substitutes for butter. On page 125 there is a recipe for homemade mayonnaise—no, it's *not* too difficult—and in other places throughout the book are scattered recipes for other delicious homemade dressings.

Your sandwich-making should be done on *purpose*. "What shall I feed them? Oh, I'll just whip up some sandwiches!" is wrong-minded thinking. Instead, "Shall I feed them Beef Fondue? No, I'll give them Supreme Sandwiches!"—that's what we're getting at in this book.

Sandwiches are the most versatile of foods. They are splendid "company refreshments" for any kind of gathering, from a meeting of Cub Scouts to an elegant wedding reception. They are a fine basis for a luncheon party, a tea. They are great to serve to evening visitors—not too heavy, but substantial enough to satisfy appetites when dinner was hours ago. They can—the best ones—serve as the main course for an exciting dinner. And, of course, no picnic can call itself that without sandwiches, any more than without deviled eggs— picnics lacking both should be against the law.

Even if you're the rankest come-lately amateur in the cooking field, you'll take a big step forward if you learn the professional approach. This goes for everything from soft-cooking an egg to creating a Gateau Saint Honoré. It applies to the recipes in this book—to every recipe in every cookbook.

No professional worth his salt would dream of tackling a job—nor would he be allowed to—if he were not equipped with the basic knowledge of the vocabulary of his trade and a basic selection of the tools of his calling. A cook is no different. If you're just starting to cook, bone up on your skills and acquire your tools—the right ones. If you've been cooking a long while and are still weak on the basics—well, shame on you . . . get cracking! General cooking know-how is outside the province of anything but a big, good cookbook (the two terms aren't necessarily synonymous). This is not a general, all-purpose cookbook. If you don't have one, get one, and start reading. Then—only then—can you afford, gastronomically, to venture into the specialized cookbooks, of which this is one.

When you think sandwich, think *good* sandwich. May this book be your guide.

IN GENERAL . . .

Begin at the beginning: Read the recipe—ingredients and method—all the way through before you do another thing. Do it early enough so that there's time to fill in supplies that may have run out—or to change your mind and decide to cook something else! Now, get out all your ingredients and the proper tools to deal with them. Then go to it, following the recipe to the letter, measuring accurately with standard measuring cups and spoons. Don't take liberties unless you're an old hand at cooking. The second, not the first time around, is the time to experiment, even if you're a splendid cook. You can't really be sure of the flavor or texture of any new recipe other than the simplest concoction until you've prepared it and tasted it in its finished form.

Tidy as you go: When you're through with the mayonnaise, wipe off the top of the jar with a damp cloth and put it back in the refrigerator promptly. When you're finished dicing vegetables, take a second to dispose of the peelings and trimmings before going on to the next step. When you've used a bowl or a pan, put it in to soak in the sink before you go back to work. I don't recommend these and like measures because I'm an innately neat soul, but because a kitchen can look like a disaster area at the end of a cooking spree.

Have the right tools and use them: You'll need knives—sharp knives—for sandwich making . . . a good paring knife, or, better yet, two; a thin-blade, serrated-edge slicer for bread; a trimmer, which does double-duty as a boner of meats and a slicer of such things as tomatoes, cucumbers, hard-cooked eggs; a carving knife for meats; a short, flexible, thin-blade spatula for spreading butter, mayonnaise, and fillings; a wire-blade cheese cutter; and—if you really want to be an old pro—a French chef's knife for chopping, dicing, and cubing. If you don't own one, why not buy yourself a present? This knife is a good cook's best friend, but be sure you learn how to use it properly—if you don't, you'll have diced fingertips in with the celery.

Those are the necessities, and you can make out nicely with them. Handy to have around as well are: an egg-slicing contraption that, by wires, divides the egg neatly into seven or eight slices; a ditto-type wire tomato slicer; a big butcher knife for heavy-duty cutting; a swivel-blade vegetable peeler; a rotary-type nut chopper. If you're a coward, get an onion chopper, too—but you'll still have a lot of trouble with the celery, carrots, green pepper, and so on that the French chef's knife would take care of so easily.

IN PARTICULAR . . .

To dice or chop with a French chef's knife: Besides the knife, you need a sturdy, steady chopping board or block. Place on the block the food to be chopped. Grasp the handle of the knife between the thumb and forefinger of your right hand, with your fingers following the curve of the handle. Put the tip of the knife blade on the board at a 45-degree angle with the surface of the board. Hold the tip of the blade firmly to the board with the thumb and forefinger of your left hand.

Move the knife up and down in a rocking position on the board while at the same time moving the handle back and forth over the board in a quarter circle.

To juice onions: Cut the onions in half across the equator. Scrape with a spoon—lightly if the juice is all you want, a bit more firmly if you can use a bit of the pulp as well.

To grind meats, etc.: Use a meat grinder, first cutting the meat —cooked or uncooked—into pieces suitable for fitting the hopper of the grinder. However, take warning—when the recipe calls for diced meat, make the effort and dice it by hand. Ground meats are fine for some purposes, but in other cases they give a nasty, pre-chewed texture to a sandwich filling. Never short-cut.

To cube: Cut into small pieces—solid little cubes—about 3/4 of an inch on all sides.

To dice: Same process, but cut in smaller pieces—cubes of less than 1/2 inch.

To flake: Pull apart—such foods as fish, chicken—following the natural grain. Do it with two forks, or, if you like, with your fingers—which, as the children say, were made before forks, and which are the best kitchen tools you'll ever own.

To sliver: Cut into long, thin strips—use a small, sharp knife on a cutting board.

To chop parsley: Strip the leaves from the heavy stems and put into a small glass. With your kitchen scissors, snip the parsley into coarse, medium, or fine bits, depending on what you're going to use it for. This way, you'll keep snippets of parsley from flying all over.

To chop chives: Again, snip with scissors, this time holding a number of strands cut from the chive plant in your left hand, snipping—into a small dish or onto waxed paper—with your right.

To blanch almonds: Pour boiling water over shelled almonds and let stand 5 minutes. Drain. Slip off skins and dry the nuts on paper toweling.

To peel tomatoes: Impale the stemmed end of a tomato on a fork and dip into boiling water for 30-40 seconds. Take from water and insert the point of a paring knife under the skin, which will strip off nicely. Cool before serving, but it's best not to refrigerate them more than an hour.

To hard-cook eggs: Eggs should be at room temperature, not straight from refrigerator. Bring water to a boil in a pan large enough to allow the water to cover the eggs. Prick the large end of each egg with a needle or a Swedish egg-pricker—but be delicate about it. Dip a spoon into the water, place an egg on the spoon and gently lower into the water. Repeat with remaining eggs. When water returns to the boil, lower the heat and cover the pan. Cook—simmering, not boiling—16 minutes longer. Pour off water and run cold water over the eggs— this stops the cooking action and insures against the unattractive green tint that sometimes surrounds the yolk.

To peel hard-cooked eggs: When the eggs are cooled, tap the entire surface gently to break the shell. Start at the wide end and take off the shell.

To fine-cut hard-cooked eggs: If you want the eggs very fine, put through a sieve—whites and yolks separately—helping them along by pressing with the back of a spoon. For larger-sized pieces, cut into chunks and mash with a fork, for pieces as coarse or as fine as you need.

TO SERVE WITH YOUR SANDWICHES . . .

For crispness: Potato or corn chips, shoestring potatoes.

For heartiness: Potato salad (hot or cold, in all its many varieties) or macaroni salad, deviled eggs or a wedge of good cheese.

For fresh taste and color: Celery, green pepper, carrot or turnip sticks, cucumber fingers or rosy radishes.

For a nice surprise: Salted nuts, pickled mushrooms, jelly-dotted broiled fruit, cinnamon-sugared fried apple slices, glazed baby carrots or onions, a heap of assorted melon balls dusted with snipped mint, cheese-stuffed celery or Belgian endive, small bunches of seedless grapes dunked in lemon French dressing, toothpick kabobs threaded with anchovy fillets alternating with tiny pickled onions, slices of orange and sweet onion happily married with a drizzle of lemon French dressing.

For variety: Olives, pickles, relishes . . . so many, many kinds you seldom have to repeat yourself.

For flavor balance: The many variations on the coleslaw theme, ditto mixed-green-salads theme, French salad, wilted lettuce, marinated beets or asparagus or thin-sliced raw cauliflower or tomatoes.

And, of course, mostly for pretty, but for taste appeal too— the sprig or sprinkle of parsley or watercress, the dusting of chopped chives, the dash of paprika—the finishing touches that dress the dish.

The Very Best Breads

Almost every one of the recipes in this book starts with bread, because—obviously—that's where you have to start before you can put together a sandwich. However, it's vital to remember that if every sandwich you make starts with two pieces of the same kind of bread, your reputation as a cook will be shocking. And there's no excuse for it, either. When a recipe says "8 slices of bread" it doesn't mean you should reach for the white bread. It means, "Now, what kind of bread will bring out the best in this filling?" And even when a recipe specifies "8 slices of whole-wheat bread" don't feel you have to follow it slavishly.

From the shelves:

White, round or square, enriched
Home-style
Whole wheat
Cracked wheat
Raisin
Cinnamon raisin
Rye
Caraway rye
Sesame rye
Swedish rye
Sour rye (Jewish rye)
Hard rolls, plain
Hard rolls, seeded
Hamburger buns
Frankfurter rolls
Small packaged rolls
English muffins
Vienna
Cheese
Pumpernickel (dark, medium, light)
Potato
Miniature salty rye (party) loaves
French—long or round
Italian—long, round, twisted
Nut
Orange-nut
Corn muffins
Bran muffins
Toaster muffins
Scones
Packaged biscuits
Brown-and-serve rolls in many varieties

From the freezer:
Homemade-style loaves (to be baked at home)

From the refrigerator case:
Packaged biscuits in many varieties

Canned:
Boston brown
Date-nut
Orange-nut
Orange-date
Chocolate
Chocolate-nut

Chicken and Other Birds

Chicken, with its good-but-mild flavor, takes to dressing up as well as little girls do. Here are good ways with such dress-ups. But don't feel that an elderly hen, long past her prime, cooked to a fare-thee-well before you can stick a fork into her resistant hide, will do just as well as a younger and juicier bird. Sandwiches—good ones—are made from roasters or fryers, oven-cooked or gently simmered.

Gingered Chicken Puffs

6 sliced hamburger buns	1/4 cup finely diced celery
2 teaspoons lemon juice	1/4 teaspoon salt
2 teaspoons finely chopped crystallized ginger	2 tablespoons mayonnaise or salad dressing
6 tablespoons well-drained crushed pineapple	2 egg whites
3/4 cup chopped cooked chicken	1 cup grated American cheese

Add lemon juice and ginger to pineapple. Let stand for about 15 minutes. Combine chicken, celery, salt, and mayonnaise. Blend in pineapple mixture. Place 1/4 cup of salad mixture on each bun half. Beat egg whites until stiff. Fold in cheese. Spread egg mixture over salad. Place on baking sheet and bake at 450° F. until browned—about 10 minutes.
Or try it this way . . . For a company luncheon, spread gingered chicken salad on medium-thick slices of French bread.

Crunchy Chicken-Cheesies

12 slices Russian rye bread	1 teaspoon salt
3/8 cup soft butter	2 teaspoons prepared mustard
2 5-ounce cans cooked chicken, drained	1/2 cup chopped parsley
1 cup applesauce	6 thin slices Swiss cheese
1 1/2 cups chopped raw cauliflower	

Butter each slice of bread. Combine chicken, applesauce, chopped cauliflower, salt, and mustard. Divide chicken mixture over 6 slices of the buttered bread, spreading to corners of each slice. Top with parsley and a slice of Swiss cheese. Cover cheese with remaining bread slices.

Chicken Éclairs

6 frankfurter rolls
1/4 cup mayonnaise or
    salad dressing
1 tablespoon milk
1 teaspoon granulated
    sugar
2 tablespoons minced
    onion
1/2 cup chopped celery
2 tablespoons diced red
    peppers or pimento

1/2 teaspoon salt
1/4 teaspoon pepper
3/8 teaspoon nutmeg
1 1/2 cups or 2 6 1/2-ounce
    jars chopped cooked
    chicken
6-8 slices cooked bacon,
    crumbled
1 3-ounce package cream
    cheese
2 tablespoons milk

Split rolls. With a fork, remove some bread from inside of roll, leaving a 3/4-inch shell. In a medium-size bowl, combine mayonnaise, milk, sugar. Add onion, celery, red peppers, salt, pepper, nutmeg, chicken, crumbled bacon. Toss to blend. Fill each roll with about 1/3-cup chicken mixture. Replace tops and wrap in foil or plastic wrap. Chill until serving time. Soften cream cheese with milk. Spread cheese mixture over top of each éclair or pipe on with pastry tube.

Or try it this way . . . Substitute 4 chopped hard-cooked eggs for chicken, or one 7-ounce can of flaked tuna or 1 cup of ground ham for the chicken and bacon.

Chicken and Ham

12 slices white bread
1/2 stick butter
1 1/4 cups chopped chicken

1 1/4 cups chopped ham
Salt
Paprika

Cream butter. Add chicken and ham. Season with salt and paprika. Mix well. Spread not too thickly on 6 slices bread, top with remaining slices.

Or try it this way . . . Finger rolls instead of white bread for a party touch.

Turkey Imperials

Buttered bread
Cooked turkey, sliced
Cooked bacon

Tomato slices
Cheddar cheese slices

For each sandwich, arrange several slices of cooked turkey on a buttered bread slice. Crisscross 2 slices cooked bacon over turkey. Top with 2 thin slices tomato and a slice of Cheddar cheese. Bake at 400° F. for 8 to 10 minutes.

17

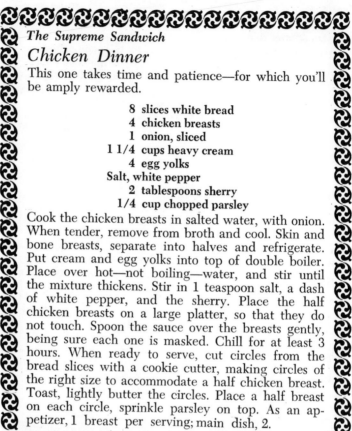

The Supreme Sandwich

Chicken Dinner

This one takes time and patience—for which you'll be amply rewarded.

8 slices white bread
4 chicken breasts
1 onion, sliced
1 1/4 cups heavy cream
4 egg yolks
Salt, white pepper
2 tablespoons sherry
1/4 cup chopped parsley

Cook the chicken breasts in salted water, with onion. When tender, remove from broth and cool. Skin and bone breasts, separate into halves and refrigerate. Put cream and egg yolks into top of double boiler. Place over hot—not boiling—water, and stir until the mixture thickens. Stir in 1 teaspoon salt, a dash of white pepper, and the sherry. Place the half chicken breasts on a large platter, so that they do not touch. Spoon the sauce over the breasts gently, being sure each one is masked. Chill for at least 3 hours. When ready to serve, cut circles from the bread slices with a cookie cutter, making circles of the right size to accommodate a half chicken breast. Toast, lightly butter the circles. Place a half breast on each circle, sprinkle parsley on top. As an appetizer, 1 breast per serving; main dish, 2.

Chicken-Almond Sandwiches

12 slices buttered white
bread
2 cups diced cooked
chicken (or 4 5-ounce
cans boned chicken)

1/2 cup slivered, blanched
almonds, toasted
2 teaspoons lemon juice
1/4 cup mayonnaise

Combine chicken, almonds. Stir lemon juice into mayonnaise; pour over chicken mixture; blend. Spread half of bread slices with filling; top with remaining slices; cut each in half. Wrap in aluminum foil until ready to serve. Makes 6 servings.

Creole Chicken Fiestas

8 frankfurter rolls	1/2 cup tomato paste
2 tablespoons butter	1/4 cup chopped stuffed
1/4 cup finely chopped onion	olives
1/3 cup finely chopped green	1/2 cup Worcestershire sauce
pepper	1/4 teaspoon chili powder
1/3 cup finely chopped celery	1/4 teaspoon salt
1 cup chopped cooked	1/8 teaspoon pepper
chicken or turkey	

Melt butter in skillet. Add onion, green pepper, and celery and sauté until soft. Add chicken, tomato paste, olives, Worcestershire sauce, chili powder, salt and pepper. Simmer 10 minutes, stirring frequently. Fill sliced rolls with creole-chicken mixture, using 1/3 cup each.

Hot Chicken-Bacon Rolls

6 finger rolls	2 teaspoons lemon juice
1/2 cup chopped cooked	1/4 cup grated process cheese
chicken	6 slices of bacon
1/2 cup finely chopped celery	

Combine chicken, celery, lemon juice, and grated cheese. Slice rolls lengthwise. Spread about 2 tablespoons chicken mixture between halves of each roll. Wrap a bacon slice around each roll, fastening it with toothpicks. Place rolls on a wire rack, set inside a shallow baking pan. Grill rolls, turning often, until bacon is crisp and rolls are heated.

Open Chicken Delight

4 crumpets	3 tablespoons sherry
4 tablespoons butter	2 cups cooked chicken cut
1/4 cup flour	into large pieces
1 teaspoon salt	Paprika
1/8 teaspoon pepper	Baked ham slices
2 cups milk	

In saucepan, melt butter; stir in flour, salt, and pepper. Gradually add milk; cook over low heat, stirring constantly until thickened. Add sherry, chicken, dash of paprika. Heat thoroughly. In lightly greased skillet, heat ham slices. Split, toast, and butter crumpets. Arrange ham slices on crumpet halves; top with hot chicken mixture. Sprinkle lightly with paprika. *Perfect partners* . . . Spiced peaches, ripe olives, scallions, or canned whole-cranberry sauce.

Chicken

The Gourmet Way
Hollandaise Sauce

Mainly—as far as this cookbook is concerned—for Eggs Benedict, Hollandaise will dress any bland flavor for a fine open-face sandwich. Try hard-cooked eggs, sliced chicken, cold broccoli.

> 2 egg yolks
> 1/4 teaspoon salt
> Dash cayenne pepper
> 1/2 cup melted butter
> 1 tablespoon lemon juice

With rotary beater, hand or electric, beat egg yolks until thick and pale golden. Add salt, cayenne. Add, 1 teaspoon at a time and beating constantly, 1/4 cup of the melted butter. Combine remaining butter with lemon juice. Add slowly, about 2 teaspoons at a time, beating constantly. Makes 1/2 cup sauce. Serve soon after making. If you must delay, it can be set in the top of a double boiler over warm water—but for no longer than half an hour. (If you slip, and the water in your double boiler is too hot, what you'll end up with is a gloriously rich variety of scrambled egg and *don't* throw it out. Use it in a sandwich.)

Or try it this way . . . To sharpen lemon flavor, add 1 teaspoon grated lemon rind; or season with about 3/4 teaspoon curry powder and/or 1 teaspoon yellow prepared mustard.

Note: Made correctly, your Hollandaise won't curdle. But just supposing it does while you are keeping it warm over water . . . well, remove from stove, add 4 drops boiling water, beat vigorously, and serve at once. Nobody will ever know.

Chicken-Cheeseburger

> 4 sandwich buns, sliced
> 1/2 cup grated process American cheese
> 1/2 cup chopped cooked chicken
> 1 1/2 tablespoons pickle relish

Combine cheese, chicken, and pickle relish. Place buns, cut side up, on a cookie sheet. Spread about 1/4 cup of cheese mixture on bottom half of each bun. Bake in 400° F. oven for about 5 minutes, or until bun tops toast and cheese melts.

20

Easter Chicken Rolls

8 oval French rolls

Filling:

1 cup chopped cooked
   chicken
1/4 cup slivered almonds,
   toasted
1/4 cup chopped celery

1/4 cup pineapple tidbits
1/4 cup flaked coconut
2 tablespoons mayonnaise
   or salad dressing

Topping:

1 egg white, stiffly beaten
2 tablespoons mayonnaise
1/4 teaspoon Worcestershire
   sauce

Coconut—pink, yellow, and
   green

Hollow out rolls. Combine chicken, almonds, celery, pineapple, coconut, and mayonnaise. Fill rolls with chicken mixture. Combine egg white, mayonnaise, and Worcestershire sauce. Spread on top of rolls. Place filled rolls on cookie sheet. Bake at 425° F. for 8 minutes. Sprinkle a different color of coconut over each roll. Serve immediately.

Devonshire Sandwich

6 slices bread, toasted
18 slices bacon
1 1/4 cups flour
2 quarts milk, scalded
1 tablespoon salt
1 teaspoon dry mustard
1/2 teaspoon poultry
   seasoning
1 teaspoon monosodium
   glutamate

1/2 pound sharp cheese,
   diced
1 1/2 pounds sliced cooked
   chicken or turkey
2 tablespoons grated
   Parmesan cheese
1 teaspoon paprika

In fry pan cook bacon slowly until crisp; drain on absorbent paper. Stir flour into hot fat; blend until smooth. Add milk gradually, stirring until sauce is smooth. Cook over low heat 10 minutes, stirring constantly. Add salt, mustard, poultry seasoning, monosodium glutamate, cheese; stir until cheese is melted. Place toasted bread in baking pan. Place 3 strips bacon on each slice of toast. Arrange chicken or turkey over bacon on each sandwich; cover completely with sauce. Combine Parmesan cheese, paprika; blend. Sprinkle over each sandwich. Bake 10 minutes at 350° F. Makes 6 servings.

The Gourmet Way
Sherry-Glazed Sandwiches

Not easy to do but not as difficult as the uninitiated think. These sherry-glazed sandwiches may be appetizer, main course, or even salad course. They look and taste as if you held a Cordon Bleu.

Beef-Sherry Glaze

    2 cups water
1/3 cup sherry
    2 envelopes unflavored gelatin
    1 10 1/2-ounce can beef or chicken consommé

Mix water and sherry in a medium-size bowl. Sprinkle gelatin over surface of mixture. Let stand 5 minutes. Bring consommé—don't dilute it—to a boil. Add gelatin mixture, stirring to dissolve completely. Refrigerate until the mixture is the consistency of unbeaten egg white—this should take about 1 hour. Makes enough to glaze 8 large sandwiches.

To glaze sandwiches: Arrange chilled, open-face sandwiches on a wire rack. Set rack on a baking sheet which has a rim on all sides. Spoon chilled glaze over surface of sandwiches lightly. Spoon up and use again any glaze that drops on the tray. If desired, chill sandwiches, then glaze again for a thicker aspic coating (for this, you'll need to double the glaze recipe). Refrigerate sandwiches at least 1 hour before serving. *Now try these* . . . Glaze chicken or beef sandwiches of any kind . . . strong-flavored vegetable sandwiches, such as those made of asparagus, artichoke hearts, cauliflower . . . mushroom or mushroom-combination sandwiches.

Quick Pâté

White bread, toasted, buttered	Salt
Chicken liver	Pepper
Chicken gizzard	Nutmeg
Stock or chicken fat	

Boil liver and gizzard. Chop gizzard fine. Mash the liver. Add a little stock or chicken fat, salt, pepper, and dash of nutmeg. Spread on toast triangles.

Corn Cranwiches

6 slices corn bread
Butter
Baked ham slices

Roast turkey slices
Jellied cranberry slices
Process American cheese slices

Toast corn bread lightly in broiler. Butter. Top each slice with ham, top ham with turkey. Place a slice of jellied cranberry sauce over meat and crisscross two strips of cheese over cranberry. Bake on a shallow baking sheet at 350° F. until well heated and cheese is melted. Serve immediately.

Even better . . . Instead of the process cheese strips, grate a layer of sharp Cheddar over the cranberry sauce and place cranwich briefly under broiler. Has to be watched—worth it!

Imperial Chicken Sandwich

8 slices toast, buttered
Cooked chicken slices
Tomato slices
Salt

1 cup grated American cheese
2 teaspoons Worcestershire
sauce

Place buttered toast in shallow baking pan. Cover with sliced chicken and top with tomato slices. Sprinkle with salt. Mix cheese with Worcestershire sauce and spread thickly over tomato slices. Place under broiler until cheese is melted and browned. Serve immediately.

The Gourmet Way

Avocado Mayonnaise

Don't hide this under a sandwich's hat—put out a bowlful and let everyone use the dressing to his own taste.

> 2 cups Homemade Mayonnaise, lemon-
>   salad oil type (page 125)
> 1 avocado, puréed
> 1 teaspoon hot pepper sauce
> 2 teaspoons lemon juice

Season puréed avocado with pepper sauce, lemon juice. Mix into mayonnaise—but not entirely—that is, leave it a lovely green-and-pale-yellow marble. Refrigerate until ready to use. Makes 2 1/2 cups.

Tahiti Chicken

16 slices raisin bread	1/4 teaspoon salt
2 cups chopped cooked chicken	2 cups pineapple chunks or tidbits
1 10 1/2-ounce can condensed cream of celery soup	1 cup shredded Münster cheese
1 tablespoon chopped onion	2 tablespoons soft butter

Combine chicken, celery soup, onion, and salt. Toast and butter 8 slices raisin bread. Place on a baking sheet. Spread each slice with 1/4 cup of chicken mixture. Arrange 5 pineapple chunks, spoke fashion, on top of the chicken. Sprinkle 2 tablespoons of cheese in center of pineapple "wheel." Broil under medium heat for about 5 minutes, or until cheese is melted and brown. Toast and butter remaining bread. Cut slices in half, diagonally. Serve 2 half slices raisin toast with each open-faced chicken sandwich.

For pretty . . . Garnish with crisp celery, fat black olives.

Chicken Liver

8 slices white bread	Salt
1 cup cooked chicken liver	Pepper
2 hard-cooked eggs, chopped	Dash of cayenne
1 teaspoon minced onion	Cream

Finely chop chicken livers, mix with eggs. Add onion, salt, pepper, cayenne. Moisten with cream. Spread thickly on bread slices. Top with second slice for hearty sandwich. For company tidbits, cut spread slice twice diagonally, making 4 triangular open sandwiches.

Or try it this way . . . Omit eggs and cream. Sauté chicken liver with onion and 1/4 cup chopped mushrooms. Combine with seasonings and dash of lemon juice.

Wonder Ways with Cold Chicken—

Sandwich the sliced chicken with one of the following: baked ham . . . Swiss cheese . . . mild Cheddar cheese . . . cucumber slices . . . thin-sliced watermelon pickle . . . olive butter . . . peanut butter . . . asparagus vinaigrette . . . marinated artichoke hearts . . . cranberry jelly . . . sesame-seed butter . . . lemon-sprinkled avocado slices.

The Gourmet Way
Cranberry-Walnut Relish

Make a plain sliced-fowl—chicken, turkey, duck, goose—sandwich into a very special dish with this relish that has such a fresh-tasting bouquet. White bread, mayonnaised rather than buttered, makes the best base for fowl-with-relish sandwiches.

> 1 pound fresh cranberries
> 2 large seedless oranges
> 2 red apples
> 2 cups sugar
> 1 cup coarsely chopped walnuts

Wash cranberries, drain and pick over to remove stems. Peel oranges; reserve peel, chop pulp coarsely. Core apples—but don't peel them. Put cranberries and apples through coarse blade of food chopper, along with the peel of 1 orange. Add oranges, sugar, walnuts. Mix well. Refrigerate at least several hours before serving—overnight is better.

Pyramids

Bread	Shredded lettuce
Butter	Tomato slices
Turkey slices	Roquefort cheese spread
Mayonnaise	Cucumber slices, unpeeled
Chili sauce	Cream cheese
Chopped egg and green pepper mixed with mayonnaise	Anchovy fillet, rolled

For each sandwich, cut 5 rounds of bread in graduated sizes, from 4 inches to 1 1/2 inches. Spread each slice with softened butter. Cover largest piece with sliced turkey and spread with mixture of mayonnaise and chili sauce. Cover next slice with chopped egg and green pepper salad and shredded lettuce. Place on top of first piece. Cover third with tomato slice spread with mayonnaise. Cover next slice with Roquefort cheese spread and cucumber slice. Spread smallest piece with cream cheese and top with a rolled anchovy fillet. Eat in layers.
Take note: This is fork food—unless you're very young or just plain don't care.

Tasty Turkey

4 buttered toast slices
1 package frozen asparagus
    spears
1 tablespoon butter
2 tablespoons flour
1 cup milk

1 cup grated process sharp
    American cheese
4 large cooked turkey slices
1 3-ounce can sliced
    mushrooms
Snipped parsley

Cook asparagus as label directs; drain. In small saucepan, melt butter. Stir in flour, then milk. Cook, stirring constantly until thickened. Stir in cheese until melted. Place toast on baking sheet. Top with asparagus spears, then with turkey slices and drained mushrooms. Spoon on cheese sauce. Broil 3 to 5 minutes, or until golden. Sprinkle with parsley. Makes 4 servings.
Or try it this way . . . Substitute chicken for turkey, crumbled crisp bacon for parsley.

Hot Chicken Salads

6 hard rolls
1 1/2 cups chopped cooked
    chicken
1/2 cup chopped celery
1/3 cup mayonnaise

1/8 teaspoon salt
2 tablespoons chopped
    stuffed or ripe olives
2 tablespoons grated
    sharp cheese

Combine chicken, celery, mayonnaise, salt, and olives. Cut thin slice from top of each roll; scoop out centers. Fill rolls, using 1/3 cup chicken mixture in each. Sprinkle cheese over top of each roll. Place filled rolls in a baking pan and broil under low broiler heat for 8 minutes.
Or try it this way . . . Add 1/4 cup chopped pecans to the salad mixture—and you may need a bit more mayonnaise.

Chicken Creams

12 slices white bread
1/3 cup butter
1/3 cup flour
1 cup chicken broth
1 1/2 cups milk

Salt, pepper
2 cups diced cooked
    chicken
12 slices sharp cheese
Crumbled cooked bacon

Melt butter; blend in flour; gradually add broth, milk. Cook over low heat, stirring constantly until thickened. Add salt, pepper, chicken. Toast bread; place in bottom of shallow baking pan lined with aluminum foil. Pile 1/3 cup creamed chicken on each slice; top with cheese slice. Slide under broiler until cheese melts; top with bacon. Makes 12 servings.

The Supreme Sandwich

Duck

If you want to make duck sandwiches, start from scratch—whoever has any leftover roast duck? However, these are worth the trouble.

16 slices dark rye bread
Rind of 1/2 orange
1 cup seeded white raisins
1/4 cup mayonnaise
1 teaspoon lemon juice
Softened butter
Thinly sliced cold duck

Remove all white membrane from orange rind; cut rind into small pieces. Put rind and raisins through fine blade of food chopper. Moisten with mayonnaise and lemon juice. Spread bread with butter, then spread 8 slices with raisin paste. Top with overlapping slices of duck, cover with remaining bread.

Pakistani Rolls

6 brown-and-serve rolls
1 teaspoon finely chopped candied ginger
1/2 teaspoon salt
1 teaspoon dry mustard
1/4 teaspoon curry powder
1 teaspoon lemon juice
1/2 cup mayonnaise or salad dressing
2/3 cup diced cooked chicken
1 cup chopped hard-cooked eggs
2 tablespoons shredded coconut

Combine ginger, salt, mustard, curry powder, lemon juice, and mayonnaise. Add chicken and eggs. Toss lightly together. Cut center out of each roll, removing top in one piece and leaving a 3/8-inch shell around edges and across bottom. Fill each roll with 1/3 cup of chicken mixture. Sprinkle 1 teaspoon coconut over top of each. Place on a cookie sheet and bake at 400° F. for about 12 minutes, or until coconut and rolls are browned. During last 5 minutes of baking time, place tops of rolls, crust side up, on a cookie sheet and brown. *To serve:* Place roll tops over filling.
For pretty . . . Garnish with green olives and parsley.

Hot Chicken Rolls au Gratin

6 white finger rolls
2 tablespoons butter
2 tablespoons flour
1/2 teaspoon salt
1 cup milk
1/4 cup chopped cooked
   celery

1 cup chopped cooked
   chicken or turkey
1/3 cup grated American
   cheese

Melt butter in saucepan. Blend in flour and salt. Add milk and cook until thick, stirring constantly. Add celery and chicken. Cut a thin slice off the top of each roll. Scoop out center. (Save sliced-off tops and centers of rolls for bread crumbs or stuffing.) Fill each roll with chicken mixture. Sprinkle cheese over top of filled rolls. Place filled rolls on a baking sheet and brown in oven at 375° F. for 15 minutes. Serve immediately.

Wonder Ways with Chicken Salad—

To 2 cups of chicken-salad sandwich filling, add one of the following: 1 tbs. snipped chives . . . 1/4 cup chopped walnuts . . . 1/4 cup slivered almonds . . . 1 cup diced ham . . . 1/2 cup diced Virginia ham . . . 1/4 cup chopped ripe olives . . . 1/4 cup chopped green olives . . . 1 tbs. chopped shallots . . . 1/2 cup shredded Chinese cabbage . . . 1/2 cup chopped celery . . . 1/2 cup chopped cucumber . . . 1/4 cup chopped peanuts . . . 2 tbs. drained capers . . . 1/2 cup halved seedless grapes . . . 1 tsp. grated orange peel . . . 1/3 cup grated carrot . . . 1/2 cup diced fresh pineapple . . . 2/3 cup mandarin orange sections . . . 2 tbs. chopped sweet gherkins . . . 2 tbs. diced dill pickle . . . 3/4 cup shredded corned beef . . . 2 tbs. chutney. Or, before mixing the salad, season the mayonnaise with one of the following: 1 tsp. curry powder . . . 1 tsp. chili powder . . . 1 tsp. turmeric . . . 1 tsp. Worcestershire . . . 1 tbs. chili sauce . . . 1/2 tsp. dill seed . . . 1/2 tsp. celery seed.

Walnut Chickenwiches

10 slices Swedish rye,
   buttered
3/4 cup diced cooked chicken
1/2 cup diced canned
   pineapple

1 teaspoon chopped green
   pepper
1/2 cup chopped walnuts
Mayonnaise

Mix chicken and well-drained pineapple. Add pepper and walnuts. Moisten with mayonnaise. Makes 5 sandwiches.

Savory Salad

8 slices white bread
1 cup cooked chopped chicken
3 ribs celery, chopped
1/2 sweet red pepper, chopped

1 teaspoon grated onion
3 teaspoons chopped black olives
Mayonnaise
Watercress

Mix chicken, celery, red pepper, onion, and olives with mayonnaise. Spread on 4 slices of bread. Top with watercress and remaining slices of bread. Makes 4 sandwiches.

Crisp Chicken

Thin-sliced light pumpernickel
1 cup cooked chopped chicken or turkey

1 cup chopped celery
1/2 cup mayonnaise
1/2 cup of minced fennel

Mix chicken, celery, mayonnaise, and fennel. Spread on pumpernickel slice, top with another slice.
Even better . . . Try substituting 1/2 cup whipped cream cheese for the mayonnaise.

California Sandwich

16 slices white or whole-wheat bread, thinly spread with mayonnaise
2 cups minced chicken (1 large can boned chicken)

2/3 cup chopped stuffed olives
2 teaspoons Worcestershire sauce
2 tablespoons mayonnaise
Salt

Mix chicken with olives. Blend Worcestershire sauce with mayonnaise and combine with chicken and olive mixture to form a paste. Salt to taste. Spread on 8 slices of bread and top with remaining slices.
Good companions . . . Celery, carrot sticks, cucumber rounds that have been crisped in salted water. Serve these garnished sandwiches with hot tea or cold milk, depending on the weather.

So Pretty, So Good

Elsewhere in this book, you will find a recipe for glazing sandwiches to a gourmet's taste—or for your most impressive parties. But why confine this delectable technique to a few extra-special occasions, when prepared flavored gelatins make it perfectly possible to give your family a lusciously different treat with little time and no trouble at all? Here's how to bejewel with a rich ruby, pale topaz, or delicate emerald glow a variety of open-face sandwich combinations listed below.

Savory Tomato Glaze

1 1/2 cups tomato juice
  1/8 teaspoon peppercorns
  1/2 bay leaf
  3/4 teaspoon salt
  1/8 teaspoon whole cloves
   1 tablespoon chopped onion

1/4 cup chopped celery
  1 3-ounce package lemon gelatin
  2 tablespoons vinegar
1/2 cup cold water

Combine tomato juice, peppercorns, bay leaf, salt, cloves, onion, and celery, and simmer in covered saucepan about 10 minutes. Strain. Dissolve gelatin in the hot liquid. Add vinegar and cold water. Chill until slightly thickened.

Lemon-Herb Glaze

1 2/3 cups water
  1/8 teaspoon peppercorns
  1/2 bay leaf
  1/2 teaspoon dried dill
   1 3-ounce package lemon gelatin

1/2 teaspoon salt
Dash of cayenne
  3 tablespoons vinegar

Combine water, peppercorns, bay leaf, and dried dill in a saucepan. Cover and simmer for about 10 minutes. Strain. Dissolve gelatin and salt in the hot liquid. Add cayenne and vinegar. Chill until slightly thickened.

To glaze sandwiches: Place 6 to 8 open-faced sandwiches on a rack and pour the slightly thickened Savory Tomato or Lemon-Herb glaze over each one, being sure to cover the entire surface evenly. Allow about 1/4 cup glaze for each sandwich. Chill until glaze is firm.

Try Savory Tomato over:
Blue Cheese and Chicken . . . on buttered whole-wheat bread, use 2 tablespoons of softened blue cheese, 2 to 4 slices chicken, 1 strip of crisp bacon. Garnish with cucumber slices.
Crab Meat and Grapefruit . . . top buttered rye bread with diced celery, flaked crab meat, and grapefruit sections (well drained if canned). Garnish with green pepper strips.
Tongue and Swiss Cheese . . . on buttered whole-wheat bread, place slices of Swiss cheese and tongue. Garnish with slivered gherkins and sliced radishes.

Try Lemon-Herb over:
Dutch Special . . . spread pumpernickel bread with mustard, and top each slice with 2 slices Swiss cheese, 1/4 cup sauerkraut, and 3 small slices corned beef. Garnish with dill pickle slices and caraway seed.
Smoked Salmon and Cream Cheese . . . on buttered pumpernickel or rye bread, arrange cucumber slices and smoked salmon. Use a pastry tube to add a design of softened cream cheese. Garnish with finely chopped chives. Add dash of freshly ground peppercorns before glazing.
Turkey and Cranberry Sauce . . . top buttered whole-wheat bread with turkey slices and jellied cranberry sauce in slices. Add thin segments of orange before glazing.
Roast Beef and Tomato . . . spread buttered rye bread thinly with horseradish sauce. Top with sliced roast beef, sliced tomatoes. Sprinkle with chopped capers.

Try either of the glazes on these combinations:
Sliced Egg and Shrimp . . . on buttered whole-wheat bread, arrange 1 sliced hard-cooked egg and about 9 jumbo shrimp, cooked. Garnish with sliced stuffed olives.
Ham and Asparagus Roll-ups . . . top buttered rye bread with 2 slices of tomato, and 2 slices of ham rolled around asparagus spears. Garnish with chopped ripe olives.
Sliced Egg, Sardine, and Tomato . . . on buttered rye bread, arrange 2 or 3 slices of hard-cooked egg, 2 or 3 slices of tomato, and fill up spaces with about 4 sardines.

So much for the ruby and topaz embellishments I promised in the opening words of this fit-for-Cartier's section. The emerald glaze is a bit more special, and deserves being set apart. Yes, it *is* a bit more complicated to organize. Are you going to let that stop you? See next recipe . . .

Cheese Buns El Paso

4 sandwich buns, split and
    buttered
4 1-ounce slices Cheddar
    cheese

1 avocado, peeled and sliced
2 tomatoes, sliced
4 lettuce leaves

Place 1 cheese slice on bottom half of each bun. Cover cheese with avocado slices. Place 2 slices of tomato and a lettuce leaf over avocado. Cover with bun tops and secure sandwich with toothpicks. Cut in half to serve. Makes 4 sandwiches.

Crisp Cheese Roll-ups

1 1-pound loaf unsliced
    white bread
1 cup grated process
    American cheese
1/4 cup chopped stuffed
    olives
1/3 cup crumbled, crisp bacon

1/4 teaspoon Worcestershire
    sauce
1 No. 1 can condensed
    cream of mushroom
    soup
1/4 cup milk

Trim crusts from loaf and cut into 6 horizontal slices. Combine cheese, olives, bacon, Worcestershire sauce, and 1/3 cup mushroom soup. Spread 3 tablespoons of the cheese mixture on each slice of bread. Roll up the spread bread, jelly-roll fashion. Place rolls on a greased baking sheet and toast in a 400° F. oven for 10 to 15 minutes, or until golden brown. Combine remaining mushroom soup and milk in a small saucepan. Heat and serve mushroom sauce over each roll. Makes 6 servings.
Perfect partner . . . A salad of watercress and little cherry tomatoes goes well with Crisp Cheese Roll-ups.

Tropical Snow Sandwich

8 slices bread
1/2 cup creamed cottage
    cheese
1/2 cup crushed pineapple,
    drained

1/4 cup shredded coconut
1/4 teaspoon ground ginger

Combine cottage cheese, pineapple, coconut, and ginger. Spread on 4 slices bread, top with remaining slices. Makes 4 sandwiches.
Or try it this way . . . Cut rounds of bread from slices with 3 1/2-inch cookie cutter, pile on Tropical Snow and serve open-face with sprinkling of toasted coconut over top. Or serve for tea or dessert on tiny bread rounds; top with 1/2 Maraschino cherry.

Cranberry-Cheese Soufflé

12 bread slices
2 tablespoons soft butter
3 egg whites
1/2 teaspoon salt
3 egg yolks
Dash of pepper
1/8 teaspoon paprika
1/2 teaspoon Worcestershire
sauce

1/2 teaspoon prepared
mustard
1/2 cup grated natural sharp
American cheese
1 cup canned whole-
cranberry sauce
6 lettuce leaves

Heat oven to 350° F. Butter 6 bread slices; place on greased cookie sheet. Beat egg whites with salt until stiff but not dry. Beat egg yolks with pepper, paprika, Worcestershire sauce, and mustard until thick; add grated cheese. Fold into beaten egg whites. Place about 1/2 cup soufflé mixture on each buttered bread slice. Bake 15 minutes, or until fluffy and brown. Meanwhile, toast remaining bread slices; spread with cranberry sauce; top with lettuce leaf, then with soufflé-spread slice, with soufflé side up. Slice diagonally. Makes 6 servings.

Cheese-Relishes

8 slices whole-wheat bread
or pumpernickel
2/3 cup grated process
American cheese

2 tablespoons pickle relish
1/4 cup commercial sour
cream

Combine grated cheese, pickle relish, and sour cream. Spread on 4 slices bread, top with remaining slices.

Cheese and Egg

8 slices whole-wheat bread
3/4 cup grated American
cheese
3 hard-cooked egg yolks

Salt
Pepper
Mustard
Butter

Mix cheese and egg yolk. Season with salt, pepper, and a little mustard. Pound to paste with enough butter to make spreadable. Spread on 4 slices bread, top with remaining slices.
Perfect partners . . . Use 1 cup cheese and extra butter to increase amount of spread. With leftover spread, fill halved whites of the hard-cooked eggs, top each with an anchovy, serve with Cheese and Egg sandwiches, cucumber slices, celery and carrot sticks, and olives.

The Gourmet Way

Cheddar-Herb Bread

Almost anything at all on this bread makes a delicious sandwich—meat, fish, eggs. My own favorite is eggs, scrambled very soft, salted and white-peppered.

    1 cup milk
    2 tablespoons sugar
    1 tablespoon salt
 1/2 cup warm water (*not* hot)
    2 packages active dry yeast
 1/4 pound grated sharp Cheddar cheese
 1/2 teaspoon each, dried oregano, basil, thyme
4 1/2 to 5 cups sifted flour
    1 tablespoon butter, melted

Heat milk just until bubbles form around edge of pan. Add sugar, salt; stir until dissolved. Cool to lukewarm. Place warm water in large bowl, sprinkle yeast over and stir until dissolved. Stir in milk mixture, cheese, herbs, and 2 cups of the flour. Beat until smooth. Gradually add remaining flour. Mix in the last of flour with your hands, using just enough so that dough leaves the sides of the bowl. Turn dough onto floured board and knead 10 minutes. Place in large, greased bowl. Brush top with melted butter. Cover and let rise in a warm place that is free from drafts until double in bulk—should take about 2 hours. Punch down dough. Turn onto lightly floured board. Shape into a smooth ball. Cover with a towel and let rest 10 minutes. Roll the ball into a rectangle 8 by 12 inches. Starting at the long side, roll—very tightly—as for jelly roll. Place, seam side down, in greased loaf pan. Cover with towel, let rise again until double in bulk—about 1 hour. Bake loaf in 400° F. oven for 20 minutes, then cover with foil and put back into oven again, for 10 to 15 minutes, or until loaf sounds hollow when knocked with your knuckle. Remove from pan and cool on a rack.

Kaasteefjes

6 slices 1/2-inch-thick white bread, crusts trimmed
2 tablespoons softened butter
2 teaspoons prepared mustard

3 slices Edam or Gouda cheese
1 egg, beaten
1/2 cup milk
1/4 teaspoon salt
1/8 teaspoon pepper

Blend butter and mustard and spread on bread. Cover 3 slices of bread with cheese slices, top with remaining bread slices. Mix beaten egg, milk, salt, and pepper. Dip sandwiches in mixture. Fry in butter until golden on both sides. Makes 3 sandwiches.

Even better . . . Plenty of crisp bacon or frizzled ham slices served with these makes them even more of a meal.

French-Fried Gruyère Sandwich

8 slices sandwich bread
1 4 1/2-ounce can deviled ham
1 tablespoon mayonnaise
1 teaspoon parsley flakes
8 slices (6-ounce package) Gruyère cheese

1/3 cup milk
1 egg
1 tablespoon sesame seeds
4 tablespoons butter

In small bowl combine deviled ham, mayonnaise, and parsley flakes. Spread equal amounts of ham mixture on one side of 4 slices of bread. Place 2 slices of Gruyère cheese on top of each spread slice of bread. Cover with plain bread slice. Beat milk, egg, and sesame seeds together. Dip each sandwich into egg-milk mixture on both sides until all mixture is absorbed. Fry each sandwich in 1 tablespoon butter until golden brown on both sides. Serve hot. Makes 4 sandwiches.

Grilled Chili-Cheese

8 slices white bread, buttered
3/4 cup chili con carne

4 1-ounce slices process American cheese

Spread 3 tablespoons chili con carne on unbuttered side of bread; top with cheese slice. Cover cheese with another bread slice, buttered side up. Grill until golden brown on both sides. Serve hot. Makes 4 sandwiches.

Chicago Special

12 slices rye bread	Mayonnaise or salad dressing
1 cup grated American cheese	2 teaspoons mustard
1 cup chopped ham	1 teaspoon Worcestershire sauce

Mix cheese and ham and moisten with mayonnaise. Season with mustard and Worcestershire sauce. Spread on 6 slices bread, top with remaining slices. Makes 6 hearty sandwiches.
Even better . . . Use sharp Cheddar cheese and add 1/4 cup finely chopped green pepper.

Waldorf Cheese

8 slices white bread	1/2 cup grated American cheese
1 apple, chopped	Mayonnaise
1/4 cup chopped nuts	

Mix chopped apple with chopped nuts and grated cheese. Moisten with mayonnaise. Spread on 4 slices bread, top with remaining slices. Makes 4 sandwiches.
Even better . . . For those who like onion, a few drops of onion juice livens this up.

Baked Swiss Supper

8 slices bread, toasted and buttered	2 tablespoons prepared mustard
2 cups shredded Swiss cheese	4 eggs, slightly beaten
2 2 1/4-ounce cans deviled ham	2 cups milk
	1 teaspoon sesame seeds
	1/2 teaspoon caraway seeds

Mix together Swiss cheese, deviled ham, and mustard. Spread mixture on 4 slices of toast, approximately 1/2 cup for each; top with remaining 4 slices of toast. Quarter sandwiches diagonally and arrange in 3 rows in buttered 8-inch-square baking dish, standing crust sides down. Combine eggs and milk; pour over sandwiches. Sprinkle sesame and caraway seeds over top. Bake in preheated 350° F. oven for 45 minutes. Makes 6 servings.
Take note: This casserole may be made ahead and refrigerated until ready to bake. It may also be baked and frozen. To serve, thaw before reheating.

Hot Salad Cheesewiches

4 slices bread, buttered
1 cup shredded Cheddar
  cheese
1/2 cup diced cucumber
1 tablespoon minced onion
1/4 cup commercial sour
  cream

1/8 teaspoon pepper
1/8 teaspoon chili powder
4 large, thick tomato slices
8 slices dill pickle
Paprika

Mix together Cheddar cheese, cucumber, onion, sour cream, and seasonings. Toast bread lightly under broiler. Arrange a tomato slice and 2 pickle slices on each slice of toasted bread; top with cheese mixture. Sprinkle with paprika. Place under broiler until cheese is melted and lightly browned. Makes 4 servings.

Crunchy Cheese

8 slices white bread
1/4 cup slivered or chopped
  toasted almonds
2 tablespoons chopped ripe
  olives

1/2 cup grated process
  American cheese
1/3 cup mayonnaise or salad
  dressing
Dash of pepper

Combine almonds, olives, cheese, mayonnaise, and pepper. Spread on 4 slices bread, top with remaining slices. Makes 4 sandwiches.

Creamy Roquefort Rounds

10 thin slices dark
  pumpernickel
1 3-ounce package cream
  cheese
1 tablespoon milk
2 tablespoons Roquefort
  cheese

1/4 teaspoon salt
2 hard-cooked eggs,
  chopped
1 teaspoon dried or fresh
  chopped parsley

Cut pumpernickel into rounds with large cookie cutter. Combine cream cheese and milk until soft. Add Roquefort cheese, salt, and chopped eggs, and blend well. Spread on all rounds, sprinkle tops with parsley and serve open-face. Or spread on 5 rounds, top with remaining rounds. Makes 10 open-face sandwiches, 5 regular sandwiches.

Even better . . . Sour cream, instead of milk, makes a richer, tastier spread. To get spreadable mixture, you may have to vary the amount according to the consistency of the cream.

The Gourmet Way

Herb Buns

Make these to add savor to cold-cut sandwiches or to dress up tag ends of baked ham. And try them with Braunschweiger and mustard butter—delicious!

1 package hot roll mix
2 teaspoons caraway seeds
2 teaspoons sage
3/4 teaspoon nutmeg
1 cup water

Mix seasonings with package contents; follow directions to make dough. When dough is ready to shape, roll or pat it on a floured board to 1/2-inch thickness. Cut out buns with a round 3-inch cutter, or into 3-inch squares. Place on greased baking sheet 3 inches apart. Cover with a towel, and let rise until double in bulk (see package directions). Bake at 375° F. for 20 to 25 minutes. Makes about 10 buns.

California Combination

8 slices white bread, buttered
3 tablespoons mayonnaise or salad dressing
4 1-ounce slices American cheese

1/4 cup pickle relish
1 avocado, peeled and sliced
2 teaspoons fresh lemon juice
Salt

Spread each buttered bread slice with mayonnaise. On 4 slices of bread, place 1 slice of American cheese, 1 tablespoon of pickle relish, and 1/4 of a peeled, sliced avocado. Drizzle a little lemon juice and sprinkle a little salt over the avocado slices. Top with another slice of bread. Makes 4 sandwiches.

Onion-Cheese Miniatures

24 slices party rye bread
1 1/2 tablespoons chopped green onion
1/2 cup grated sharp cheese

1/4 cup chopped cooked bacon
2 tablespoons mayonnaise or salad dressing

Combine onion, cheese, bacon, and mayonnaise. Spread 2 teaspoons cheese filling on half of the slices of bread. Top with remaining slices. Makes 12 sandwiches.

40

✳✳✳✳✳✳✳✳✳✳✳✳✳✳✳✳✳✳✳✳✳✳✳✳✳✳✳

The Basic Way with

French-Fried Sandwiches

French-frying is the sneaky way of turning a common garden variety sandwich into something worth eating—and worth looking at.

Try first . . . FRENCH BUNWICHES

> 6 sandwich buns, split
> 2 cups any soft, moist sandwich filling
> 1/2 cup milk
> 1/2 cup fine, dry bread crumbs
> Hot, deep fat for frying

Fill each bun with 1/3 cup of filling. Roll buns in milk, 1 at a time, then in bread crumbs, being sure to coat all over. Fry in deep hot fat at 375° F. until brown on both sides—takes about 1 minute. Makes 6 sandwiches.

Then experiment with . . .

Salad-sandwich fillings—chicken, egg, seafood—with crisp, crumbled bacon and/or chopped pecans added . .˙. ham salad with finely cubed Swiss cheese, or with chopped peanuts added.

✳✳✳✳✳✳✳✳✳✳✳✳✳✳✳✳✳✳✳✳✳✳✳✳✳✳✳

Swiss-and-Slaw

> 8 slices white or rye bread
> 1 cup coarsely shredded cabbage
> 1/4 teaspoon caraway seed
> 1/4 teaspoon salt
> 1 tablespoon creamy French dressing
>
> 1 1/3 tablespoons soft butter
> 1/2 teaspoon prepared mustard
> 1/2 teaspoon prepared horseradish
> 4 slices Swiss cheese

Combine shredded cabbage, caraway seed, salt, and French dressing. Blend butter with mustard and horseradish. Spread bread with butter mixture. Place about 3 tablespoons of cabbage slaw on 4 of the bread slices. Top each with a cheese slice and another slice of bread. Makes 4 sandwiches.

Perfect partner . . . Slices of tomato aspic, each topped with a spoonful of French dressing and sprinkled with fresh chopped chives.

Cheddar and Vitamins

8 slices whole-wheat
   bread, buttered
1/2 cup chopped raw
   cabbage
1/4 cup chopped raw carrot
1/4 cup 1/2-inch Cheddar
   cheese cubes

1 1/2 tablespoons mayonnaise
   or salad dressing
1/2 teaspoon salt
1/2 teaspoon prepared
   mustard

Combine cabbage, carrot, cheese, mayonnaise, salt, and mustard. Spread on 4 slices bread, top with remaining slices. Makes 4 sandwiches.

Cheese Devils

6 slices of bread
2 cups sharp Cheddar,
   shredded
1/4 cup soft butter
1/4 teaspoon dry mustard

Dash of cayenne
1 teaspoon scraped onion
1 tablespoon ketchup or
   chili sauce

Toast bread on one side. Combine all other ingredients. Spread cheese mixture on untoasted side of bread. Broil until bubbly. Makes 6 servings.

Savory Cheesewiches

4 slices white or whole-
   wheat bread
1 2 1/4-ounce can deviled
   ham
1 tablespoon sweet pickle
   relish

4 slices sharp cheese
1 egg, beaten
1/4 cup milk
2 tablespoons butter

Spread one side of each slice of bread with 1/4 of the deviled ham. Set aside 2 slices. Spread half of the pickle relish on 2 ham-spread slices. Place 2 slices cheese on top of pickle relish. Top with remaining slices of bread, placing ham-spread side down. Beat egg and milk slightly. Place each sandwich in egg-milk mixture, turning once to absorb all mixture. Melt butter over low heat in large skillet. Fry slowly so that bottom slice browns evenly and egg mixture "sets." Turn carefully to brown other side. Serve hot. Makes 2 sandwiches.

✳✳✳✳✳✳✳✳✳✳✳✳✳✳✳✳✳✳✳✳✳✳✳✳✳✳✳✳✳
✳ *The Basic Way with*

Grilled Cheese Sandwiches

This is an easy way to dress up a simple sandwich that says you've put a little—and it takes only a very little—time and effort into the luncheon or snack you're serving.

> 8 slices white bread
> 2 tablespoons mayonnaise
> 1 tablespoon hot prepared mustard
> 4 1/4-inch slices sharp American cheese
> 6 tablespoons soft butter

Mix mayonnaise and mustard and spread on one side of each slice of bread. Put spread slices together with a slice of cheese between. Butter the outsides of the sandwiches, top and bottom. Sauté on a griddle or in a frying pan until nicely browned on one side; turn and grill the other side.

Even better . . . A slice of ham improves these, so does a slice of tongue. Never be sparing with the pickles when you serve grilled sandwiches. In fact, never be sparing of the grilled sandwiches—almost any simple sandwich, including one with salad-type filling if not too wet, is likely to be better grilled.

✳✳✳✳✳✳✳✳✳✳✳✳✳✳✳✳✳✳✳✳✳✳✳✳✳✳✳✳✳

Bermuda Grill

12 slices rye bread
2 cups chopped Bermuda
   onion
1 teaspoon salt
1/4 teaspoon pepper
1/2 cup Sauterne
12 slices Swiss cheese

To marinate onion: Place chopped onion in a shallow dish. Sprinkle with salt and pepper. Add Sauterne. Cover and let stand for at least 1 hour, stirring onions every 15 minutes.

To make sandwiches: Place a slice of cheese on 6 of the bread slices. Top with marinated onion and another slice of cheese and bread. Grill sandwiches on both sides or place in a folding long-handled wire rack and toast on both sides over hot coals. Makes 6 sandwiches.

Good companions . . . Pickle chips, stuffed olives, tomato wedges, cucumber slices.

Sandwich by the Yard

French or Vienna loaf,
  unsliced
Butter

Prepared mustard
Sweet onion slices
American cheese slices

Slice into loaf at 1/2-inch intervals, but do not cut through to the bottom. Combine equal quantities of butter and mustard and spread on cut surfaces of bread. Insert thin slices of onion and cheese into cuts. Bake in 350° F. oven on baking sheet for 15 minutes. Count on 2 slices for each serving.
Even better . . . Slip thin slices of ham or meat loaf into cuts in bread loaf, along with onion and cheese. Pass tomato sauce.

Swiss Toast Emmental (Croûte)

6 slices white bread
1/2 pound Swiss cheese,
  grated

2 eggs, separated
1 scant teaspoon grated
  onion

Mix cheese with egg yolks and onion. Beat the egg whites lightly and add to mixture. If the mixture is too stiff, add 1 tablespoon of cream or evaporated milk. Spread the mixture liberally on one side of each bread slice and sauté in butter, spread side first, until both sides are golden brown. Makes 3 servings.
Keep in mind . . . These croûtes can be warmed over, and make wonderful appetizers or coffee-time "bites" when cut into triangles or fingers.

Butter-Grilled Cheese Triples

12 slices bread
1/2 cup (1 stick) butter,
  softened
4 slices Cheddar cheese
4 slices ham

4 slices sweet onion
4 slices tomato
4 slices Swiss cheese
8 slices bacon, cooked

Butter both sides of bread. In a skillet, slowly brown 4 slices on one side. Turn. While underside is browning, top each slice with a slice of Cheddar cheese, ham, and sweet onion and a second slice of bread. When underside is brown, turn sandwiches over. Top with a slice of tomato and Swiss cheese and 2 slices of bacon. Place a third slice of bread on each sandwich. When bottom slice is brown, turn whole sandwich over and brown. Cut sandwiches in half diagonally. Secure with toothpicks garnished with pimento olives. 4 sandwiches.

Baked Asparagus-Cheese

6 slices of bread, crusts trimmed
1 package frozen asparagus, thawed
12 slices Swiss cheese, 3 by 2 inches
4 eggs
2 1/2 cups milk
1/4 teaspoon nutmeg
1 1/2 teaspoons salt
1/8 teaspoon pepper
1 tablespoon finely chopped onion
1/2 cup shredded Cheddar cheese

Cut asparagus spears in half lengthwise. Arrange 6 slices of bread on bottom of 13 by 9 by 2 inch baking dish. Cover each bread slice with a slice of cheese; top with 2 asparagus spear halves. Repeat layers, arranging the remaining asparagus over 6 sandwiches. In a bowl beat eggs until light; add milk, nutmeg, salt, pepper, and onion; blend thoroughly. Pour over sandwiches; bake 25 minutes in preheated 350° F. oven. Sprinkle with Cheddar cheese; continue to bake 10 to 15 minutes or until custard is set and top is golden brown. Allow to stand 10 minutes; cut in 6 squares to serve. Makes 6 servings.
Even better . . . A thin layer of ham under each cheese slice upgrades this into an elegant supper or buffet specialty.

Pizza Hero

2 French rolls
2 to 3 tablespoons butter
4 tomato slices, cut in half
3 tablespoons grated Parmesan and Romano cheese
3/4 teaspoon oregano
1/2 cup sliced fresh mushrooms or 1 4-ounce can button mushrooms, drained
4 slices mozzarella cheese

Cut each French roll in half lengthwise. Butter cut sides of roll. For each sandwich, place 4 half-slices tomato on bottom part of each cut roll, overlapping each slice. Combine grated Parmesan and Romano cheese and oregano. Sprinkle half the mixture on top of tomato slices. Cover with mushroom slices. Top with 2 slices mozzarella cheese. Sprinkle with remaining grated cheese-oregano mixture. Cover with top half of roll. Wrap each sandwich in aluminum foil, place on baking sheet. Bake at 350° F. until cheese melts, about 15 minutes. Serve at once. Makes 2 individual heroes.
Even better . . . A layer of leftover meat loaf or tiny meatballs, covered with 2 tablespoons of good tomato sauce, makes these sandwiches even more heroic. In this variation, omit the sliced tomatoes.

Cheddar Bunboats

6 frankfurter buns	1/3 cup chopped ripe olives
1 cup shredded Cheddar cheese	1/2 teaspoon grated onion
1/2 cup mayonnaise	1/2 teaspoon Worcestershire sauce

Split buns and hollow out slightly. Combine cheese, mayonnaise, olives, onion, and Worcestershire sauce and spoon into buns. Wrap each sandwich in aluminum foil. Heat in 325° F. oven 15 to 20 minutes. Makes 6 sandwiches.

Good companion . . . Small sweet gherkins are a nice extra.

Tacos

12 tortillas, canned or packaged	2 cups kidney beans
1 bunch green onions, chopped, including some of the green	1 1/2 cups shredded Cheddar cheese
2 tomatoes, peeled and diced	2 tablespoons chili sauce
1 teaspoon chopped green chili	1/4 teaspoon chili powder
1 1/3 cups tuna	Fat or oil
	1/2 medium head lettuce, shredded
	3 cups shredded brick cheese

Combine onions, tomatoes, and green chili; set aside. In saucepan heat together tuna, kidney beans, Cheddar cheese, chili sauce, and chili powder; keep warm. In skillet heat 1/2 inch of fat or oil until very hot. Brown tortillas until slightly crisp. Remove from skillet, fold and place on absorbent paper to drain. Fill inside of folded tortilla with generous portion of tuna-cheese mixture. Spoon tomato mixture over filling and top with lettuce and brick cheese. Pile Tacos on platter and serve immediately.

Note: Tacos may be kept warm in oven before adding lettuce and cheese.

Gruyère Savories

4 slices of bread	1/2 tablespoon mustard
1 tablespoon of butter	4 slices Gruyère cheese

Blend mustard with butter, spread evenly on bread and cover with thick slices of cheese. Fry lightly in butter until the cheese is melted. Do not turn. Serve piping hot. Makes 4 servings.

Or try it this way . . . While savories are frying, sauté until crisp, 2 strips of bacon for each sandwich. Drain well, crumble, sprinkle over melted cheese. Garnish with watercress.

Fruit-and-Cheese

8 slices of bread
1 cup shredded process
   American cheese
1/2 cup raisins, chopped
1/2 cup dates, chopped

1/4 cup mayonnaise
2 eggs, slightly beaten
1/2 cup milk
1/8 teaspoon salt
Butter

Combine cheese, raisins, dates, and mayonnaise. Spread on 4 bread slices, and top with remaining slices. Combine eggs, milk, and salt. Dip sandwiches in batter and brown on both sides in hot butter in heavy skillet. Makes 4 sandwiches.

Olive-American Sandwiches

8 slices white bread,
   buttered
1/4 cup olive butter

4 slices process American
   cheese

Spread 1/4 cup olive butter over 4 slices buttered bread. Place cheese slices over olive butter. Top with remaining slices of buttered bread. Makes 4 sandwiches.

Or try this . . . Add 1/4 cup coarsely chopped pecans to olive butter. Moisten with a little mayonnaise.

Zesty Swiss Eggs

8 slices white or whole-
   wheat bread
1/2 cup grated Swiss cheese,
   tightly packed
1/2 cup chopped, hard-
   cooked egg
1/4 teaspoon dry mustard

1/8 teaspoon salt
3 tablespoons mayonnaise
   or salad dressing
Few grains of paprika
1 tablespoon finely chopped
   green pepper

Combine cheese, egg, mustard, salt, mayonnaise, paprika, and green pepper. Spread on 4 slices bread, top with remaining slices. Makes 4 sandwiches.

The Gourmet Way

Roquefort Cheese Dressing

1/4 cup Homemade Mayonnaise (page 125)
1/4 cup French dressing
1/4 cup (or more) crumbled Roquefort
1 teaspoon Worcestershire sauce

Mix all ingredients well. Refrigerate until ready to serve.

Vegetable Logs

2 lengthwise slices whole-
wheat bread (cut from
unsliced 1 1/2-pound
loaf)
3/4 cup chopped cabbage
1/2 teaspoon chopped green
pepper

2 tablespoons chopped
celery
2 tablespoons mayonnaise
or salad dressing
1 tablespoon ground
Roquefort cheese
1/4 cup soft butter

Combine cabbage, green pepper, celery, mayonnaise, and
Roquefort cheese. Spread each slice of bread with butter.
Spread half of the Roquefort-vegetable filling on each slice.
Cut each lengthwise slice into 4 crosswise sections. Roll each
section up tightly as for jelly roll. Wrap in waxed paper or
foil and place on a cookie sheet so that roll rests on last turn
of bread; chill. *To serve:* Cut each roll in half. Makes 16
servings.

Piccalilli Dillies

6 slices molasses-corn bread
Mayonnaise
2/3 cup cottage cheese

3 tablespoons drained
piccalilli
3 tablespoons chopped stuffed
olives

Spread bread with mayonnaise. Combine cottage cheese, piccalilli, and olives. Divide filling over 3 slices of bread, top
with remaining slices. Makes 3 sandwiches.

Pepper-Swiss

6 slices white bread
1/2 cup grated Swiss cheese
1/2 cup soft butter

1/4 teaspoon cayenne pepper
Lemon juice

Combine cheese and butter. Season with cayenne pepper and
a few drops of lemon juice. Divide over 3 slices bread, top
with remaining slices. Makes 3 sandwiches.

Ranchburgers

6 split sandwich buns
1 1/2 cups grated process
cheese (firmly
packed)
2 tablespoons finely
chopped onion

1/3 cup chopped cooked
bacon
1/4 cup ketchup
1 tablespoon prepared
mustard

Combine cheese, onion, bacon, ketchup, and mustard. Spread
3 tablespoons cheese mixture on bottom half of each bun
and cover with bun top. Place buns on shallow baking pan.
Cover pan with foil. Heat in a 350° F. oven for 10 minutes.

Broiled Bunwiches

6 hamburger buns, split,
  buttered
6 large tomato slices
Seasoned salt

2 tablespoons minced onion
1 package process American
  cheese slices
12 bacon slices, crisp

Place tomato slices, sprinkled with seasoned salt, on bottom halves of buns. Sprinkle with minced onion. Top with cheese slices. Broil until cheese is lightly browned and tops of buns are lightly toasted. Top each bun with 2 crisp bacon slices. Makes 6 bunwiches.
Perfect partners . . . Ripe olives, relishes.

Belgian-Swiss Partners

8 slices rye bread
1/4 cup mayonnaise or salad
  dressing
1/2 pound cooked smoked
  tongue, sliced

12 pieces Belgian endive
4 slices Swiss cheese

Spread mayonnaise on bread. Place sliced tongue on 4 slices of bread. Cover tongue with sliced Swiss cheese. Top with 3 pieces endive, then with remaining bread slices. Makes 4 sandwiches.

Raisin-Olive

1 can Boston brown bread,
  sliced, buttered
1 cup ripe olives, chopped

1/2 cup seedless raisins,
  chopped
1/2 cup grated Münster cheese

Combine ingredients; moisten to spreading consistency with mayonnaise. Spread on half of bread slices, top with the remaining slices.

Ham-Salad Grillwiches

10 slices bread, buttered
1/2 pound ham, chopped
1/2 cup grated American
  cheese
1/4 cup stuffed olives, sliced

1/4 teaspoon dry mustard
2 tablespoons chopped dill
  pickles
2 tablespoons mayonnaise
Butter, softened

Combine ham, cheese, olives, mustard, dill pickles, mayonnaise. Blend thoroughly. Make sandwiches, using ham mixture. Spread outside of each sandwich with softened butter. Brown on both sides on hot griddle. Makes 5 sandwiches.

Beanwiches

6 slices of bread	6 slices American cheese
2 cups baked beans	6 strips bacon, partially cooked
1 large onion, finely chopped	
1 1-pound can jellied cranberry sauce	

Toast bread on one side under broiler. Spread other side with beans. Sprinkle on chopped onion. Cut cranberry sauce into 6 slices. Place 1 slice atop onions on each sandwich. Top with slices of cheese and a strip of bacon cut in half. Broil for 10 minutes or until bacon is done and cheese is melted. Makes 6 servings.

Toasty Cheese Surprise

8 slices white bread, toasted	8 slices sharp Cheddar cheese
8 slices canned pineapple, well drained	(6-ounce package)

Cover each slice of toast with 1 slice of pineapple, top with a slice of cheese. Place sandwiches in a shallow baking pan, about 4 1/2 inches below heat. Broil until cheese is melted and starts to bubble, about 5 minutes. Serve at once. Makes 8 servings.
Good companions . . . Mustard pickles for flavor contrast and potato chips for crunchy texture.

Cottage-Cheese Color Wheel

4 slices rye bread, buttered	1 tablespoon chopped chives
2 cups cottage cheese	1 1/2 teaspoons salt
1/2 cup finely grated carrots	1/4 teaspoon pepper
1/4 cup chopped green pepper	4 large tomato slices
2 tablespoons chopped pimento	Lettuce 1/4 cup chopped parsley

Several hours ahead: Mix cottage cheese with carrots, green pepper, pimento, chives, 1 teaspoon salt, pepper. Refrigerate.
To serve: Sprinkle both sides of tomato slices with 1/2 teaspoon salt. Butter bread. Arrange lettuce and 1 tomato slice on each rye bread slice. Top with large scoopful of cottage-cheese mixture; sprinkle with chopped parsley. 4 servings.
Good companions . . . This salad-on-rye goes especially well with soup. Try it with onion soup for a hot meal, jellied madrilène for a cold one.

Cranberry-Cheese Toastwich

12 slices white bread, buttered	2 eggs, slightly beaten
12 slices process American cheese	1/3 cup milk
	1/4 cup butter
3/4 cup canned whole-berry cranberry sauce	

On each of 6 bread slices lay a slice of cheese and top it with 2 tablespoons of cranberry sauce. Place a second slice of cheese over the sauce and finish sandwich with a slice of bread. Combine beaten eggs and milk and dip each sandwich into it on both sides. Brown sandwich, on both sides, in butter in a skillet. Serve immediately. Makes 6 sandwiches.

Or try it this way . . . Substitute thin slices of peeled tomato for the cranberry sauce.

Easter-Bonnet Sandwiches

20 slices white bread	16 slices unpeeled cucumber about 1/8 inch thick and 1 1/2 inches wide
1 cup creamed cottage cheese	
2 teaspoons lemon juice	
Dash of salt	16 small sprigs watercress
2 drops yellow food coloring	24 fresh red raspberries
2 drops green food coloring	24 fresh blueberries
2 drops red food coloring	

Whip cottage cheese until creamy. Add lemon juice and salt. Cut circles from 16 bread slices, using a 3-inch cookie cutter. Cut 4 circles from each remaining bread slice, using a 1 1/2-inch cookie cutter. Divide cottage-cheese mixture into 4 equal parts and add 1 color to each of 3 parts, leaving the fourth part white. Spread 4 large and 4 small circles of bread with each color of cottage-cheese mixture. Place a cucumber slice in center of each large bread circle. Top with small bread circle spread with same color of cottage cheese, spread side up. Decorate "bonnets" by arranging a watercress sprig and 3 or 4 raspberries or blueberries on one side of each hat. Makes 16 sandwiches.

Onion Miniatures

24 slices party rye bread	1/4 cup chopped cooked bacon
1 tablespoon finely chopped onion	Mayonnaise
2 tablespoons grated Cheddar	

Combine onion, cheese, bacon, and mayonnaise. Spread cheese filling on half of the slices of bread. Top with remaining slices. Makes 12 sandwiches.

Flying Dutchmen

16 slices caraway rye bread,
  buttered
16 slices corned beef

16 slices Swiss cheese
1 1/3 cups sauerkraut, drained

Arrange bread slices in pairs on a cookie sheet. Cut each slice of corned beef in half and place on 8 slices of bread; top with a slice of Swiss cheese. Fork about 3 tablespoons sauerkraut on remaining slices of bread; top with a slice of Swiss cheese. *To serve:* Heat both sandwich halves, open-face, in a 350° oven for 5 to 8 minutes, or until cheese melts. Close sandwiches, cut in half, and serve immediately. 8 sandwiches.

Seaside Smokies

8 frankfurter buns, split,
  buttered
2 cups diced Cheddar
  cheese
1 7-ounce can tuna, drained
1/2 cup sour cream

1/3 cup chopped stuffed olives
1/4 cup diced celery
3 tablespoons smoke-
  flavored ketchup
1/2 teaspoon onion salt

Combine cheese, tuna, sour cream, olives, celery, ketchup, onion salt; blend well. Fill buns with cheese mixture. Place each bun in center of a 12-inch square of aluminum foil; wrap, using double fold over top, twisting ends. Place on baking sheet; bake at 350° F. for 20 minutes. Serve in opened foil packages. Makes 8 sandwiches.

Clam-Lobster Cheesies

12 slices toast, buttered
2/3 cup finely diced celery
1 tablespoon minced green
  pepper
1 tablespoon mayonnaise
1/4 teaspoon salt

1/8 teaspoon pepper
1 5-ounce container
  Neufchâtel cheese
  spread with clam and
  lobster
6 lettuce leaves

In small bowl combine celery, green pepper, mayonnaise, and seasonings. Trim crusts from toast. Spread one side of 6 slices of the toast with the clam-lobster cheese. Cover with equal amounts of the vegetable mixture. Top with lettuce leaves. Cover with remaining toast. Makes 6 sandwiches.

A Fine Foundation

Cream cheese, like plastic bags and telephones, is something no one should try to keep house without. Its bland charms enhance almost anything you combine it with; it gives authority (protein, too, but we're thinking in terms of good taste, not good nutrition, just now) to dozens of sandwich makings. And, if you're backed into a corner, a *plain* cream cheese sandwich is not to be despised (salt it—or, if you're feeling venturesome, sugar it). Come out of the corner, though, and try the sandwiches ahead for flavor—all with a cream cheese base.

Pink Cheese

8 slices white bread
1 3-ounce package cream
    cheese

1/2 cup chopped walnuts
2 tablespoons tomato sauce

Mix cream cheese with chopped walnuts, and color with tomato sauce. Spread on 4 slices of bread, top with remaining slices. *Take note:* These, plus creamy scrambled eggs, add up to a luncheon children love.

Hawaiian Roll-ups

8 slices sandwich bread,
    crusts removed
1 6-ounce package cream
    cheese
8 slices boiled ham
8 spears pineapple

1/3 cup milk
1 egg
1/2 teaspoon cinnamon
1/4 teaspoon nutmeg
1/4 cup (4 tablespoons)
    butter

Flatten each slice of bread with a rolling pin to approximately 1/8-inch thickness. Carefully spread equal amounts of cream cheese on one side of each bread slice. Cover with a ham slice and pineapple spear. Roll up each bread slice around pineapple spear, jelly-roll fashion. Fasten with a toothpick at each end. Beat milk, egg, and spices. Dip each roll into this mixture. Fry in butter, in a large skillet, until golden brown on all sides. Place on absorbent paper to remove excess butter. Serve warm. Makes 8 rolls.
Or try it this way . . . When ready to serve, sprinkle with confectioners' sugar mixed with a dash of powdered ginger.

The Gourmet Way

Orange Marmalade Bread

Fruity, chewy, crunchy with nuts, this tea-type bread, sliced thin and buttered, makes perfect sandwiches.

2 1/2 cups sifted flour
1 tablespoon baking powder
1 teaspoon salt
1/2 cup honey
2 tablespoons soft butter
3 eggs, beaten
1 cup orange marmalade
1 tablespoon grated orange rind
1 cup finely chopped pecans

Sift flour with baking powder and salt. In bowl, beat together honey, butter, and eggs until smooth. Stir in marmalade and orange rind. Mix well. Add flour mixture, stirring until well blended. Stir in nuts. Bake in greased loaf pan, in 350° oven, about 1 hour, or until cake tester inserted in center of loaf comes out clean. Cool 10 minutes in pan, then remove and cool completely on a wire rack—it won't slice well unless completely cooled.

Cream Cheese Alsatian

14 slices white bread
2 3-ounce packages cream cheese
1/4 cup creamy French dressing
1/4 cup chopped celery

1/4 cup chopped pecans
2 tablespoons chopped ripe olives
4 teaspoons chopped parsley

Soften cream cheese and blend with French dressing until smooth. Add celery, pecans, olives, and parsley. Spread on 7 slices bread, top with remaining slices.

Good companions . . . Well-drained canned peach and pear halves, with dabs of bright jelly in their centers, can rest on a ring of lettuce leaves around a platter of these sandwiches and turn them into quite a dish. Or omit the jelly and pass a sauceboat of French dressing for the fruit.

Walnut-Pimento Sandwich

6 slices brown or nut bread,
  buttered
1/2 cup chopped walnuts
1/2 cup chopped pimentos

1 3-ounce package cream
  cheese
1/2 cup mayonnaise
1/8 teaspoon salt

Combine all ingredients except bread. Spread on 3 slices bread, top with remaining slices.

Nut Pinwheels

2 lengthwise slices
  whole-wheat bread
  (cut from unsliced
  sandwich loaf)
1 3-ounce package cream
  cheese
3 tablespoons milk

3 tablespoons chopped
  parsley
1/8 teaspoon minced onion
1 3-ounce package cream
  cheese
3 tablespoons milk
1 cup chopped nut meats

Combine cream cheese and milk until soft. Add parsley and onion. Remove crusts from bread and spread 1/2 cup cheese-parsley mixture on each slice. Cut each slice crosswise into equal halves. Roll each half slice of bread up, jelly-roll fashion. Combine cream cheese and milk until soft. Cover the outside of each roll with a thin coating of cream cheese, then roll in chopped nut meats. Wrap each roll in waxed paper, twisting ends of paper. Place on a flat surface so that roll rests on last turn of bread; chill. *To serve:* Unwrap and cut each roll into 6 slices. Makes 24 sandwiches.

Rich and Rosy

12 slices buttered nut bread
1 cup cream cheese,
  softened

1/2 can jellied cranberry
  sauce, crushed
6 orange slices

Spread softened cream cheese on 6 slices buttered nut bread. Then spread thinly with crushed jellied cranberry sauce. Top with remaining bread slices. Garnish with orange slices.

Keep in mind . . . This combination can be quieted down or fancied up. To quiet down, serve on toasted white bread. To go all out, serve open-face on Boston brown bread, and instead of crushing the cranberry jelly try cutting it into shapes with a small cookie cutter before laying it atop the cream cheese.

The Gourmet Way

Banana-Walnut Bread

Make "social occasion" sandwiches of thin slices of this delicious bread, spread with butter or cream cheese, with honey butter or—marvelous surprise—lime marmalade.

2 1/2 cups sifted flour
3 teaspoons baking powder
1/2 teaspoon salt
1 cup sugar
1/4 cup soft butter
1 egg, beaten
1 cup mashed ripe bananas
2 tablespoons grated orange rind
1/2 cup milk
1 cup chopped walnuts

Sift flour with baking powder and salt. In a bowl, beat sugar, butter, and egg together until smooth. Add bananas, orange rind, milk; mix well. Add flour mixture. Beat until just smooth. Stir in nuts. Bake in greased loaf pan, in 350° oven, about 1 hour, or until cake tester inserted in center of loaf comes out clean. Cool 10 minutes in pan. Remove to rack and cool completely before serving. Cuts better if you restrain your impatience until the following day; when cooled, wrap in foil to keep the loaf fresh.

Mushroom-Chive Cheese

6 slices white or
whole-wheat bread
1/2 tablespoon butter

1/4 cup chopped mushrooms
1/3 cup chive cream cheese

Melt butter in a skillet; add mushrooms and sauté until done. Combine with chive cream cheese. Spread on 3 slices bread, top with remaining slices.
Good companions . . . These are fine company for a meat salad—beef in aspic, perhaps.

Cheese and Anchovy I

12 slices bread	1/2 teaspoon dry mustard
3/4 cup cream cheese	Lemon juice
1/4 cup anchovy butter	

Mix cream cheese and anchovy butter and mustard. Add lemon juice to taste. Spread on 6 slices bread, top with remaining slices.

Anchovy Butter: Cream together 1/4 cup softened butter, 1 to 2 teaspoons anchovy paste, few drops onion juice, few drops lemon juice, dash of cayenne pepper.

Cheese and Anchovy II

Thin-sliced bread	Chopped capers
Cream cheese	
Anchovies, pounded, or anchovy paste	

Mix 2 parts of cream cheese with 1 part pounded anchovies or anchovy paste. Add capers. Spread on bread, serve open-face, cut in fingers or triangles.

Or try this . . . Don't use the capers in the filling, but instead sprinkle over tops of sandwiches before serving.

Creamy Anchovies

12 slices white bread	1/4 cup chopped stuffed olives or ripe olives
1 small can anchovy fillets	
1 cup softened cream cheese	

Mash anchovy fillets into cream cheese. Mix in olives. Spread on 6 slices bread, top with remaining slices.

Even better . . . For dress-up serving, spread Creamy Anchovies on tiny rolls. Garnish with radishes, watercress, parsley.

Pimento Cream

6 slices bread	2 pimentos, finely chopped
1 3-ounce package cream cheese	Salt
1 teaspoon Worcestershire sauce	

Thoroughly blend cream cheese with Worcestershire sauce and mix with pimentos to a smooth paste. Spread on 3 slices bread, top with remaining slices.

Even better . . . Try these browned on a waffle iron.

Cheese-Ham Ribbons

2 lengthwise slices
   whole-wheat bread (cut
   from unsliced
   1 1/2-pound loaf)
1 lengthwise slice white bread
   (cut from unsliced
   1 1/2-pound loaf)

1 3-ounce can deviled ham
1 3-ounce package cream
   cheese
3 tablespoons soft butter

Combine deviled ham and cream cheese. Spread each slice of bread with butter. Spread half of the cheese-ham mixture on 1 slice of whole-wheat bread. Top with white bread slice, buttered side down; spread with remaining mixture. Top with second slice of whole-wheat bread, buttered side down. Wrap in waxed paper, twisting ends of paper; chill for several hours. *To serve:* Unwrap and cut sandwich loaf crosswise into 16 sections.

Jack-O'-Lanterns

18 slices whole-wheat bread
1/2 cup apple butter
3/4 cup pimento cream cheese
   spread

2 teaspoons lemon juice
Raisins
6 strips green pepper

Cut each slice of bread into a 3-inch circle with a round cookie cutter. Spread 2 teaspoons apple butter on 12 circles. Stack 2 circles together; top with plain circle. Press each stack of 3 together gently. Combine pimento cream cheese and lemon juice. Frost top and sides of each loaf with cheese mixture. Decorate top of loaves with raisins placed so they represent the eyes, nose, and mouth of a Jack-O'-Lantern. Press on green-pepper strips to represent the stem of each pumpkin. Makes 6 servings.

Cream Cheese Stand-bys

Mix cream cheese with one of the following.

1. chili sauce
2. 1/4 of small clove of garlic, minced
3. chopped nuts
4. chopped walnuts plus a small amount of tomato sauce to color
5. chopped olives, black or green
6. tomato chutney
7. watercress
8. mustard, salt, and cayenne pepper
9. chopped olives and chopped nuts
10. chopped cooked ham and a pinch of dry mustard

New Ham-and-Cheese

8 slices rye bread, buttered	1/2 cup cream cheese
1/2 teaspoon dry mustard	1 cup chopped cooked ham

Cream mustard and cheese together. Add ham and mix well. Spread on 4 slices bread, top with remaining slices. Makes 4.

Orange-Mince

16 slices whole-wheat bread, buttered	2 3-ounce packages cream cheese
1 9-ounce package mincemeat	2 tablespoons orange juice
1/2 cup water	1/2 teaspoon grated orange rind

Crumble mincemeat into saucepan, add water. Stir over low heat until lumps are thoroughly broken. Bring to a boil and boil briskly, stirring often, until mixture is almost dry, about 3 minutes. While mincemeat cools, let cream cheese stand at room temperature until softened. Mash cheese with a fork and gradually blend in orange juice and rind. Spread cream-cheese mixture generously on 8 slices of bread. On remaining 8 slices of bread, spread cooled mincemeat. Put cheese-spread bread, filling side down, on mincemeat-spread bread. 8 sandwiches.

Make-Ahead Wafflewiches

8 slices rye sandwich bread	Melted butter
1 8-ounce package cream cheese	

Divide cheese in quarters. Spread on 4 slices bread, top with remaining bread. Brush outside of sandwiches with melted butter. Toast in waffle iron until golden. Wrap and freeze. *To serve:* Heat oven to 400° F. Unwrap frozen sandwiches. Bake 10 minutes, turning once. Or toast twice in toaster.

Cherry-Cream Cheese Pinwheels

1 loaf unsliced day-old white bread	12 green Maraschino cherries, drained
2 3-ounce packages cream cheese	or
2 tablespoons milk	3 pineapple spears

Let cream cheese stand at room temperature until softened. Gradually blend in milk. Remove crusts from bread loaf; cut lengthwise into 3 equal slices. Divide cream-cheese mixture into 3 parts. Spread a portion on each bread slice. At one end of each bread slice lay 4 cherries or a pineapple spear. Beginning at this end, roll bread as for jelly roll. Spread a little cream-cheese mixture on the last lap of bread to make it stick. Wrap each roll and refrigerate. *To serve:* Slice into 1/4-inch sandwiches. Makes 30.

The Good Garnishes

You don't bring a roast to the table without its little complement of added attractions . . . vegetable, potato, salad. Why treat a sandwich any less generously? From the most casual children's-lunch variety to one of our gourmet-worthy Supremes, a sandwich worth serving is worth serving well, which means with garnishes. They add decoration, vitamins, texture contrast, taste-appeal, and altogether up-grade your offering into the real meal it ought to be.

Straight from the market shelves come olives, relishes, pickles, potato chips, potato- and cheese-stick crisps, jams, jellies, preserves, nuts, pickled and spiced peaches, and crabapples (and how about kumquats?)—any number of yours-for-the-opening tidbits to dress up your sandwich plates. These are fine for times when you're hurried, often just right for what you're serving even when time is not a factor. Don't forget whole-berry cranberry sauce as well as the jellied variety. Keep an eye out for elegant marinated artichoke hearts and wonderful Italian eggplant appetizer in cans and jars.

Then turn to the vegetable bins for new ideas: thin-sliced radishes or radish roses (make 4 or 6 cuts into radishes from the root end toward the leaf end, but not through; crisp in water in refrigerator, and the sections will open out into flower-like form) . . . cucumber slices or spears . . . green-pepper circles or spears . . . tiny beets, cooked, drained, and seasoned, or marinated in French dressing . . . small, white raw mushroom caps, as they come or French-dressed . . . thin-sliced turnips, carrot curls crisped in cold water . . . celery stalks cut into narrow strips down toward, but not through, the leaf end, then crisped in cold water so that they fan out decoratively . . . and now you take it from here!

For special occasions, here are three marvelous make-ahead relishes that taste as though days, and not minutes, had gone into their preparation. The big secret is not the time you put into making them, but the length of time you leave them to "marry" their flavors. Make them your specialties-of-the-house.

Added thought . . . Almost any cooked vegetable, marinated in a zippy French dressing, makes a delightful go-with for your sandwiches. And never forget deviled eggs to add taste and substance to your sandwich-based meal. Devil them in the usual way—with mayonnaise to moisten the yolks and mustard and cayenne to perk up the flavor—or work added wonders with capers, deviled ham, mashed skinless and boneless sardines, some snipped chives or chopped shallots. Chopped mushrooms add a what's-that? texture. Shredded smoked salmon lends delightful taste as well as eye-appeal in the combination of coral salmon and golden egg yolk.

Cider-Bean Relish

1 cup sugar	1/4 teaspoon salt
1/2 cup cider vinegar	1 1-pound can wax beans,
3 tablespoons prepared	drained, or 9 ounces
mustard	fresh wax beans,
1/2 teaspoon minced onion	cooked

Combine all except beans in saucepan; bring to boil. Stir until sugar is dissolved. Add beans, simmer 5 minutes. Refrigerate overnight or longer, covered.

Tarragon Mushrooms

2/3 cup tarragon vinegar	Dash fresh-ground pepper
1/2 cup salad oil	2 tablespoons water
1 clove garlic, finely	1 medium onion, sliced
chopped	2 pints fresh mushroom
1 tablespoon sugar	caps (no stems)
1 1/2 teaspoons salt	

Combine, cover, refrigerate several hours or overnight.

Honey Beets

1/4 cup honey
1/2 to 1 teaspoon shredded
 orange peel
1/4 cup orange juice
1/4 cup lemon juice
Dash salt
 1 1-pound can miniature
 whole beets, drained

Combine all except beets, mix well. Add beets, making sure there is enough liquid to cover them completely. Refrigerate several hours or overnight, stirring occasionally.

Mainstay Meats

Most substantial meals, from snack to banquet and all the infinite variations between, are built around a meat dish of some kind. And there is a corollary to that premise: any kind of meal—yes, from snack to banquet—can be built around a meat *sandwich* . . . the right one. Here are sandwiches of intriguing variety. Some are simple, some elaborate. Some will appeal to young tastes, while others should be saved to offer only to more educated palates.

Italian Beef

1 1-pound loaf Italian or French bread	1 teaspoon salt
1 1/2 cups beef stock	1 bay leaf
1 cup water	1/4 teaspoon instant granulated garlic
3 tablespoons tomato paste	20 slices cooked beef (1/8 inch thick)
1/2 teaspoon dry red pepper, crushed	

Combine beef stock, water, tomato paste, crushed red pepper, salt, bay leaf, and garlic in a 10-inch skillet; cover and simmer for 45 minutes to 1 hour. Add sliced cooked beef to seasoned stock in skillet and heat together an additional 15 minutes. While meat is heating through, cut Italian bread in half lengthwise. Then cut crosswise into 10 sections. *To serve:* Dip each bread piece into stock. Arrange 2 beef slices on the bottom half, completing with top half of bread slice. Serve hot. Makes 10 sandwiches.

Barbecued Steakettes

10 sliced sandwich buns	2 teaspoons soy sauce
1/2 cup French dressing	10 cube steaks
1/4 cup chili sauce	1 can French-fried onions

Combine French dressing, chili sauce, and soy sauce. Place cube steaks on a grill over hot coals. Dip 1 1/2 tablespoons barbecue sauce onto steak. Grill steak on one side, turn, and dip 1 1/2 tablespoons sauce onto other side. Grill steak on other side. *To serve:* Place a Barbecued Steakette and some French-fried onions in each heated roll. Makes 10 sandwiches. *Or try this* . . . Use frozen cooked onion rings, heating according to package directions.

The Supreme Sandwich

Pot Roast of Beef

Pot roast of beef sandwiches served with a delicious jellied relish loaf—they will make your reputation as a cook. These are lots of trouble, and worth every bit of it! Fortunately, it's the kind of trouble that can be coped with the day before—by serving day you'll be in fine shape.

For Beef:

4-5 pound top-quality beef pot roast
2 carrots, scraped and quartered
2 onions, quartered
2 ribs celery, cut in chunks
2 cloves garlic, minced
1/2 cup chopped parsley
1 bay leaf
Salt

For Red Relish Layer:

2 envelopes unflavored gelatin
1 cup tomato juice
1 cup pan gravy from pot roast
2 tablespoons tomato paste
1 tablespoon prepared mustard
2 teaspoons onion juice
3 drops Tabasco sauce
1 cup chopped celery
1/4 cup chopped sweet pickle

For White Relish Layer:

1 envelope unflavored gelatin
1/2 cup dill pickle juice
1 cup pan gravy from pot roast
1/2 cup mayonnaise
2 tablespoons prepared horseradish, drained
Salt, white pepper
2 tablespoons chopped chives
1 cup chopped cucumber (seeds and pulp removed)
1/2 cup chopped dill pickle

(Continued)

(Continued)

Brown pot roast on all sides. Put into a Dutch oven with carrots, onions, celery, garlic, parsley, bay leaf, 2 cups water. Season with salt. Cook at low simmer until fork tender. Remove meat and cool, then refrigerate. Reserve pan gravy for next steps.

For Red Relish Layer: Soften gelatin in 1/2 cup of the tomato juice. Measure pan gravy from roast, add water to make 2 cups. To 1 cup of this gravy, add softened gelatin in tomato juice, remaining 1/2 cup tomato juice, tomato paste, mustard, onion juice, and Tabasco. Heat until gelatin is dissolved. Cool, refrigerate until consistency of unbeaten egg white. Add celery, pickle. Pour into loaf pan. Refrigerate.

For White Relish Layer: Soften gelatin in pickle juice. Place remaining cup pan gravy in saucepan, add softened gelatin, heat until gelatin is dissolved. Cool, stir in mayonnaise, horseradish; season with salt and white pepper. Refrigerate until consistency of unbeaten egg white. Stir in chives. cucumber, dill pickle. Pour over stiffened layer of Red Relish and refrigerate overnight.

To make sandwiches: Place overlapping slices of pot roast on buttered slices of bread. Season with salt and pepper. Cover with a 1/2-inch slice of jellied relish. Surround bread with curly greens (chicory, lettuce, escarole) and serve brightly open-face, so that the jewel-like jellied layer gets a chance to show.

Beef Tartare

4 slices white bread, buttered	2 tablespoons capers
1 pound beef sirloin, raw	2 tablespoons chopped parsley
2 tablespoons chopped onion	4 egg yolks
2 tablespoons chopped pickled beetroot	1 teaspoon salt
	Pinch pepper

Scrape beef, or put once through meat grinder. Divide among the slices of bread and spread evenly. Garnish with onion, beetroot, capers, and parsley. Serve with yolks of egg, ensconced each in its shell, in the middle of each piece. Sprinkle with salt and pepper. Makes 4 servings.

Jumbo Steakwiches

Sandwich:

1 loaf round, unsliced sourdough bread	Instant meat tenderizer
1 to 1 1/2 pounds round steak, 3/4 inch thick	Zesty Sauce

Zesty Sauce

> 2 8-ounce cans tomato sauce with mushrooms
> 1 small onion, chopped
> 1/4 cup red wine
> 2 tablespoons brown sugar
> 2 cloves garlic, mashed
> 1 teaspoon salt
> 1/2 teaspoon seasoned pepper

Start coals for barbecueing. Combine all sauce ingredients and simmer 15 minutes. Set aside. Slice bread loaf horizontally so as to have 2 large slices for sandwich. (Note: If loaf is thick, slice 1 1/2-inch thick slices horizontally from top and bottom —save center section for toasted garlic bread, cheese bread, etc.) Set aside while grilling steak. When coals are ready, apply instant meat tenderizer to steak, following package directions. Place on rack 2 to 3 inches from coals. Grill 3 to 4 minutes on each side. Brush with Zesty Sauce and grill 2 minutes; turn, brush with sauce and continue grilling 2 minutes more. (This cooking time yields a medium steak—cook longer for well done, or less time for rare.) Slice steak diagonally into strips. Brush bottom bread slice generously with Zesty Sauce. Arrange strips of steak in overlapping layers over bread; spread on more sauce. Top with second bread slice. Cut in wedges. *Afterthought* . . . To hold sandwiches together and to add a good measure of good taste, spear each wedge with a skewer threaded with olives, cherry tomatoes, onion rings, or your choice of relishes. And, of course, if you're not an outdoor-grill addict, these sandwiches can be easily accomplished in the broiler of your kitchen stove.

Beef-and-Onion

4 hamburger rolls, buttered and grilled	1 medium onion, chopped and browned in butter
1 can chopped beef	Lettuce
	1 tomato, sliced

Lightly brown chopped beef in skillet with onion. Arrange on grilled rolls with lettuce and sliced tomatoes.

Teriyaki Kabobs

6 sliced frankfurter buns
2 pounds boneless sirloin
   steak, 1 inch thick
1 cup soy sauce

1/4 cup granulated sugar
2 cloves garlic, thinly sliced
2 small pieces ginger root

Cut meat into strips 1/4 inch wide. To make a marinade, combine soy sauce, sugar, sliced garlic, and ginger root. In a flat, oblong casserole, place meat strips, add marinade, and let stand for at least 2 hours. Thread meat onto skewers. Broil kabobs at 500° F. or grill over hot coals, turning them so they will cook on all sides. *To serve:* Place a grilled kabob in each heated bun. Makes 6 kabobs.
Note: These kabobs freeze well, and may be prepared up to a month in advance.

Steak Plus

6 sliced sandwich buns,
   heated
1/2 cup ketchup
1/2 cup salad oil
3 teaspoons smoke flavor

2 teaspoons Worcestershire
   sauce
1 teaspoon salt
1/8 teaspoon pepper
6 cube steaks

Combine ketchup, salad oil, smoke flavor, Worcestershire sauce, salt and pepper. Place cube steaks in marinade, and turn meat over after an hour. Continue marinating another hour. Grill on each side, serve in buns. Makes 6 sandwiches.

Cheese-and-Beef Sandwich

8 slices whole-wheat bread,
   buttered
3/4 cup snipped dried beef,
   firmly packed

1/3 cup mayonnaise
1/2 cup grated process
   American cheese

Rinse dried beef well. Dry. Combine beef, mayonnaise, cheese. Spread on 4 slices of bread and top with remaining slices.
Afterthought . . . These are make-aheads which can profitably spend some time in the freezer.

The Gourmet Way
Roast Beef for Sandwiches

Roast beef, rare—is there any other way?—makes the best of the man-hearty sandwiches.

1 8-pound boneless sirloin roast

Wipe meat with a damp cloth. Place on a rack in a shallow pan. Roast, uncovered, at 325° F. until meat thermometer reaches 140° F. Slice thinly, serve hot —several slices per serving—on hard rolls, sandwich buns, or rye bread. Makes 16-20 big sandwiches.

Point to remember . . . If you're going to serve the beef cold, take it out of the oven a few minutes before the thermometer reaches the 140°, or "rare," mark—the meat cooks a bit more, out of the oven.

Longshoreman's Special

8 slices rye or white bread, buttered	Pepper
1 cup cooked chopped roast beef	2 tablespoons onion, minced
1/4 to 1/2 cup mayonnaise	1/2 cup chopped celery
Salt	Parsley or watercress

Combine all ingredients except bread. Spread on 4 slices bread, top with remaining slices. Makes 4 hearty sandwiches.

Keep in mind . . . Chopped tongue, ham, veal, or corned beef may replace the roast beef. Mustard may be added to the seasonings, chopped green pepper to the celery. Make it as you like it! And serve it with tomato wedges, thick cucumber rounds, dill pickle spears. This is a real-meal sandwich.

Curry-Beef

8 slices bread	Cucumber slices
1/2 stick butter	Watercress
Curry powder	Salt
Roast beef, sliced	Pepper
Tomato slices	Vinegar

Knead butter with curry powder to taste, and spread on bread. Cover 4 slices of bread with thinly sliced roast beef, tomato slices, cucumber slices, and watercress leaves. Season with salt, pepper, vinegar. Top with remaining slices of bread.

Barbecued Beef Sandwiches

8 sandwich buns, toasted   2 cans chopped beef

Barbecue Sauce

1/4 cup chopped onion
1 tablespoon butter
1/8 teaspoon pepper
4 teaspoons sugar
1 teaspoon dry mustard
4 teaspoons Worcestershire sauce
1/2 cup ketchup
1/4 cup vinegar
1/4 cup water

To make barbecue sauce, cook onion in butter until clear, add remaining ingredients and bring to a boil. Slice chopped beef and brush with the barbecue sauce. Broil slices approximately 3 minutes, turn, brush again with the sauce and broil an additional 3 minutes. Serve barbecued beef on toasted·buns. Makes 8 servings.

Afterthought . . . Do these on the grill outdoors if you like—cook approximately the same length of time.

French-Roll Beef

8 French rolls, split, toasted, and buttered
1 cup chopped onion
2 tablespoons vegetable oil
2 8-ounce cans tomato sauce
1/4 cup water

1 teaspoon salt
1 to 2 teaspoons chili powder
2 cups thinly sliced cooked roast beef, pot roast, or barbecued beef

Sauté onion in vegetable oil. Add tomato sauce, water, salt, and chili powder. Simmer 10 minutes. Add beef and heat. Serve on toasted French rolls. Serve hot or wrap in foil and freeze for future use. If frozen, do not defrost, heat in 400° F. oven for 20 minutes, opening foil for last 3 minutes.

Chutney-Lamb

8 slices white bread
1 cup chopped cooked lamb
1/4 cup chopped chutney

3 tablespoons mayonnaise or whipped cream cheese

Mix lamb, chutney, and mayonnaise and spread on 4 slices bread. Top with remaining slices. Makes 4 sandwiches.

Leftovers Lunch

8 slices bread
1 pound leftover roast veal
   (2 cups)
1/2 small onion
2 tablespoons melted butter

1 teaspoon dry mustard
3 tablespoons mayonnaise
1/2 teaspoon celery salt
Pinch of cayenne pepper

Several hours ahead: Put meat and onion through food chopper, using fine blade. Mix in remaining ingredients. Refrigerate.
To serve: Spread on 4 slices of bread, top with other slices.

Uitsmijter

1 or 2 slices of white bread,
   buttered
Cold roast veal
1 or 2 fried eggs

Salt
Pepper
Capers

On 1 or 2 slices of white bread place liberal portion of cold, cooked, thinly sliced veal. Top with 1 or 2 fried eggs. Season. Sprinkle 2 or 3 capers on each egg.
On the run . . . In Holland, *"uitsmijter"* is what you order if you have 5 minutes flat in which to eat something substantial. With 1 egg it is called a *"halve"* (half) *uitsmijter,* and can be eaten even more quickly.

Lamb à la Russe

8 slices rye or pumpernickel
   bread
1 cup sour cream
2-3 teaspoons packaged
   dehydrated onion salad
   dressing mix

2 teaspoons prepared
   horseradish, well
   drained
12 slices cooked roast lamb
Lettuce leaves
Pickle slices

Blend sour cream, salad dressing mix, and horseradish. Spread on 4 slices bread, using about 1 tablespoon for each slice. Arrange meat on bread. Top with remaining dressing, using about 2 tablespoons for each sandwich. Cover with lettuce and remaining bread. Cut sandwiches diagonally into 2 or 4 pieces. Serve with pickle slices. Makes 4 sandwiches.
Or try it this way . . . Make open-face sandwiches with this combination. Prepare dressing mixture, spreading about 1 tablespoon on each slice of bread. Place 2 bread slices on each plate. Arrange meat and lettuce on breads. Top with remaining dressing. Serve with pickle slices. Makes 4 servings.

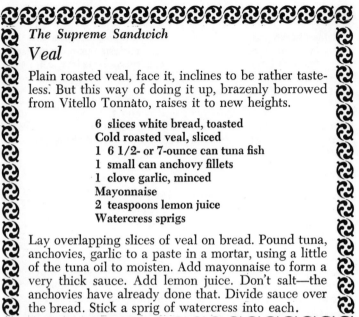

The Supreme Sandwich
Veal

Plain roasted veal, face it, inclines to be rather taste-less. But this way of doing it up, brazenly borrowed from Vitello Tonnàto, raises it to new heights.

6 slices white bread, toasted
Cold roasted veal, sliced
1 6 1/2- or 7-ounce can tuna fish
1 small can anchovy fillets
1 clove garlic, minced
Mayonnaise
2 teaspoons lemon juice
Watercress sprigs

Lay overlapping slices of veal on bread. Pound tuna, anchovies, garlic to a paste in a mortar, using a little of the tuna oil to moisten. Add mayonnaise to form a very thick sauce. Add lemon juice. Don't salt—the anchovies have already done that. Divide sauce over the bread. Stick a sprig of watercress into each.

Barbecued Lamb Buns

8 sesame sandwich buns,
   split
1 pound ground lamb
1/2 teaspoon garlic salt
1/4 teaspoon curry powder
3/4 cup tomato paste

2 tablespoons brown
   sugar
3 tablespoons lemon juice
1 1/2 tablespoons chopped
   parsley
1 teaspoon Worcestershire
   sauce

Combine lamb, garlic salt, and curry powder; brown in a skillet. Combine tomato paste, brown sugar, lemon juice, parsley, and Worcestershire sauce. Add to meat; simmer 10 minutes. Heat buns. Fill each bun with 1/4 cup hot barbecued lamb. Makes 8 sandwiches.

Minted Lamb

8 slices white bread, buttered
1 cup cold cooked lamb, finely
   chopped

1 tablespoon chopped mint
Mayonnaise

Combine lamb and mint with enough mayonnaise to make spreadable. Spread on 4 slices bread, top with remaining slices.

Swiss Porkies

8 slices bread
1/2 pound Swiss cheese,
    grated
1 teaspoon dry mustard
1/4 cup chopped stuffed green
    olives

1/3 cup mayonnaise
8 strips bacon, fried crisp
1/2 cup butter or margarine,
    softened

Combine cheese, mustard, olives; toss lightly with fork. Add mayonnaise; blend well. Spread 4 slices bread with cheese mixture; top each with 2 strips crisp bacon; top with remaining slices of bread. Spread outside of each sandwich with butter. Brown sandwiches on both sides on griddle or in fry pan over medium heat—about 7 minutes. Makes 4 servings.

Ham on a Waffle

1 1/3 cups ground, cooked
    ham
2 tablespoons prepared
    mustard

1 package frozen waffles
1 egg
1/3 cup of milk
2 tablespoons butter

Mix ham with prepared mustard. Spread ham mixture on unthawed frozen waffles, pressing 2 together to make sandwich. Beat egg slightly. Stir in milk. Dip waffle sandwiches into egg-milk mixture. In hot butter in skillet, sauté sandwiches until golden on both sides. Makes 3 servings.
Added attraction . . . Serve with fresh-fruit salad platter for Sunday-night supper. A fork makes eating easier.

Bacon-Corn Scramble

3 round buns, split, toasted,
    and buttered
1/2 pound bacon
2 tablespoons bacon
    drippings
2 tablespoons finely
    chopped onion

1 tablespoon chopped green
    pepper
1 8-ounce can cream-style
    corn
1/4 teaspoon celery salt
1/8 teaspoon pepper
3 eggs, well beaten

Fry bacon until crisp. Remove from skillet and keep hot. Sauté onion and green pepper in drippings. Add corn and seasonings. When corn is hot and bubbling, turn heat to low. Mix some corn mixture into beaten eggs and add eggs to corn in skillet. Stir frequently until eggs are set. Spoon onto buttered bun halves. Top each serving with crisp bacon slices. Makes 6 servings.

Bacon-Avocado Crisps

24 slices white bread,
  toasted
24 slices bacon
 1 medium avocado
1/2 cup commercial sour
  cream

1 tablespoon chopped
  chives
2 teaspoons grated lemon
  rind
1/8 teaspoon salt
 3 medium tomatoes, each
  cut into 4 slices

Fry bacon slices until crisp; drain on paper toweling. Peel avocado and remove seed; cut into chunks. Blend avocado and sour cream, using electric mixer or blender, until smooth; add chives, lemon rind, and salt. Spread about 4 teaspoons avocado-cream mixture on each of 12 toast slices. Top avocado with 2 slices of bacon, a tomato slice, and another piece of toast. *Take note:* Make avocado mixture as close to serving time as possible—not more than an hour ahead.

Frilled Bacon Buns

 6 hamburger buns, split,
  buttered
1 1/2 cups (6 ounces) grated
  process American
  cheese
 2 tablespoons minced
  onion

6 to 8 crumbled crisp
  bacon slices
1/4 cup ketchup
 1 tablespoon prepared
  mustard
 3 cups tossed green salad
French dressing

Mix cheese with onion, bacon, ketchup, mustard. Spread bottom half of each bun with cheese mixture. Place both halves of buns on cookie sheet. Broil about 5 minutes, or until cheese is melted and tops are toasted. Heap green salad, tossed with dressing, on top halves of buns. Makes 6 servings.

Green Bean Buns

 5 hamburger buns, split,
  buttered
5-6 strips crisp bacon,
  crumbled
3/4 cup finely chopped cooked
  green beans
 1 tablespoon chopped
  pimento

2 teaspoons minced onion
2 tablespoons French
  dressing
2 tablespoons mayonnaise
  or salad dressing

Combine bacon, beans, pimento, onion, French dressing, and mayonnaise. Spread between bun halves. Makes 5 sandwiches.

The Gourmet Way

Herb Jellies

These jewel-bright jellies are an Epicurean delight. They are wonderful with fowl, game, meats.

Basic ingredients for all recipes:

> 3 1/4 cups sugar
> 1/2 bottle liquid pectin

Also, for Basil Jelly:

> 2 tablespoons basil
> 1 cup tomato juice
> 1/4 cup lemon juice
> 1/4 cup water

Also, for Sweet Marjoram Jelly:

> 2 tablespoons sweet marjoram
> 1 cup pineapple juice
> 1/4 cup lime juice
> 1/4 cup water

Also, for Lemon Thyme Jelly:

> 1 1/2 tablespoons lemon thyme
> 1 cup red Bordeaux
> 1/2 cup water

Also, for Sage Jelly:

> 1 tablespoon sage
> 1 1/4 cups red Burgundy
> 1/4 cup water

Also, for Rosemary Jelly:

> 1 1/2 tablespoons rosemary
> 1/4 cup orange juice
> 1/4 cup lime juice
> 3/4 cup water

To make any one of these jellies: Wash the leaves of the fresh herb—and be sure to use the fresh. Spread them out to dry for a few minutes. Crush the leaves thoroughly with 1/4 cup of the sugar. Stir in the liquid. Simmer for 8 minutes. Bring to a rolling boil. Add the liquid pectin, stirring constantly for 1/2 minute. Skim the jelly. Pour through a fine sieve into glasses. Cover with melted paraffin.

Hot-and-Cold Buns

4 hamburger buns, split
2 cups ground cooked ham
2 tablespoons prepared
    mustard
1/4 chopped green pepper
2 eggs, slightly beaten
2 tablespoons mayonnaise

2 cups Special Potato Salad
4 fresh or canned peach
    halves
1/4 cup brown sugar, packed
2 tablespoons butter
Shredded lettuce

Several hours ahead: Hollow out bun halves slightly. Mix crumbled bread with ham, mustard, green pepper, eggs, and mayonnaise; refrigerate. Rewrap buns to keep fresh. Make Special Potato Salad (see below); refrigerate. *About 10 minutes before serving:* Place lower halves of buns on cookie sheet; heap in meat filling. Sprinkle peach halves with sugar; dot with butter; place on cookie sheet beside buns. Broil slowly, about 5 minutes. Meanwhile, fill top halves of buns with Special Potato Salad. Arrange a hot and cold open sandwich on each plate. Garnish with peach half set in nest of shredded lettuce. Makes 4 servings.

Special Potato Salad

6-8 potatoes, boiled in jackets (about 2 pounds)
1/2 cup oil-and-vinegar dressing
Paprika
4-5 green onions, finely chopped
Mayonnaise
Commercial sour cream
Salt

While potatoes are still hot, peel and slice into deep bowl, adding dressing and sprinkling with paprika and onions as you go. Chill until potatoes are cold. When ready to serve, add mayonnaise, sour cream to the consistency you like. Salt to taste.

Crispy Bananas

8 slices white bread toast
2 bananas, ripe
8 thin slices tomato

8 slices crisp bacon
8 teaspoons mayonnaise or
    salad dressing

Slice bananas twice lengthwise, and once through the center. Place 3 pieces banana on each of 4 slices toast; top each with 2 slices tomato, 2 bacon slices, and 2 teaspoons mayonnaise. Cover with second slice of toast. Makes 4 sandwiches.

Cottage Cheese Hamwiches

8 slices whole-wheat bread, buttered	1 tablespoon finely chopped green pepper
1/2 cup cottage cheese	4 slices boiled ham
1/2 teaspoon minced onion	4 lettuce leaves

Combine cottage cheese, onion, and green pepper. Spread 2 tablespoons cheese mixture over each slice of buttered bread. Place a slice of ham and a lettuce leaf on 4 slices of bread. Top with remaining slices of bread. Makes 4 sandwiches.

Pickle-Pusses

8 slices rye bread, buttered	2 dill pickles
1/2 pound slice of ham	Salad dressing
1 large onion	

Sauté ham until tender, about 20 minutes. Mince ham with onion and pickles. Moisten with salad dressing. Spread on four slices of bread, top with remaining slices.

Sautéed Junior Clubs

12 slices of bread	2 eggs, slightly beaten
6 thin slices boiled ham	1/4 cup milk
Prepared mustard	1/4 teaspoon salt
6 slices Münster cheese	Maple-blended syrup
1/4 cup butter	

Trim crusts from bread. Top half of the bread with ham slices. Spread lightly with mustard; cover with cheese slices, then with remaining bread. Melt butter in large skillet. Blend eggs, milk, and salt. Dip sandwiches quickly into egg mixture. Sauté in butter, turning to brown both sides. Serve hot with syrup. Makes 6 servings.

Baked Beans and Bacon

8 slices of toast	1 medium onion, sliced
1 can baked beans	8 slices of bacon, cut in half
3 large tomatoes, sliced	

Heat beans. Cover toast with a layer of hot beans. Top with tomato and onion slices and 2 strips of bacon. Broil until bacon is crisp under medium heat. Serve immediately. Makes 8 open-face servings.

Or try it this way . . . Canadian bacon instead of regular, and sweet pickle relish on the side.

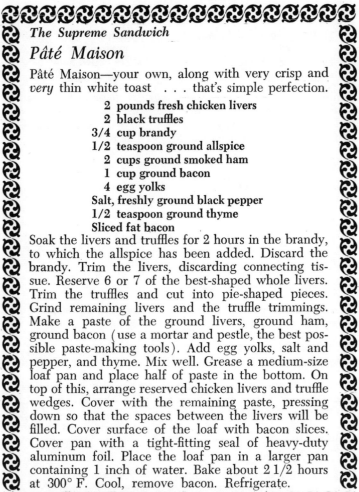

The Supreme Sandwich
Pâté Maison

Pâté Maison—your own, along with very crisp and *very* thin white toast . . . that's simple perfection.

2 pounds fresh chicken livers
2 black truffles
3/4 cup brandy
1/2 teaspoon ground allspice
2 cups ground smoked ham
1 cup ground bacon
4 egg yolks
Salt, freshly ground black pepper
1/2 teaspoon ground thyme
Sliced fat bacon

Soak the livers and truffles for 2 hours in the brandy, to which the allspice has been added. Discard the brandy. Trim the livers, discarding connecting tissue. Reserve 6 or 7 of the best-shaped whole livers. Trim the truffles and cut into pie-shaped pieces. Grind remaining livers and the truffle trimmings. Make a paste of the ground livers, ground ham, ground bacon (use a mortar and pestle, the best possible paste-making tools). Add egg yolks, salt and pepper, and thyme. Mix well. Grease a medium-size loaf pan and place half of paste in the bottom. On top of this, arrange reserved chicken livers and truffle wedges. Cover with the remaining paste, pressing down so that the spaces between the livers will be filled. Cover surface of the loaf with bacon slices. Cover pan with a tight-fitting seal of heavy-duty aluminum foil. Place the loaf pan in a larger pan containing 1 inch of water. Bake about 2 1/2 hours at 300° F. Cool, remove bacon. Refrigerate.

Ham Walnutwich

8 slices white bread, buttered
1 cup cooked ham, finely chopped

1/2 cup walnuts, chopped
1 teaspoon mustard
4 tablespoons thick cream
Salt and pepper

Combine ingredients and spread between slices of bread.

Bacon-Cheese Special

4 sandwich buns, split,
 buttered
8 strips bacon
2 eggs, well beaten
2 cups (1/2 pound)
 shredded Swiss cheese
1/2 teaspoon salt
1/8 teaspoon pepper
1/2 teaspoon paprika
1/2 teaspoon Worcestershire
 sauce
1 teaspoon lemon juice
Dash of garlic salt
Dash of celery salt

Cut bacon strips in half and cook partially. Toast buns under broiler until lightly browned. In a bowl combine eggs, cheese, salt, pepper, paprika, Worcestershire sauce, lemon juice, and salts. Spread on toasted sides of buns; top each with 2 pieces of bacon. Place on baking sheet; broil until cheese is lightly browned and bacon crisp.

Bacon Brunch

4 English muffins
2 red apples
8 slices bacon, halved and
 fried crisp
1 cup shredded sharp Cheddar
 cheese

Core apples but do not peel. Cut each into 4 slices crosswise. Cook halved bacon strips until crisp. Sauté apple rings in bacon fat over low heat until soft, turning to brown each side lightly. Cut English muffins in half and toast lightly. Place an apple ring on each muffin half and cover with shredded Cheddar cheese. Top with bacon strips and broil until cheese melts. Serve hot. Makes 4 servings.

Big-Boy Hero

1 individual French roll
2 tablespoons mayonnaise
2 tablespoons grated
 Parmesan and Romano
 cheese
1/4 teaspoon dried mustard
1/4 teaspoon instant minced
 onion
2 slices fresh tomato
2 slices boiled ham
2 slices mozzarella cheese
2 slices salami

Cut French roll in half, lengthwise. Combine mayonnaise, grated Parmesan and Romano cheese, mustard, and onion. Spread mixture on split roll. On the bottom half of the roll arrange tomatoes, ham, mozzarella cheese, and salami. Cover with top of roll, gashed vertically for easier slicing. Wrap sandwich in aluminum foil and place in 350° F. oven until cheese has melted, about 15 minutes. Serve hot. Makes 1 hero.

Ham Sandwich

4 slices of bread, buttered	Thin slices cucumber
4 slices boiled ham	Parsley
4 tablespoons French Salad (page 191)	

On each piece of buttered bread place a slice of ham, rolled in the shape of a cornet. Fill each cornet with French Salad. Garnish with cucumber and parsley. Makes 4 servings.

Poor-Boy Sandwich

4 hard rolls, sliced in half	12 thin slices cucumber
1 tablespoon vinegar	4 1-ounce slices American
2 tablespoons salad oil	cheese
4 1-ounce slices smoked ham	8 thin slices tomato

Combine vinegar and salad oil; brush on cut surfaces of buns. On each bottom half, place 1 slice ham, 3 slices cucumber, 1 slice cheese (cut to fit bun), and 2 slices tomato. Replace tops of buns. Makes 4 sandwiches.

Ham Savories

4 sandwich buns	1 teaspoon salt
1/4 cup chopped onion	1/2 teaspoon liquid or
2 8-ounce cans tomato sauce	powdered smoke
1/4 cup water	flavoring
2 tablespoons vinegar	1/2 pound cooked ham, diced
1 tablespoon sugar	1/4 pound process cheese,
1 teaspoon prepared mustard	diced

Combine onion, tomato sauce, water, vinegar, sugar, mustard, salt, smoke flavoring. Simmer 20 minutes. Add to ham and cheese, and serve on hot buns. Makes 4 servings.

Yard-Longs

1 loaf French bread	1 cup shredded Cheddar
1/4 cup butter	cheese
2 tablespoons mustard	1/4 cup minced onion
2 cans deviled ham	Dill pickle slices

Cut French bread into 3/4-inch slices down to the bottom crust. Cream together butter and mustard and spread between bread slices. Spread alternate slices with deviled ham and sprinkle shredded cheese on remaining slices. Spoon chopped onion onto the deviled ham and insert pickles into the cheese. Wrap loaf in aluminum foil. Heat in 400° F. oven for 15 minutes. Six to 8 servings.

Ham-Mushroom Specials

6 slices toast, buttered
6 mushrooms, sautéed
3/4 cup finely minced baked ham
1 teaspoon Worcestershire sauce

Mayonnaise
Salt
Pepper

Chop mushrooms and mix with ham. Moisten with Worcestershire sauce and mayonnaise, season with salt and pepper. Spread on 3 slices toast, top with remaining slices. Makes 3 sandwiches.

Party Berrywiches

1 package refrigerator biscuits
1 can deviled ham

1 can jellied cranberry sauce
10 cheese strips

Bake packaged refrigerator biscuits until golden. Split biscuits. Spread with deviled ham. Top with rounds of jellied cranberry sauce, cut to fit the biscuit tops. Add cheese strips. Bake on cookie sheet in medium oven until heated and cheese melts.

Westburger

8 slices toast
1/2 cup coarsely chopped green pepper
1/4 cup chopped onion
2 tablespoons butter
1 cup chopped cooked ham

1 10 1/2-ounce can condensed cream of mushroom soup
6 eggs, slightly beaten
Dash of pepper

Cook green pepper and onion in butter until tender. Add ham; cook until lightly browned. Blend soup, eggs, and pepper; add to ham and vegetables. Cook over low heat, stirring occasionally, until eggs are set. Serve on toast. Makes 8 servings.

Ham Zesties

8 slices bread, buttered
2 teaspoons Worcestershire sauce
1 tablespoon mayonnaise

1 cup chopped ham
3 tablespoons mixed pickle relish

Blend Worcestershire sauce with mayonnaise. Add ham and pickle relish and mix thoroughly. Spread on buttered bread. *Even better* . . . Try toasted or browned in waffle iron.

The Gourmet Way

Homemade Egg Bread

What better company for your best sandwich filling than this egg-rich, moist, flavorful homemade bread?

2 packages active dry yeast
1/2 cup warm water
1/3 cup sugar
1/2 cup shortening
4 teaspoons salt
2 cups milk
1/2 cup cold water
4 eggs, beaten
9 (or more) cups all-purpose flour
Melted butter

Soften yeast in warm water. Combine sugar, shortening, salt in large bowl. Scald milk. Add to bowl, stirring to melt shortening. Add cold water, cool to lukewarm. Add eggs and yeast. Add flour gradually until a stiff dough is formed. Knead on a floured board until satin-smooth—5 minutes or more. Place in a greased bowl; cover. Let rise in a warm place—about 85° F.—until doubled in bulk (1 1/2 to 2 hours). Punch down, let rise again, this time for 1/2 hour. Divide dough into 3 parts, shape into 3 loaves on a floured surface. Place in greased bread pans. Let rise again, in a warm place, about 1 1/4 hours, or until light. Bake in a 375° F. oven 35 to 40 minutes. Brush tops of loaves with melted butter when you take them from the oven—makes a glowing brown crust.

Chewy Ham Sandwiches

8 slices of bread, buttered
3/4 cup cooked ham, finely
  chopped
1/4 cup diced celery
1/2 teaspoon chopped onion
1 1/2 teaspoons prepared
  mustard
1 ripe banana

Combine ham, celery, onion, and mustard. Dice banana and mix lightly with ham mixture. Spread on 4 slices of bread and cover with remaining bread.

Poppy Swiss

6 hamburger buns, split	6 slices packaged process
1/2 cup soft butter	swiss cheese
1/4 cup minced onion	6 slices boiled ham
1/4 cup prepared mustard	Monosodium glutamate
1 tablespoon poppy seeds	

Mix butter with onion, mustard, poppy seeds. Spread cut surfaces and tops of hamburger buns with butter mixture. Put buns back together with Swiss cheese and boiled ham slices, sprinkled with monosodium glutamate, as filling. Place on cookie sheet. Bake 15 minutes in 350° F. oven. 6 servings.

To top it off . . . Serve with a big fresh-fruit plate to double as dessert.

Super Submarines

2 cans Southern-style biscuits	1 to 2 packages (4 ounces
Melted butter	each) Liederkranz cheese
Sesame seeds or poppy seeds	2 medium-size red onions,
4 to 6 slices boiled ham	thinly sliced

Remove biscuits from cans; press 5 biscuits together and re-shape into a small French-bread-type loaf. Place on baking sheet. Repeat 3 more times. (This makes 4 small loaves.) Brush each biscuit loaf with melted butter and sprinkle generously with seeds. Bake in a 450° F. oven until loaves are browned, about 15 minutes. Cool. Split each loaf in half, lengthwise; spread each half with butter. On bottom half of each loaf, place a slice of ham and spread it with Liederkranz cheese; top with sliced onion. Place seeded half atop each. Makes 4 sandwiches.

Added thought . . . Serve these with assorted relishes and man-size mugs of hot coffee.

Chopped Ham and Cheese Waffle Sandwiches

8 slices of bread	1/2 cup shredded Cheddar
8 thin slices chopped ham	cheese
Mustard	

Butter 8 slices of bread on both sides. Place 2 thin slices of chopped ham on each of 4 pieces of bread. Spread with mustard and sprinkle lightly with freshly shredded Cheddar cheese. Top with remaining bread slices and bake in waffle iron until bread is golden brown and cheese is melted. Makes 4 sandwiches.

Note . . . These can also be done under the broiler, but they're more fun the waffle way.

✿✿✿✿✿✿✿✿✿✿✿✿✿✿✿✿✿✿✿✿✿✿✿✿

The Gourmet Way

Pan Bagna

A favorite in Monaco, Pan Bagna is marvelous in summer with a glass of wine or beer. Try serving with a Parmesan-sprinkled green salad.

1 loaf of Italian bread	Basil or parsley
Garlic	Fillet of anchovies
Olive oil	Black olives
Tomato slices	Onion rings
Hard-cooked eggs, sliced	

Cut bread in half lengthwise. Rub with garlic, then turn over and soak in olive oil. Fill with tomato slices (not too ripe) and egg slices; sprinkle with basil or parsley. Add layer of fillets of anchovies, black olives, onion rings. Top with other half of bread. Cut in thick diagonal chunks.

✿✿✿✿✿✿✿✿✿✿✿✿✿✿✿✿✿✿✿✿✿✿✿✿

Ham and Cheese Savory

8 thin slices of stale bread, crusts trimmed	4 slices ham (1/2 ounce each)
4 slices (1/4 ounce each) Gouda or Edam cheese	Butter

Cut the cheese and the ham to the size of the bread slices. Put 1 slice of ham and 1 slice of cheese between two slices of bread. Spread the outside of the sandwiches with butter. Fry until golden brown and crisp. Makes 4 sandwiches.
Perfect partner . . . Potato salad with chopped chives.

Simple Supper

8 slices of bread	4 slices Gruyère cheese
4 slices of boiled ham	Butter

Remove the crusts from the bread, and butter evenly. Place a slice of ham on 1 piece of bread, and a piece of cheese on the other, and sandwich the two together. Fry in butter until the bread is crisp and the cheese melts. Makes 4 sandwiches.
Even better . . . Mustard butter on the bread perks this up.

Sunshine Sandwich

4 slices of bread, buttered
4 slices of boiled ham
1 onion, chopped

4 egg yolks
1 bunch chives, finely chopped

Chop ham, mix with onion, and spread on buttered bread. Make a "well" in center of each spread slice, and slide in a raw egg yolk. Sprinkle with chives. Makes 4 servings.

Saucy Pork Buns

6 hamburger buns, split, toasted, and buttered
1 8-ounce can tomato sauce
1/2 cup water
1/2 cup finely chopped onion

1/4 cup chopped green pepper
1 teaspoon salt
1 1/2 teaspoons dry mustard
1/8 teaspoon bottled hot pepper sauce
3-4 cups shredded cooked pork

Combine tomato sauce, water, onion, green pepper, salt, mustard, and hot pepper sauce. Simmer 15 minutes. Add pork and simmer 10 minutes. Spread between hot bun halves.

The Gourmet Way

Amish Dressing

This tangy, sweet-sour dressing is the basis for that wonderful Pennsylvania Dutch Wilted Lettuce—reason enough, believe me, to make it.

1 teaspoon salt
2 tablespoons dry mustard·
1 cup sugar
4 tablespoons flour
1 teaspoon onion powder

2 eggs
2 cups milk
1 cup vinegar
1 tablespoon butter

Mix the dry ingredients well with the eggs. Gradually add milk and vinegar. Cook, stirring, until thickened. Stir in the butter. Refrigerate. Makes 1 quart.

Cranwiches

6 sandwich roll halves
6 slices boiled or baked ham
1 1-pound can jellied
   cranberry sauce

6 slices process American
   cheese, halved

Lightly toast and butter sandwich roll halves. Top each with sliced ham, ring of jellied cranberry sauce, and 2 cheese strips. Place under broiler until cheese is melted. (Cranwiches may be baked, instead of broiled, until cheese melts.) Makes 6 servings.

Afterthought Sandwich

8 slices bread
1/2 cup slivered ham
1/4 cup grated raw carrots
1/4 cup finely chopped celery
1/4 cup grated cabbage

1/4 teaspoon salt
2 teaspoons chili sauce
2 teaspoons mayonnaise or
   salad dressing

Combine ham, carrots, celery, cabbage, salt, chili sauce, and mayonnaise. Spread between bread slices. Makes 4 sandwiches. *Keep in mind* . . . You *can* sneak meat leftovers, like lamb or beef or tongue into this sandwich (instead of the ham) without anyone's being the wiser. That's why it's an afterthought.

Wonder Ways with Ham Salad—

To 2 cups of ham salad sandwich filling, add one of the following: 1/4 cup toasted sesame seeds . . . 1 tbs. chopped shallots . . . 1/4 cup chopped cashews . . . 1/3 cup chopped pistachio nuts . . . 1/4 cup chutney . . . 1/4 cup chopped dates . . . 1/3 cup chopped raisins . . . 2 chopped hard-cooked eggs . . . 1/4 cup chopped sweet gherkins . . . 1/4 cup chopped dill pickle . . . 1/2 cup diced pineapple . . . 1/4 cup chopped green pepper . . . 1/2 cup chopped celery . . . 1/2 cup chopped cucumber . . . 1/2 cup diced Swiss cheese . . . 1/2 cup diced sharp Cheddar . . . 1/2 cup shredded cabbage . . . 2 tbs. drained capers . . . 1/4 cup chopped pecans . . . 1/4 cup chopped peanuts . . . 1/4 cup diced preserved kumquats. Or season the mayonnaise, before mixing salad, with one of the following: 1 tsp. curry powder . . . 1 tbs. currant jelly . . . 1 tbs. crabapple jelly . . . 1 tbs. honey . . . 1 tsp. grated orange rind . . . 1/4 tsp. ground ginger . . . 1/4 tsp. ground cloves . . . 1 tsp. prepared mustard . . . 1/2 tsp. dill seed . . . 2 tbs. chili sauce.

Raisin Rounds

12 slices round sandwich
  bread
1/2 cup seedless raisins
1/2 cup shredded coconut
1/2 cup grated raw carrots

1/2 cup julienne ham
2 tablespoons chopped
  pickled green pepper
2 tablespoons creamy
  French dressing

Combine all ingredients except bread. Spread on 6 slices
bread, top with remaining slices. Makes 6 sandwiches.
Take note: If you happen to be fresh out of ham, just leave
meat out of this sandwich. It's good that way, too.

Canadian Cooler

8 slices dark rye bread,
  buttered
1 cucumber, thinly sliced
Commercial sour cream

8 thick slices cold, cooked
  Canadian bacon
Watercress
Cherry tomatoes

Marinate cucumbers in sour cream for at least an hour before
serving time. Place 2 slices cold bacon on each of 4 slices of
bread. Top with marinated cucumbers and cover with remaining ·bread slices. Serve with watercress and cherry-tomato
garnish. Makes 4 sandwiches.

Denver Special

8 slices white bread
1 cup cooked ham, diced
1 tablespoon butter
1/4 cup chopped onion

1/4 cup chopped green pepper
4 eggs, slightly beaten
Salt
Pepper

Dice luncheon meat and brown in the butter along with the
onion and green pepper. Add eggs, season, and cook over low
heat until light and fluffy, lifting mixture from bottom of pan
with broad spatula as eggs are set. Divide mixture over 4 slices
bread, top with remaining slices. Makes 4 servings.
Even better . . . You might sneak 1/4 cup cooked, leftover
vegetables into the pan along with the green pepper—peas,
cut-up green beans, Italian beans—not to get rid of the leftovers, mind you, but because they really do make a better
Denver Special. Add a pinch or two of onion salt as well.

Wonder Ways with Cold Ham—

Sandwich the sliced ham with one of the following: caraway-
seed cheese . . . sliced turkey . . . sliced hard-cooked egg
. . . shredded Chinese cabbage . . .French Salad (page 191)
. . . coleslaw . . . peanut butter . . . slice of canned pineapple . . . Swiss cheese . . . marinated artichoke hearts.

Pork

Submariners

1 16-inch loaf French or
    Vienna bread
4 tablespoons salad oil
4 teaspoons vinegar
8 1-ounce slices process
    American cheese
3 dill pickles, thinly sliced
    lengthwise

2 12-ounce cans chopped ham,
    each sliced into 13 slices
2 medium onions, thinly sliced
1 green pepper, thinly sliced
    crosswise
3 radishes, thinly sliced
    lengthwise

Slice French loaf in half lengthwise. Combine oil and vinegar; brush cut sides of loaf with oil mixture. Cut cheese slices in half and arrange across bottom half of loaf, one next to the other, slanting them in one direction. Top cheese with pickle slices, 13 slices ham, onion slices, 13 slices ham, green-pepper rings, and radish slices. Place top half on loaf over filling and secure with toothpicks to prevent bread from slipping. Slice crosswise into 4-inch lengths. Transfer to a large piece of foil, keeping loaf intact. Cover the sides and ends with foil, leaving the top exposed. Heat in a 400° F. oven for 8 to 10 minutes. May be served hot or cold. Makes 4 sandwiches.

Rainbow Rolls

6 oval French rolls
1 1/2 cups chopped cooked
    ham
1/3 cup sweet-pickle relish
1/4 cup mayonnaise or salad
    dressing
1 8-ounce package cream
    cheese

1/3 cup of milk
Few drops of red or green food
    coloring
3 radishes
12 thin strips green pepper

Cut thin slices from top of each roll and scoop out bottom halves. Combine ham, pickle relish, and mayonnaise. Fill rolls, using 1/4 cup ham filling in each roll. Place tops on rolls. Blend cream cheese and milk. Spread about 2 tablespoons cream cheese over top and sides of each roll. Tint remaining cheese with food coloring. Force it through a pastry bag and make a border around side of each roll. Cut each radish in half lengthwise, and cut it to form 3 flower petals. Place a radish flower on each roll. Use green-pepper strips to make stems for radish flowers. Cut remaining green-pepper strips in half to make leaves for radish flowers. Makes 6 rolls.

Triple Treats

18 slices bread, buttered	3 eggs, slightly beaten
12 slices baked ham	1/4 cup milk
.6 slices cooked chicken	1/4 teaspoon salt
6 thin slices Swiss cheese	

Use 3 slices of bread for each sandwich. Butter first slice and cover with a slice of ham and a slice of chicken. Butter both sides of second slice of bread and top with ham and Swiss cheese. Cover with third slice of bread. Press slightly and hold together with toothpicks. Trim crusts. Cut in half diagonally. Combine eggs, milk, and salt. Dip sandwich halves in egg mixture. Fry in butter in skillet until golden brown on both sides, adding butter when necessary. Remove toothpicks. Makes 6 sandwiches.

To top it off . . . Serve these—piping hot—with cranberry sauce or currant jelly.

Corned Beefies

8 slices brown bread, buttered	Horseradish
Mustard	1/2 pound corned beef, shredded

Cream butter with mustard and horseradish to taste. Spread on brown bread. Cover 4 slices with layer of shredded corned beef. Top with remaining slices.

Afterthought . . . If you'd like to add something crisp, layer thin-sliced cucumbers over corned beef before putting on the top slice of bread.

Waffled Sandwich Reuben

12 slices rye bread	12 slices (1 pound) corned beef
3 tablespoons prepared mustard	12 slices Swiss cheese
6 tablespoons sauerkraut	6 tablespoons butter

On each of 6 slices of bread, spread 1/2 tablespoon mustard; top with 1 tablespoon sauerkraut. Arrange 2 slices of corned beef and 2 slices of Swiss cheese on each, then top with remaining slices of bread. Butter outside of each sandwich, using 1/2 tablespoon of butter; grill until cheese begins to melt.

Or try this . . . Substitute commercial sour cream, flavored to taste with chili sauce and prepared horseradish sauce, for the mustard.

The Supreme Sandwich
Corned Beef

This is a kind of super-delicatessen special, guaranteed to scare away picky eaters (Are there any, if everyone told the truth?) and bring joy to the hearts of honest trenchermen.

8 slices dark rye bread	4 slices tomato
Butter, softened	8 leaves lettuce
1 cucumber, sliced thin	Watercress
1 pound sliced corned beef	2 hard-cooked eggs,
2 cups coleslaw	deviled

Butter bread. On half the slices, arrange cucumbers, overlapping. Top with corned beef, then coleslaw, then tomato, finishing with lettuce leaves. Put on the remaining slices of bread. Top each sandwich with a few sprigs of watercress and a deviled-egg half—hold in place with a toothpick if you fear slippage. *Perfect partners* . . . Mustard should be passed with these. The beverage? Beer, naturally.

Coleslaw Corned Beef

2 slices rye bread	Brisket corned beef, sliced
Mustard butter	Coleslaw

Spread rye bread with mustard butter. Cover one slice of bread with thin slices of brisket corned beef. Cover the other with sharply flavored coleslaw.

Double-Decker Corned Beef

3 slices rye bread, buttered	1 slice Cheddar cheese
2 slices corned-beef loaf	Mustard
2 tablespoons sliced stuffed olives	

On 1 slice of bread, layer meat and olives; add second slice of bread and cheese. Spread with mustard and top with third slice. Makes 1 sandwich.

Dinty-Burgers

8 hard rolls, split and buttered	1 can (2 cups) sauerkraut
1 can corned beef	1/2 cup finely chopped onion
	1 tablespoon horseradish

Break corned beef into pieces and heat with sauerkraut, onion, and horseradish. Pile corned beef onto bottom halves of rolls and top with the remaining halves. Wrap in aluminum foil and heat in 350° F. oven for 10 minutes.

Spicy Corned Beef

8 slices white or rye bread	1/4 cup mayonnaise or salad dressing
1 cup chopped corned beef	
1/2 cup chopped gherkins or drained chopped relish	

Mix all ingredients except bread. Spread on 4 slices bread, top with remaining slices.

Or try this . . . Use slightly less mayonnaise and mix it with 1 or 2 teaspoons good prepared mustard before adding to other ingredients.

Big Wheel Sandwich

2 1-pound loaves long narrow French bread	24 slices process Swiss cheese
3 Bermuda or Spanish onions, medium-size	24 slices corned beef
	8 dill pickles, sliced into thirds

Cut loaves into alternate 3/4-inch and 2-inch slices, almost to bottom crust. Start cutting 1/2-inch from end of loaf, making 24 slices in all. Remove narrow sections in each loaf, but do not cut through crust. Cut each onion into 8 slices. Fold slices of Swiss cheese, placing 1 in each bread cavity so that fold is on bottom. Wrap a corned beef slice around a slice each of dill pickle and onion; insert between folds of cheese slices. Cut each loaf into thirds. Place in shallow baking pan. Heat in 400° F. oven for 10 minutes. To serve, place 1/3 loaf on a flat wood serving platter and use a sharp bread knife for slicing bread between filled sections to make sandwiches for easier eating. Makes 6 servings of 1/3 loaf per serving.

Another idea . . . To pretty-up the serving of these, for each person, place 1/3 loaf in a long narrow wicker basket, placing relishes and potato chips at ends of basket.

Horseradish Corned Beef

8 slices rye bread, buttered
1 cup of chopped cooked
   corned beef
1 tablespoon prepared
   horseradish

3 tablespoons mayonnaise or
   whipped cream cheese
Dry mustard, to taste

Mix together and spread on 4 slices of bread, top with remaining slices.
Top off with . . . Mustard pickles—the good, old-fashioned chunky kind—and a pile of crisp julienne potato sticks.

Corned-Beef Fry

8 slices white bread,
   buttered
3/4 cup minced, cooked
   corned beef

1/2 teaspoon Worcestershire
   sauce
1 egg
1/2 cup milk

Mix corned beef with Worcestershire sauce. Spread on buttered bread and cover with second slice. Beat egg with milk. Dip sandwiches into egg-milk mixture and fry in melted butter until golden brown on both sides. Makes 4 sandwiches.
Or try it this way . . . Vary the flavor by adding horseradish, prepared mustard, or a spoonful of pickle relish to the meat.

Corned-Beef Doubles

4 frankfurter rolls
2 cups chopped, cooked or
   canned corned beef
1 cup crisp coleslaw
1/4 cup horseradish
1 3-ounce package cream
   cheese

2 tablespoons milk
1/4 cup well-drained canned
   crushed pineapple
1/4 cup snipped, pitted dates
4 gherkins
4 pitted dates
Large romaine leaves

Several hours ahead: Mix corned beef, coleslaw, horseradish. Mix cream cheese with milk, pineapple, snipped dates. Refrigerate both. *At serving time:* Split frankfurter rolls lengthwise; hollow out both sections slightly. Fill about 2/3 of the length of the bun with corned-beef filling; fill remainder of bun with cheese-pineapple filling. Close sandwich. Put each pickle and date on end of toothpick; stick pickle into top of meat end of sandwich, date into top of other end. Serve each roll on romaine leaf. Makes 4 servings.

Breakfast in a Bun

4 sandwich buns	4 corned beef slices
1 tablespoon butter	4 eggs

Split, toast, and butter the buns. Grill the meat lightly. Fry the eggs once over lightly. On each bun, place the grilled meat and the hot fried eggs. Makes 4 servings.

Onion Corned Beef

10 slices rye bread, buttered	2 tablespoons prepared
1 cup chopped, cooked	mustard
corned beef	1/4 cup salad dressing
1/2 cup chopped celery	
2 tablespoons chopped	
onion	

Combine corned beef, celery, onion, mustard, and salad dressing. Spread 1/4 cup corned-beef mixture over 5 slices buttered bread. Top with remaining slices. Makes 5 sandwiches.

Bermuda-Burgers

4 hamburger buns, toasted	Bermuda onion, sliced
1 can corned beef hash,	Butter
chilled	

Cut contents of 1 can of corned-beef hash into 4 slices. Brown hash rounds with slices of Bermuda onion in butter. Place each hash round on a toasted bun half and top with an onion slice and remaining bun half. Makes 4 burgers.

Hamburgers Stroganoff

6 brown-and-serve club or	3/4 cup sliced mushrooms
French rolls	1 teaspoon salt
1 tablespoon shortening	1/2 teaspoon paprika
3/4 pound hamburger	1/2 cup commercial sour
1/2 teaspoon minced garlic	cream

Melt shortening in a skillet. Add beef and brown it on all sides. Add garlic, mushrooms, salt, and paprika and sauté until meat is cooked. Remove from heat. Add sour cream. Cut thin slice from top of rolls and scoop out bottom halves. Fill rolls with meat mixture, 1/3 cup of filling for each roll. Place filled rolls and top slices separately on an ungreased baking sheet. Bake in a hot oven (400° F.) until rolls and tops are lightly browned, about 12 minutes. Place tops on meat to serve. Serve immediately. Makes 6 sandwiches.

Sweet-Sour Hamburger Sandwiches

8 Kaiser rolls, split	1 tablespoon
1 1/4 pounds ground beef	Worcestershire sauce
1/4 pound ground pork	1/2 teaspoon ground cloves
1 teaspoon salt	1/3 cup wine vinegar
1/4 teaspoon pepper	1/2 medium green pepper,
8 slices pineapple	sliced crosswise into
1 tablespoon soy sauce	8 rings
1/3 cup brown sugar (firmly packed)	

Combine beef, pork, salt and pepper. Shape into 8 patties; brown well on both sides in a large skillet. Place a slice of pineapple over each browned patty. Combine soy sauce, brown sugar, Worcestershire sauce, cloves, and wine vinegar; pour over patties. Cover and simmer 20 minutes. Place green pepper slices on pineapple; cover and simmer an additional 10 minutes. Place 1 patty between each sliced roll and serve while hot. Makes 8 sandwiches.

Hobgoblin Hamburgers

4 brown-and-serve French rolls	8 1/4-inch-thick slices Cheddar cheese, 4 by 2 inches
Butter, softened	
4 teaspoons prepared mustard	2 pounds ground beef
8 teaspoons ketchup	1 teaspoon salt
16 tomato slices	Pepper to taste
Onion rings	Cheddar cheese for garnish

Split rolls in half, butter and lightly toast under preheated broiler. Spread each half with 1/2 teaspoon mustard; then 1 teaspoon ketchup. Top each half with 2 tomato slices and several onion rings; cover with slice of cheese. Mix together beef, salt, and pepper; divide into 8 parts. Shape into oblong patties; place on top of cheese, spreading and sealing to edge of roll (this prevents cheese from running out). Place on baking sheet; bake 25 minutes in preheated 350° F. oven or until beef is desired degree of doneness. When sandwiches are removed from oven, Cheddar cheese may be grated or placed sliced on top as garnish.

Or try it this way . . . Partify these by cutting cheese for garnish with cookie cutters. This is where the Hobgoblins come in—a circle of Cheddar cheese with round eyes and crescent mouth cut out is just right for a children's Halloween party.

Minipizza

3/4 pound ground chuck
1/4 teaspoon Worcestershire
    sauce
1/8 teaspoon garlic salt
1/8 teaspoon salt
Dash of pepper
  1 package refrigerated pan-
    ready biscuits (10
    biscuits)

1/4 cup ketchup
  5 large tomato slices,
    sprinkled with salt
  5 large onion slices
  5 slices process American
    cheese
Watercress

Mix beef, Worcestershire sauce, salts, pepper. On cookie sheet, flatten out each biscuit to make 3-inch circles. Spread each of 5 biscuits with ketchup; top with beef mixture, tomato slice, onion slice. Heat oven to 425° F. Let filled and plain biscuits stand at room temperature 15 to 20 minutes. Then bake biscuits 10 to 15 minutes. Top each filled biscuit with plain biscuit, then with cheese slice. Bake 5 minutes longer, or until cheese is melted and golden. Serve with sprigs of watercress. Makes 5 sandwiches.

Perfect partners . . . Anything cold and not too spicy, like frozen limeade, orangeade, lemonade.

The Supreme Sandwich
Meat Loaf

This is the substantial kind, firm-textured and easy-slicing, that makes the best sandwiches.

    2 pounds ground round
1 1/2 pounds ground veal
  1/2 pound ground lean pork
    2 large eggs
2 1/2 cups milk
    1 onion, diced fine
    2 teaspoons salt
    1 cup soft white bread crumbs

Grind all meats together a second time. Combine with all other ingredients and mix well. Bake in a loaf pan about 1 1/4 hours at 350° F.

Perfect partners . . . This loaf—don't be miserly in slicing it—paired with your favorite bread, dressed up with a crisp lettuce leaf and a good, old-fashioned tomato-onion relish, or chili sauce if you prefer.

Vastburgers

When I was a little girl, the cookout, as a suburban institution, had not been thought of. (Or, if thought of, would have been dismissed with a sharp, "Whatever for? Go to all that trouble?") However, porch suppers on Sunday night were an acceptable summer-evening treat, and to set them apart from ordinary dining-room suppers, Aunt Hazel invented Vastburgers—never mind that she called them simply "those big beef patties." Along with a bowl of her turmeric-tasty potato salad and a platter of sliced beefsteak tomatoes with fresh basil in the oil-vinegar dressing, they were cause for rejoicing. Nowadays, Vastburgers—and why not with the same accompaniments?—can hold up their heads at any cookout. Do the big burgers on the grill, make their giant-size buns ahead of time, from the keeps-beautifully recipe below. What makes Vastburgers superior to the ordinary hamburger? Homemade rolls, for one thing. Their size, for another—they can be juicy-rare within, appetizingly brown on the outside. Besides, they're fun.

Vastburger Buns

3/4 cup hot water	2 packages active dry
1/2 cup sugar	yeast
1 tablespoon salt	1 egg, beaten
1/4 cup shortening	5 1/4 cups sifted flour (more
1 cup warm water	or less)

Combine hot water, sugar, salt, shortening. Cool to lukewarm. Measure warm water into large bowl. Sprinkle yeast over and stir until dissolved. Stir in lukewarm sugar-shortening mixture. Add egg and 2 1/2 cups flour. Beat smooth. Stir in remaining flour; beat 1 minute. Place dough in greased bowl. Brush top with soft shortening. Cover tightly with aluminum foil. Place in refrigerator; leave until doubled in bulk. (It can be kept there as long as a week if you wish.) *To make buns:* Form dough into a roll about 15 inches long. Divide in quarters. Form each quarter into a big bun, smooth on the surface. Place on greased baking sheet, at least an inch apart. Cover. Let rise in warm place, out of the way of drafts, until doubled in bulk. Brush with melted butter. Bake, in a 375° F. oven 35-45 minutes, until plump and brown.

Vastburgers

1 Vastburger Bun, split, oven-heated, buttered	3 drops garlic juice
	1 teaspoon salt
	1/2 teaspoon pepper
1 1/2 pounds ground sirloin	2 teaspoons powdered mushrooms
1 small onion, chopped fine	

Mix meat and seasonings together, using a light hand—heavy-handed mixing makes for tough burgers. Broil or pan-broil to the desired degree of doneness. Place on the bottom half of the heated Vastburger Bun, put its hat on, and cut into pie-shaped wedges—makes 4 hearty servings, 6 smaller ones.

Of course you'll want . . . sauces and relishes—the ever-present ketchup, a zippy mustard, brown steak sauce, a good pepper relish, thin-sliced dill pickle rounds. If you prefer, omit the onion in the burgers and serve a plate of thin-sliced sweet onions, Bermudas or the red Italian kind. And, of course, there's no law against making a cheese Vastburger—just top the burger with slices of nippy Cheddar. But do it while the burger's hot, put the heated bun-top on at once, and slip into the oven for a brief time, so the cheese will relax a little.

There's no law against using fillings other than the simple broiled or fried hamburger in the Vastburger Bun. Vastburgers take kindly to what was known inelegantly in our family as "Sloppy Meat Loaf"—ground beef sautéed with onion and a whiff of garlic, then mixed with a thick, richly-flavored tomato sauce, the homemade kind that has simmered a long time to bring out the best in it. Diced cheese—some kind that's co-operative about melting, such as Münster or Swiss or wonderful California Jack—can be stirred into the mixture just before piling it on the buns, and adds delightful taste and texture. But don't wait too long after the addition of the cheese, or the texture you'll end up with will be gluey rather than chewy. Another fine filling for the versatile Vastburger is London broil, very rare indeed, sliced thin and laid on the bun with the slices overlapping. Some of the good pan juices sprinkled over the meat add moisture. Salt and pepper—all the seasoning you need.

Added thought . . . If you are going to use only 1 or 2 Vastburger Buns, divide the dough, make your buns with part of it, and save the remainder of the dough to use—as much as a week later—for a batch of delicious dinner rolls to turn an ordinary meal into a feast. There's nothing, absolutely nothing, that says "topnotch cook" like the glorious smell of baking homemade bread!

Gourmet Party Burgers

12 small sandwich buns
1/4 cup crumbled blue cheese
1/4 cup soft butter
1/2 teaspoon prepared
    mustard

Dash of Worcestershire sauce
3/4 pound hamburger
1/4 teaspoon salt
1/8 teaspoon pepper

Combine blue cheese, butter, mustard, and Worcestershire sauce. Cut buns in half, crosswise. Spread 1 teaspoon cheese mixture on each bun half. Combine hamburger, salt and pepper. Shape into 12 small patties; broil or pan fry. Place buns, spread side up, on a cookie sheet and toast them until bubbly and brown. Place cooked hamburger patty between toasted bun halves. Serve hot. Makes 12 burgers.

Stack-a-Burger

6 hamburger buns, split
1 1/2 pounds ground chuck
2 tablespoons minced
    onion
1 1/2 teaspoons salt
1/8 teaspoon pepper

6 slices process American
    cheese
6 tomato slices
Seasoned salt
Soft butter

A few hours ahead: Mix beef with onion, salt, pepper. Shape into 12 thin patties. Put cheese slice between each 2 patties, pressing edges together to seal cheese inside. *At mealtime:* In greased skillet, cook cheeseburgers to desired rareness. Meanwhile, sprinkle tomato slices with seasoned salt. Toast split buns; spread with butter. Insert cheeseburger and tomato slice between each split bun. Makes 6 servings.

Keep in mind . . . Add something green (like a tossed green salad), plenty of milk, and a plateful of homemade brownies and this meal has everything to delight the appetites of kids.

Burgundy Burgers

3 sandwich rolls, split
1 pound ground beef
1 teaspoon salt
1/4 cup Burgundy

Freshly ground pepper to taste
1 tablespoon minced
    parsley
1 tablespoon minced chives

Mix all ingredients except rolls, and shape into 3 patties. Broil. Serve between halves of sandwich rolls. Makes 3 servings.

Smokyburgers

6 sandwich buns, split	1/2 teaspoon salt
1/3 cup smoky cheese spread	1/8 teaspoon pepper
3 teaspoons finely chopped onion	1/4 cup milk
	1 egg, slightly beaten
1/2 cup soft bread crumbs	1 pound ground beef

Combine cheese spread and 1 teaspoon onion; set aside. Combine soft bread crumbs, salt, pepper, 2 teaspoons onion, milk, beaten egg, and beef. Shape into 6 patties, using about 1/3 cup of mixture for each one. Make a well in the center of each patty by pressing down with the back of a tablespoon. Place patties on a moderately hot greased griddle (350° F.) with the "well" side turned down. When browned on underside, turn and fill "well" with about 1 tablespoon of the cheese mixture. Continue grilling until browned on second side. Toast cut surface of buns on grill. Place 1 patty in each toasted bun. Makes 6 burgers.

Midnight Burgers

8 sliced sandwich buns	1 tablespoon Worcestershire sauce
1 pound ground beef	
2 tablespoons minced onion	1/2 teaspoon salt
2 tablespoons prepared mustard	Dash of pepper
3 tablespoons ketchup or chili sauce	

Combine beef, onion, mustard, ketchup, Worcestershire sauce, salt and pepper. Place about 2 tablespoons meat mixture on each sandwich bun half. Place on a shallow baking pan. Broil under moderate heat for about 10 minutes, or until meat is cooked. Serve hot. Makes 8 servings of 2 bun halves per serving.

Hamburgers Parmigiana

3 hamburger buns, split	3 tablespoons ketchup
1 pound ground chuck	1 1/2 tablespoons Worcestershire sauce
2 tablespoons chopped onion	
3/4 teaspoon seasoned salt	1/4 cup grated Parmesan cheese
1/8 teaspoon pepper	1/4 cup snipped parsley

Mix beef, onion, salt, pepper. Spread meat mixture about 1/4 inch thick on each bun half. Mix ketchup with Worcestershire. Spread lightly over meat. Sprinkle with Parmesan and parsley. Broil until of desired rareness. Makes 3 servings of 2 halves.

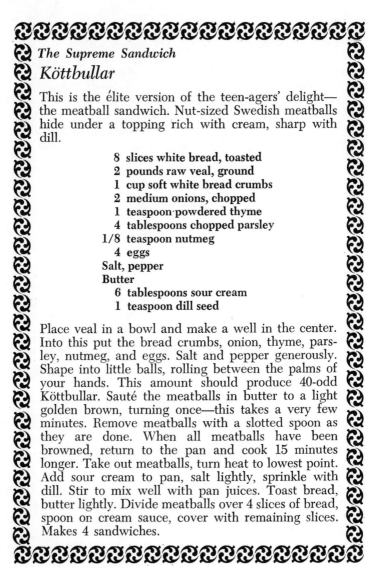

The Supreme Sandwich

Köttbullar

This is the élite version of the teen-agers' delight—the meatball sandwich. Nut-sized Swedish meatballs hide under a topping rich with cream, sharp with dill.

8 slices white bread, toasted
2 pounds raw veal, ground
1 cup soft white bread crumbs
2 medium onions, chopped
1 teaspoon powdered thyme
4 tablespoons chopped parsley
1/8 teaspoon nutmeg
4 eggs
Salt, pepper
Butter
6 tablespoons sour cream
1 teaspoon dill seed

Place veal in a bowl and make a well in the center. Into this put the bread crumbs, onion, thyme, parsley, nutmeg, and eggs. Salt and pepper generously. Shape into little balls, rolling between the palms of your hands. This amount should produce 40-odd Köttbullar. Sauté the meatballs in butter to a light golden brown, turning once—this takes a very few minutes. Remove meatballs with a slotted spoon as they are done. When all meatballs have been browned, return to the pan and cook 15 minutes longer. Take out meatballs, turn heat to lowest point. Add sour cream to pan, salt lightly, sprinkle with dill. Stir to mix well with pan juices. Toast bread, butter lightly. Divide meatballs over 4 slices of bread, spoon on cream sauce, cover with remaining slices. Makes 4 sandwiches.

Beef 'n' Pickle

4 slices bread, buttered
1/2 cup beef, minced
1 ounce sweet pickles

Salt and pepper
2 teaspoons tomato sauce

Mince beef with sweet pickles. Season with salt and pepper, mix with tomato sauce. Spread on 2 slices bread, top with remaining slices.

Better still . . . Dress each sandwich with crispy, paper-thin slices of radish.

Stateside Hero

1 loaf Italian bread (oval-shaped)
Italian Meatballs
2 tablespoons salad oil
2 thinly sliced onions
1 thinly sliced green pepper
1 can (8 or 10 3/4 ounces) spaghetti sauce with meat

1/2 pound sliced mozzarella cheese
6 slices process American cheese
1/2 cup soft butter

Make, then brown, Italian Meatballs. In hot salad oil in same skillet, sauté onions, green pepper. Slice bread lengthwise, horizontally, into 3 even layers. Spread bottom bread slice with half of spaghetti sauce. On top, arrange meatballs, then mozzarella and American cheese. Spread second bread slice with rest of sauce; place, with sauce side down, on cheese. Spread top of this slice with some of butter; cover with onions and green pepper. Top with buttered crust slice, gashed for easier slicing. Place on greased cookie sheet. Wrap cookie sheet and loaf in aluminum foil. Bake loaf at 375° F. 1 hour, or until heated through and cheese melts. Keep wrapped until ready to serve. With scissors and knife, cut gashes all the way through; serve with pie server. Eat with knife and fork. Makes 8 servings.

Italian Meatballs
3/4 pound ground chuck
1/2 cup packaged bread crumbs
Pinch oregano
3/4 teaspoon cornstarch
1 egg, beaten
1/2 cup light cream
1/2 teaspoon salt
1/2 teaspoon garlic salt
2 tablespoons salad oil

Combine beef with bread crumbs, oregano, cornstarch, egg, cream, salts. Shape into 40 small balls. Brown balls on all sides in hot oil in skillet; set aside while assembling other ingredients.

Picnic Beefburgers

6 sliced sandwich buns	2 tablespoons crumbled
1 1/2 pounds ground beef	blue cheese
1 tablespoon salt	1 large tomato, cut into 6
1/2 teaspoon pepper	slices
1 large Bermuda onion	Parsley sprigs

Combine beef, 1 teaspoon salt, and 1/4 teaspoon pepper; form into 6 meat patties. Place each patty on a 12-inch square of heavy foil. Slice onion into 6 equal slices. Place 1 teaspoon crumbled cheese and an onion slice on top of each meat patty. Sprinkle remaining salt and pepper over onion, then wrap each patty securely in its foil square, fastening and folding foil over. Cook over hot coals on grill, turning foil packets every 10 minutes. Open foil, place a tomato slice on each patty and insert in a warm sandwich bun. Garnish with parsley sprigs. Makes 6 burgers.

Keep in mind . . . To make secure foil packages, bring edges of foil together at top, then fold down once or twice, creasing well, until foil touches patty.. Smooth and tuck ends under. Reverse process to open, and there will be no accidents.

Party Patties

1 1-pound loaf unsliced	1 teaspoon garlic salt
bread	2/3 cup water
1 pound ground beef	4 tomatoes
1 cup soft bread crumbs	1 green pepper
1/2 teaspoon salt	1 onion
1/4 teaspoon pepper	

Trim crusts from loaf of bread. Cut the loaf, horizontally, into 4 layers. Cut each layer in half, crosswise, to form 8 slices. Combine ground beef, soft bread crumbs, salt, pepper, garlic salt, and water. Cut each tomato into 12 thin wedges. Place 6 wedges around the edge of each bread slice. Pile meat on bread in center of tomato wedges. Cut green pepper into 16 thin strips. Place a strip of green pepper on each lengthwise side of each sandwich. Cut onion into thin slices. Put 2 onion rings on top of each sandwich. Place sandwiches on shallow baking pan. Bake in a moderate oven (350° F.) for 25 minutes. Makes 8 open-face servings.

Even better . . . Brush each slice of bread with chive or garlic butter before topping with tomatoes and meat.

Sweet-Sour Beefloaf

12 slices white bread,
    buttered
1 pound (2 cups) ground
    beef
1 teaspoon salt
Dash of pepper

1 cup soft bread crumbs
1 egg
1/2 cup milk
1 tablespoon
    Worcestershire sauce
Sweet-Sour Sauce

Combine beef, salt, pepper, soft bread crumbs, egg, milk, Worcestershire sauce. Press meat mixture into a 1-quart loaf pan. Bake in a 400° F. oven for 1 hour. *To serve:* Slice, place on 6 slices of bread. Spoon sauce over. Top with remaining bread. Makes 6 sandwiches.

Sweet-Sour Sauce

1 8-ounce can tomato sauce
1 teaspoon onion flakes
2 tablespoons brown sugar
4 teaspoons cider vinegar
2 whole cloves
1/2 bay leaf

Combine ingredients. Simmer 10 minutes. Remove cloves and bay leaf.

Squareburgers

1 pound ground beef
1 tablespoon instant minced
    onion
1 teaspoon salt
1/2 teaspoon celery seed
1 teaspoon pepper
1 egg

1/4 cup seasoned bread
    crumbs
1 12-ounce package sharp
    Cheddar cheese,
    cut into 8 slices
1 10-ounce package
    corn-bread mix

In medium-size bowl, combine ground beef, onion, salt, celery seed, pepper, egg, and bread crumbs. Mix until thoroughly combined. Press mixture into a 9 by 13 1/4 inch pan. Place 4 cheese slices over the meat mixture. Prepare corn-bread mix according to package directions, but do not bake. Spread on top of the cheese. Bake in 475° F. oven for 15 minutes. Remove from oven, place remaining cheese slices on top. Bake until cheese melts, about 5 minutes. Cut into 9 portions.

Note: This is only a sandwich by courtesy (it *is* bread with meat, if you stretch your definitions a bit!) but it's so tasty I thought you ought to know about it anyway. Serve with sliced peaches and you won't have to call it anything—except good.

Skillet Stroganoffs

10 sandwich buns, sliced
2 tablespoons butter
1/4 cup chopped onion
1 teaspoon finely chopped garlic
1 pound ground beef
2 tablespoons flour
1 teaspoon salt

1/4 teaspoon paprika
1/4 teaspoon nutmeg
1/2 cup chopped cooked mushrooms
1 can condensed cream of mushroom soup
1 cup prepared sour cream

Melt butter in skillet. Add onion, garlic, and ground beef. Sauté meat until browned. Combine flour, salt, paprika, and nutmeg. Sprinkle over meat mixture and stir until blended. Add mushrooms and mushroom soup to meat mixture. Simmer for 10 minutes. Pour sour cream over top and simmer 5 minutes longer. *To serve:* Place 1/3 cup Stroganoff in each bun.

Frikadeller Sandwiches

9 slices rye bread, buttered
2 cucumbers, sliced thin
1 recipe Frikadeller

2 jars pickled beets with onion, drained
3 hard-cooked eggs, chopped

Divide cucumber slices over bread. Place 4 Frikadeller on each slice of bread. Top with several slices of pickled beets with onions. Sprinkle tops of sandwiches with chopped egg.

Frikadeller (Danish Meatballs)

1 pound beef, ground twice
1 pound pork, ground twice
1 tablespoon finely chopped onion
1/2 cup sifted flour
1 teaspoon salt
1/4 teaspoon pepper
1 egg, beaten
1 cup milk
1/4 cup water
3 tablespoons butter

Mix meats well in a large bowl, with onion. Combine flour, salt and pepper and add to meat mixture; beat well. Combine milk, egg, and water and add gradually, mixing well. Beat until smooth and well-blended. Melt butter in heavy skillet. Drop meat mixture into butter by rounded tablespoonful. Cook over medium heat until browned, turning once with a slotted spoon. Makes about 3 dozen meatballs.

Super Supper Sandwich

3 slices rye bread, buttered	1 teaspoon vinegar
1 thick slice	1/4 cup shredded cabbage
Braunschweiger	Lettuce leaves
2 teaspoons sugar	Tomato slices
1/8 teaspoon salt	Thousand Island Dressing
1/16 teaspoon pepper	(page 145)

Spread Braunschweiger on one slice of bread. Blend sugar, salt and pepper; stir in vinegar and pour over cabbage. Mix thoroughly. Fork cabbage over meat. Top with bread, lettuce, and tomato. Spread with Thousand Island Dressing. Cover with remaining bread slice. Makes 1 sandwich.

Cervelat Bars

2 lengthwise slices white bread (cut from unsliced 1 1/2-pound loaf)	1 cup ground cervelat sausage
1/2 cup chopped cucumber	2 tablespoons pickle relish
Dash of salt	3 tablespoons mayonnaise or salad dressing
2 3-ounce packages cream cheese	2 tablespoons butter

Combine cucumber, salt, and cream cheese. Combine cervelat sausage, pickle relish, and mayonnaise. Spread each slice of bread with butter. Spread center strips of bread with cervelat sausage filling. Spread outside strips with cucumber-cheese filling; chill. Cut crosswise into individual bars. Makes 20 bars.

Fruited Sausage au Gratin

8 slices toast, buttered	1 cup of jellied cranberry sauce, crushed
2 dozen (approximately 1 1/2 pounds) sausage links	American cheese, grated

Fry sausage links until brown. Spread 2 tablespoons cranberry sauce on each slice of toast. Place sausages over cranberry sauce, using 3 for each slice. Sprinkle grated American cheese over sausage on each sandwich. Place sandwiches on cookie sheet and broil at 400° F. for 5 minutes, or until cheese melts. Makes 8 open-face sandwiches.

Sandwich-in-a-Casserole

9 slices white bread	1 package brown-and-serve
4 eggs	sausages
1 quart milk	2 sliced tomatoes
1/2 teaspoon salt	1 cup grated process
1 teaspoon dry mustard	American cheese

Start heating oven to 325° F. Beat eggs lightly; mix in milk, salt, mustard. Make three 2-decker sandwiches, using sausages for first layer, tomato slices sprinkled with grated cheese for second layer. Halve each sandwich diagonally. Arrange, cut sides down, in 12 by 8 by 2 inch baking dish. Pour milk mixture over all. Bake 1 1/2 hours, or until mixture is set in center. Makes 6 servings.

To top it off . . . These, with a plate of crispy assorted relishes and tall glasses of iced tea, make a meal. Fruit and cookies for dessert.

Grinders

6 hard rolls	12 thin slices sweet Bermuda
1/2 pound (36 slices) hard	onion
cervelat, thinly sliced	12 slices sharp process cheese
18 slices tomato	

Cut each roll in half lengthwise. On bottom halves of rolls, place sliced cervelat, sliced tomato, sliced onion—broken into rings—and 2 slices cheese. Replace roll tops. Place on baking sheet. Bake in 400° F. oven for about 5 minutes, or until cheese melts. Makes 6 sandwiches.

In-a-hurry note . . . Skip the baking—this sandwich is good served cold, too.

Little Porky Pizzas

4 English muffins, split	8 1-ounce slices mozzarella
1 pound pork sausage meat	cheese
1/2 cup canned pizza sauce	

Brown pork sausage in a skillet, breaking it into small pieces as it browns. Place buns, cut sides up, on a baking sheet. Spread 1 tablespoon of pizza sauce on each bun half; top this with about 2 tablespoons crumbled, browned sausage and 1 slice of cheese. Warm pizza buns in a 375° F. oven for 5 minutes, or until cheese begins to melt. Serve with pickle fans. Makes 4 servings, 2 pizza bun halves per serving.

****

The Basic Way with

Grilled Sandwiches

These make substantial fare, the kind men like, and growing boys can consume more of them than anyone cares—or dares—to count.

Grilled Swiss-Bacon

8 slices rye bread	4 slices Swiss cheese
3 tablespoons soft butter	12 slices cooked bacon

Butter bread lightly. Place 1 slice of cheese on the unbuttered side of 4 bread slices. Top with 3 pieces of bacon. Cover with remaining bread, buttered side up. Brown sandwiches on both sides in a frying pan or on a griddle.

Now experiment with: Ham, bacon, or Canadian bacon in combination with Swiss, Münster, or American cheese—in any case, spread the unbuttered side of the bread lightly with prepared mustard if your men are mustard fanciers . . . Sliced chicken with mild cheese, Münster or mozzarella . . . Turkey with Swiss . . . Beef with sharp Cheddar . . . or almost anything-with-anything, as long as there's cheese that will benefit from the heat of the grill.

****

Pizzarino Grill

8 slices of bread	3/4 cup shredded mozzarella cheese
1/2 cup tomato sauce	Melted butter
1/2 pound salami, sliced thin	Oregano

Spread tomato sauce on 4 slices of bread. Top with salami slices and shredded mozzarella cheese, then with remaining bread slices. Brush with melted butter seasoned with a little oregano. Broil until lightly browned, and cheese is melted. Makes 4 sandwiches.

Or try it this way . . . Use 1/4 pound thin-sliced Italian sausage instead of salami. Add 1/4 cup sliced mushrooms, preferably fresh. Or substitute 4 English muffin halves for the bread. In this case, layer the ingredients on the muffin halves as above, but omit the melted butter, sprinkling a bit of oregano on the cheese instead. Broil these, open-face, well below the heat. Serve with crisp, cold greens—romaine, endive, fennel, celery.

Egg Salad Plus

4 white hard rolls, buttered
3 tablespoons soft butter
2 hard-cooked eggs, chopped
2 tablespoons finely chopped celery
1/2 cup chopped cervelat sausage

1 teaspoon minced onion
1 tablespoon mayonnaise or salad dressing
1/2 teaspoon salt
1/8 teaspoon pepper

Cut thin slice from top of rolls and scoop out bottom halves. Spread butter on insides of rolls. Combine chopped eggs, celery, cervelat sausage, onion, mayonnaise, salt and pepper. Fill rolls with mixture. Makes 4 servings.
Added thought . . . Wilted Cucumbers (page 202) go beautifully with these.

Dagwiches

4 frankfurter buns
1 tablespoon French dressing
8 1-ounce slices American cheese, cut in half, diagonally

1 tomato, thinly sliced
4 1-ounce slices bologna
1 small carrot, cut into 4 lengthwise slices
1/2 cup chopped lettuce

Slice each bun in half lengthwise; brush cut sides with French dressing. Place 4 triangle slices of cheese across bottom half of each bun. Cut tomato and bologna slices in half. Top cheese with 3 tomato halves, 2 bologna pieces, 1 slice carrot, and 2 tablespoons chopped lettuce. Cover with bun tops. Secure sandwiches with toothpicks. Makes 4 sandwiches.
Better . . . Instead of bologna, try sliced meat loaf, liverwurst, ham, or tongue. Old-fashioned corn or tomato relishes go well with these Dagwiches.

Wonder Ways with Liverwurst—

To 1 cup mashed liverwurst, add one of the following, and moisten with mayonnaise or sour cream: 1/2 cup chopped pistachio nuts . . . 1/2 cup chopped walnuts . . . 1/4 cup chopped sweet pickle . . . 1/4 cup chopped radishes . . . 1/4 cup coarsely ground hazel nuts . . . 2 chopped hard-cooked eggs . . . 1/3 cup chopped celery . . . 1 tbs. prepared horseradish . . . 1/4 cup diced Swiss cheese . . 1 tsp. grated lemon rind . . . 1/4 cup chopped raw cauliflower . . . 1 large fresh dill pickle, chopped . . . 1/4 cup crumbled crisp bacon.

Bologna Broil

4 English muffins, split	8 slices process American
1/3 cup ketchup	cheese
16 slices bologna	Caraway seeds
1/2 cup chopped onion	

Broil muffins, cut side up, 5 1/2 inches from heat until well browned. Remove from broiler. Spread with ketchup, lay 2 bologna slices on each half. Sprinkle with onion. Top with cheese slices and sprinkle with caraway seeds. Return to broiler until cheese is melted and lightly browned. Serve immediately. Makes 8 open-face sandwiches.

The Gourmet Way

Onion Bread

Combine this with rare roast beef for a sandwich so special the men you serve it to will pass the hat to buy you a medal. Oh—and be sure not to forget plenty of big, fresh dill pickles.

    Warm water
1 package active dry yeast
1 cup commercial sour cream
1 envelope onion soup mix
1/4 teaspoon baking soda
2 tablespoons granulated sugar
2 teaspoons salt
2 tablespoons soft butter
2 eggs, beaten
6 1/2 cups sifted flour—or a little more

Measure 1/4 cup warm water; sprinkle yeast into it to soften. In large bowl combine sour cream, soup mix, baking soda, sugar, salt, butter, eggs, 1 cup warm water. Gradually add flour to form a soft dough. Turn out on floured board and knead 5 minutes. Place in greased bowl and cover with towel. Let rise in warm place, free from drafts, until doubled in bulk. Punch dough down. Divide in half. Roll each half into rectangle; then, starting at long side, roll tightly, as for jelly roll. Place in 2 greased loaf pans; cover, let rise until light. Bake about 45 minutes, until loaf sounds hollow when rapped, in 350° oven. Brush tops with melted butter while loaves are hot. Cool on wire racks.

Date-Bait Sandwiches

6 Italian "Poor Boy" loaves
(about 8 inches)
1/2 cup chili sauce
1 teaspoon prepared
mustard
2 tablespoons piccalilli

2 tablespoons thinly sliced
green onion
1/8 teaspoon Worcestershire
sauce
2 dozen thin slices bologna
or salami sausage

Slice into each loaf, almost to bottom crust, making 8 equal-size sections. Combine chili sauce, mustard, piccalilli, onion, and Worcestershire sauce. Spread about 1/2 tablespoon chili mixture into alternate cuts of bread. Fold each slice of bologna and insert 1 slice into same cut. Arrange filled loaves on baking sheets. Brown loaves in a 400° F. oven for 12 minutes, or until heated through. *To serve:* Break loaves into sections and eat as small sandwiches. Makes 6 servings.

Good companions . . . Wedges of iceberg lettuce or separated leaves of romaine, fennel sliced thinly into spears.

Lunchtime Treat

12 round buns or hard rolls
1 package bologna slices
1 small green pepper
6 stuffed olives
1/2 pound Old English cheese,
grated

1/4 cup ketchup
2 tablespoons chopped
onion

Chop bologna, green pepper, and olives together. Add cheese, ketchup, and onion; mix thoroughly. Spread on bottom halves of buns; cover with top halves. Wrap each sandwich in aluminum foil and bake 20 minutes in 300° F. oven. 12 sandwiches.

Or try it this way . . . With 1/2 pound of chopped tongue or ham substituting for the luncheon meat. Add 1/2 teaspoon chili powder or dry mustard to the ketchup to sharpen things up.

Sweet Sausage Towers

8 toast rounds
2 pounds pork sausage meat
8 slices canned pineapple

Prepared mustard
Pineapple syrup

Form sausage into 8 flat patties, a little larger than the pineapple slices. Partially cook patties in a skillet, browning lightly on both sides. Spread pineapple slices lightly with prepared mustard and on them lay sausage cakes. Bake in 350° F. oven for half an hour. Baste during cooking with a little pineapple syrup. Remove from oven, place on hot toast rounds. Makes 8.

Paul Bunyan

4 French rolls, split	8 slices chopped ham
lengthwise, buttered	4 slices Swiss cheese
8 slices salami	Lettuce leaves

Cut meat and cheese to fit sandwich and layer with lettuce leaves between halves of roll. Makes 4 sandwiches.

Double Sausage Delight

2 slices whole-wheat bread,	Thinly sliced onion
buttered	Thinly sliced dill pickle
1 thick slice Braunschweiger	2 slices bologna

Spread Braunschweiger on 1 slice of bread. Top with onion, pickle, and bologna slices and cover with remaining bread slice. Makes 1 sandwich.

Sunshiners

4 sandwich buns, split,	1/8 teaspoon salt
buttered	Dash of pepper
1 teaspoon lemon juice	1 large orange, peeled,
1 tablespoon evaporated	diced
milk	1 cup chopped or shredded
1/2 teaspoon prepared	cabbage (medium fine)
horseradish	4 slices bologna
1/2 teaspoon sugar	

Slowly stir lemon juice into milk. Blend in horseradish, sugar, salt and pepper. Drain juice from diced orange. Add orange and cabbage to milk mixture. Place a slice of bologna and 1/3 cup slaw in each bun. Makes 4 sandwiches.

Vienna-Burgers

4 hamburger buns, split and	Prepared mustard
toasted	Ketchup
2 tablespoons butter	Pickle relish
2 cans Vienna sausage	

Melt butter in heavy fry pan. Add drained Vienna sausage and brown lightly over low heat, turning occasionally. Place two halves of buns on each plate. On half of the bun arrange 3 or 4 Vienna sausages. Spread other bun half with mustard, ketchup, and pickle relish. Makes 4 servings.

Added thought . . . Serve mugs of hot soup—cream of tomato would be fine—with these on a cold night.

International Heroes

6 brown-and-serve hard
  rolls
1/4 cup French dressing
1 teaspoon dill seeds
6 1-ounce slices American
  cheese, cut in half

6 tablespoons chopped black
  olives
18 thin slices salami, about
  1/2 pound
12 slices bread-and-butter
  pickles
18 strips pimento

Cut each roll in half lengthwise, and place, cut side up, on a
cookie sheet. Brown in 400° F. oven for 12 minutes. Combine
French dressing and dill seeds; brush on cut sides of rolls. On
each bottom roll half, place 2 half slices cheese, top with a
tablespoon chopped olives, 3 salami slices, 2 bread-and-butter
pickles, and 3 pimento strips. Cover with top half of roll.
Secure sandwiches with toothpicks. Makes 6 sandwiches.
Even better . . . Give these Heroes wider international cover-
age by using Italian salami, and serving English chutney relish.

Frankfurter-Sauerkraut

6 frankfurter buns, split
3 tablespoons soft butter
3/4 teaspoon caraway seeds

6 frankfurters
1 can sauerkraut

Combine butter and caraway seeds; spread mixture on buns.
Wrap each bun in aluminum foil. Place wrapped rolls on
skewer, along with a frankfurter. Turn frequently over hot
coals until frankfurter is cooked and bun is hot. Remove label
and top from sauerkraut can and place over the grill to heat.
To serve: Place 1 frankfurter and 1/4 cup drained, heated
sauerkraut in each roll. Makes 6 franks.

Whiskery Dogs

8 slices bread
1 cup canned sauerkraut,
  drained
8 frankfurters

4 teaspoons prepared
  mustard
1/2 cup butter, softened

Chop sauerkraut. Cook frankfurters and drain; split lengthwise. Spread 4 slices bread with mustard; place 2 frankfurters,
approximately 1/4 cup sauerkraut on each slice of bread; top
with remaining slices of bread. Spread outside of each sandwich with butter. Brown sandwiches on both sides in fry pan
over medium heat for about 7 minutes. Makes 4 servings.

110

The Supreme Sandwich
Potted Meat

When I was growing up, I read many novels about England, in which the characters were forever gathered at the tea table, eating cucumber sandwiches, potted meat sandwiches or both. The cucumber I figured out at an early age, but it took me much longer to corner potted meat. It was worth the effort. This is what you use when you'd like to make a meat-loaf sandwich—only much, much better.

> 1 pound boneless beef for stew
> 2 cups water
> 1 onion, sliced
> 2 ribs celery, cut in large pieces
> 2 carrots, scraped and cut in half
> 1/2 bay leaf
> Salt
> Dash cayenne pepper
> 1/4 teaspoon mace
> 1/4 teaspoon dry mustard

Dice meat into 1-inch pieces. Put into a saucepan with water, onion, celery, carrots, bay leaf, and 1 teaspoon salt. Cover and simmer until meat is tender —about 1 hour or a bit more. Take meat from broth and cool; discard bay leaf, carrot, and celery, but reserve broth. Put meat through meat grinder, then mix with remaining ingredients and enough broth to hold together. Salt to taste. Press firmly into cups or other molds; cover and refrigerate. When ready to serve, unmold and slice thin. Use as much as you need, refrigerate the rest.

Sausage Fruit Kabobs

Buttered buns, toasted
Frankfurters cut bite-size

Pineapple chunks

On small skewers, alternate pieces of frankfurters with chunks of pineapple. Broil about 3 inches from source of heat until meat is lightly browned. Serve in toasted, buttered buns.

Savory Dogs

8 frankfurter buns, split
lengthwise
2 cups finely chopped
frankfurters
1/2 cup grated sharp cheese
2 hard-cooked eggs,
chopped

1/4 cup chili sauce
2 tablespoons pickle relish
1 teaspoon prepared
mustard
1/2 teaspoon garlic salt

Combine frankfurters, cheese, eggs, chili sauce, pickle relish, mustard, garlic salt; blend well. Pile mixture into split buns. Wrap each bun in a 6-inch square of aluminum foil, using tight double folds; twist ends securely. Place on a cookie sheet and bake in a 400° F. oven for 15 or 20 minutes. Serve in opened packages. Makes 8 servings.

Take note: These can be prepared ahead; stored in refrigerator; heated at serving time.

Frankfurter Rockets

6 frankfurter rolls, split
2 cups sauerkraut
1/2 teaspoon salt
2 tablespoons mayonnaise
or salad dressing
1/3 cup sliced radishes
6 frankfurters

2 tablespoons prepared
mustard
1 medium green pepper,
sliced into 2-inch strips
1 medium onion, thinly
sliced

Combine sauerkraut, salt, mayonnaise, and radishes; place over low heat for about 15 minutes to warm completely. While sauerkraut is heating, broil frankfurters; slice them lengthwise. Brush cut sides of rolls with mustard. Place several green-pepper strips over bottom of each roll; top with sauerkraut, broiled frankfurter, and onion rings. Cover each sandwich with roll top. Serve immediately. Makes 6 sandwiches.

Italian Sausagewiches

8 sesame or poppy-seed hard
rolls
1 pound thinly sliced Italian
sausage

1 cup shredded lettuce
8 slices mozzarella cheese

Put just enough water in a large shallow skillet to cover bottom of pan. Place sliced meat in skillet. Cover and steam over low heat for 8 minutes. Slice rolls lengthwise. Place 5 or 6 slices sausage on bottom half of each roll; cover with shredded lettuce, then a slice of cheese. Cover with top half of roll. Makes 8 sandwiches.

Stuffed Franks

6 frankfurter rolls, split	2 tablespoons mayonnaise
1/4 cup chopped dill pickle	or salad dressing
2 tablespoons chopped	6 frankfurters
peanuts	
2 tablespoons chopped	
green onion	

Combine dill pickle, peanuts, green onion, and mayonnaise. Cut frankfurters lengthwise. Place 1 tablespoon filling mixture between frankfurter halves. Place stuffed frankfurters into rolls, and set rolls in shallow baking pan. Cover top of pan with foil. Heat in 400° F. oven for 10 minutes. Makes 6 servings.

Frankfurter Bake

5 frankfurter rolls	1/4 cup grated onion
10 frankfurters	1/2 teaspoon salt
1/2 cup evaporated milk	1/4 teaspoon paprika
2 tablespoons horseradish	
2 tablespoons prepared	
mustard	

Cut frankfurters and rolls in half lengthwise. Butter a flat baking dish or jelly-roll pan. Place rolls in dish cut side up. Blend milk and seasonings. Spoon sauce generously over rolls, reserving about 1/3 cup. Lay each frankfurter cut side down on a roll half. Spoon remaining sauce over frankfurters. Bake 20 minutes in 350° F. oven. Makes 5 generous servings.

Franks-and-Beans Savory

6 split frankfurter rolls	2 tablespoons minced onion
1/2 cup chopped kidney	2 tablespoons chopped
beans, drained	green pepper
1/2 cup chopped frankfurters	1 cup drained, snipped
1 teaspoon minced onion	sauerkraut
2 tablespoons chopped	1 cup (1/4 pound) grated
sweet pickle	process American
1 tablespoon mayonnaise or	cheese
cooked salad dressing	Softened butter

Several hours ahead: Mix kidney beans with frankfurters, 1 teaspoon onion, pickle, mayonnaise. Refrigerate. *At serving time:* In 1 tablespoon hot butter in skillet, sauté 2 tablespoons onion and green pepper until onion is golden. Add sauerkraut; cook 5 minutes; stir in grated cheese. Toast frankfurter rolls in broiler; butter. Arrange frankfurter mixture on half of each roll, sauerkraut mixture on other half. Makes 6 servings.

Barber Poles

10 frankfurter rolls, split	10 bacon slices
10 frankfurters	5/8 cup Barbecue Sauce
2 large dill pickles, cut into 5 lengthwise strips	(page 68)

Slit frankfurters lengthwise. Place a dill pickle strip in each slit. Wrap a bacon slice diagonally around each filled frankfurter and fasten bacon with dampened toothpicks. Grill in a closed wire rack over hot coals, turning often, until bacon is crisp, or about 10 minutes. Heat or toast rolls; spread cut sides of rolls with Barbecue Sauce, then insert a grilled frankfurter. Remove toothpicks and serve immediately with black olives. Makes 10 sandwiches.

Keep in mind . . . You don't have to cook outdoors to enjoy these. They do just as well if you broil them about 3 inches below the heat, turning to do bacon on all sides. Omit toothpicks; if you tuck the bacon strip neatly around the frankfurter it will crisp that way.

Chili Hot Dogs

6 buttered buns	6 tablespoons chili sauce
6 frankfurters	

Broil frankfurters; heat buttered buns in oven. Tuck hot frankfurters into warmed buns. Spoon heated chili sauce over the frankfurters.

Good companions . . . Splendid with corn chips and scallions.

Frankfurter-Cheese Rolls

6 unsliced frankfurter rolls	1 tablespoon prepared mustard
3/4 cup thinly cut frankfurters	1/3 cup mayonnaise or salad dressing
3/4 cup diced process American cheese	
3 tablespoons sweet pickle relish	

Hollow out frankfurter rolls, from end to end, with an apple corer. Combine frankfurters, cheese, pickle relish, mustard, and mayonnaise. Fill center of each roll with 1/3 cup of frankfurter-cheese mixture. Wrap rolls in aluminum foil and heat in a 350° F. oven for 15 minutes. Makes 6 rolls.

Perfect partners . . . Thick slices of chive-sprinkled tomato, or a molded lime gelatin salad made with shredded cabbage and cucumber.

Bacon-Frankfurter Roll-ups

8 slices of bread   8 frankfurters
8 bacon strips   ketchup

Cook bacon slices slightly. Cut crusts from bread and tips from frankfurters. Lay frankfurter at one end of bread slice and spread with ketchup. Roll bread around frankfurter; roll bacon slices around bread and fasten with a toothpick. Finish cooking bacon under broiler, turning once.

Space Dog

6 frankfurter rolls, split   6 frankfurters
1/4 cup hot-dog relish

Spread 2 teaspoons hot-dog relish in each roll and wrap individually in heavy foil. Place wrapped rolls and frankfurters alternately on long skewers. Turn frequently over hot coals until frankfurters are cooked and buns hot. *To serve:* place a hot frankfurter in each roll. Makes 6 sandwiches.

French Franks

6 frankfurter buns, split,   French Salad (see page 191)
    toasted, buttered   3/4 cup grated Swiss cheese
6 frankfurters

Skin frankfurters and split three-quarters through. Place on bottom halves of buns. Fill split in each frankfurter with French Salad. Sprinkle with cheese. Heat under broiler until cheese melts. Cover with bun tops. Makes 6 sandwiches. **Perfect partner** . . . Coleslaw perked up with a helping of caraway seeds.

Frank Frizzles

6 frankfurter buns, split,   2 tablespoons butter
    toasted, buttered   3 tablespoons chopped onion
6 frankfurters   Prepared mustard

Skin frankfurters and chop coarsely. Melt butter in heavy skillet. Frizzle franks and onions in butter until franks are lightly browned, onion soft and yellow. Spread bottom halves of buns with prepared mustard, and divide frank mixture over. Cover with top halves. Makes 6 sandwiches. **Perfect partners** . . . Pickles—almost any kind of pickles you can name!

Taco Dog

1 frankfurter roll, split	Shredded lettuce
1 frankfurter	Shredded Cheddar cheese
Chili sauce	Potato chips

For each sandwich, place 1 hot frankfurter on a roll. Add chili sauce. Sprinkle with shredded lettuce and shredded Cheddar cheese. Serve with potato chips.

Tongue-and-Eggs

10 slices white bread, buttered	4 eggs
2 tablespoons butter	3/4 cup cold diced tongue
2 tablespoons chopped onion	Salt and pepper
2 teaspoons chopped green pepper	1/2 cup shredded Swiss cheese

Melt butter in heavy skillet. Sauté onion and green pepper until soft but not browned. Break eggs into bowl and whip briefly with a fork. Stir in tongue. Add to skillet, season, scramble—as for plain scrambled eggs—until softly done. Stir in cheese. Divide over 5 slices bread, top with remaining bread. Makes 5 sandwiches.

Variation on the Benedict Theme

2 English muffins, split, toasted, buttered	4 eggs, soft poached
4 slices cooked tongue	Hollandaise Sauce (see page 20)

Place a slice of tongue on each muffin half, and top with a poached egg. Spoon Hollandaise Sauce over eggs—about 2 tablespoons for each. Makes 4 servings.

Perfect partners . . . For a wonderful brunch: honeydew melon wedges with lime, extra toasted muffins, a selection of preserves, lots of coffee.

Tongue-on-Wheat

8 slices whole-wheat bread, buttered	8 sweet pickles, sliced thin
8 slices cooked tongue	Salad dressing

Arrange tongue on bread, cover with pickle. Spread with salad dressing and cover with remaining slices. Makes 4 sandwiches.

Tongue Cranwiches

6 slices white bread,
   buttered
12 slices cooked tongue
Mayonnaise

12 slices cooked turkey
1 can jellied cranberry sauce,
   cut into 7 slices

Place 2 slices tongue on each slice of bread. Spread lightly with mayonnaise and cover each slice with 2 turkey slices. Top each with a slice of cranberry sauce. Decorate with a dab of mayonnaise. Cut the seventh slice of cranberry sauce into 6 pie-shaped sections. Place one on each mound of mayonnaise. Makes 6 open-face sandwiches.

Tongue Salads

6 rye rolls, split, buttered
1 1/4 cups ground tongue
1/2 cup chopped celery
2 tablespoons chopped
   sweet pickle

2 tablespoons chopped
   shallots
1/2 cucumber, peeled,
   seeded, chopped
Mayonnaise

Mix together all ingredients, using just enough mayonnaise to moisten. Taste, and season if necessary. Spread on bottom halves of rolls, cover with top halves. Makes 6 sandwiches.
For pretty . . . Skewer a cocktail onion, then a stuffed olive, on a toothpick. Stick one of these in the top of each sandwich.

Tongue for Sandwiches

1 3- to 4-pound smoked
   beef tongue
1 large onion, quartered
10 whole peppercorns

1/4 teaspoon mustard seed
2 bay leaves
4 whole cloves

Wash tongue. Pat dry with paper towels. Combine tongue and remaining ingredients in a 6-quart kettle, with water to cover. Bring to a boil. Reduce heat and simmer, covered, until tongue is tender—about 3 hours. Drain tongue, reserving stock. (Use it in sauces, soups.) Plunge tongue into cold water. With a sharp knife, slit skin on underside of tongue. Peel off skin. Remove root and discard small bones. (Don't throw the root end away—this is the "schlung"—a perfect substitute for a ham bone in split-pea or lentil soup.) Refrigerate. For sandwiches, slice thin.

Brandied Tongueburgers

6 hamburger buns, split, toasted, buttered	1 1/4 cups diced cooked tongue
2 tablespoons butter	3 tablespoons brandy
2 tablespoons chopped onion	Heavy cream

Melt butter in heavy skillet. Sauté onion in butter until soft but not brown. Add tongue to skillet. Put brandy into flamer or into a small metal cup and set alight. Pour flaming brandy over tongue, and stir until flame subsides. Add enough cream to bind lightly. Heat, but do not allow to come to a boil. Spoon the filling over the bun bottoms, cover with bun tops.

Ginger Tonguewiches

8 slices rye bread, buttered	Gingersnap Sauce
16 slices cooked tongue	

Arrange tongue on 4 slices of bread. Top generously with Gingersnap Sauce. Cover with remaining bread.

Gingersnap Sauce

2 slices bacon
1/4 cup chopped onion
5 gingersnaps, crumbled
1/4 cup wine vinegar
1/4 cup light brown sugar, firmly packed
3/4 cup tongue stock
1/2 bay leaf
1 teaspoon grated lemon rind
1 teaspoon Worcestershire sauce

Sauté bacon until crisp. Drain, crumble. Add onion to bacon fat in skillet, sauté until tender. Stir in gingersnaps, vinegar, sugar, tongue stock, bay leaf. Bring to a boil and cook about 5 minutes. Taste, and add salt if needed. Take out bay leaf. Remove from heat, add bacon, lemon rind, and Worcestershire sauce. Mix well.

Cover Girls

4 poppy-seed hard rolls	12 slices cooked tongue
Mayonnaise	4 slices Swiss cheese
Boston lettuce	French Salad (see page 191)

Cut each roll into 3 slices. Spread cut surfaces with mayonnaise. On bottom of each roll place two pieces of lettuce, top with 3 slices tongue, 1 slice cheese. Cover with middle slice of roll. Pile on French Salad generously, cover with top of roll.

Sandwich + Soup = Supper

A bowl of soup—or a cup for the lighter eaters—steaming hot in the cold weather, icy cold or jellied when summer's heat wilts appetites, plus a delicious sandwich, adds up to a very acceptable meal indeed. Dessert should follow the dictates of the rest of the meal—light, such as fruit, if the soup and sandwich are hearty, sturdier—what's better than homemade cake?—if the sandwich and soup are on the light side.

If the soup is homemade, make it ahead of time. Do the same with dessert. Then getting this supper to the table becomes a cinch. Here are some suggestions:

First snow of the season:

Cream of Tomato Soup
(serve with a dollop of chive-topped sour cream)
Curry-Beef Sandwich (page 67)

Fudge Cupcakes   Beverage

Friday night in autumn:

Corn-Clam Chowder
(make it with canned corn, canned clams—easy!)
Crunchy Cheese Sandwich (page 39)

Boysenberry Tarts   Beverage

Unexpected company:

Black Bean Soup
(the canned variety—lace it liberally with sherry)
Sunshine Sandwich (page 83)

Mandarin Oranges with Sour Cream
and Candied Ginger, Macaroons   Beverage

Pretty impressive—in no time:

Superb Pea Soup
(a believe-it-or-not wonder—see this section for how-to)
Supreme Scrambled Egg Sandwich (page 123)

Lemon Bavarian   Beverage

Men's hot-and-hearty fare:

Philadelphia Pepper Pot
(don't mention the tripe until everyone's tasted)
Cheese-and-Beef Sandwich (page 66)

Hot Apple Pie   Beverage

Not the heat, but the humidity:

Special Jellied Madrilène
(canned—add chopped cucumber, chives; in the morning, refrigerate)
Chesapeake Bay (page 124)
Pineapple Sherbet   Beverage

On Dad's night out:

Chicken-Rice Soup
(take it easy—the canned kind is so good!)
Waldorf Cheese Sandwich (page 38)
Chocolate Pudding   Beverage

Summer supper—invite the next-door neighbors:

Cucumber Soup
(delicate chilled Danish hot-weather specialty)
French-Roll Beef (page 68)
Lemon Layer Cake   Beverage

Cold-day country home-style:

Vegetable Soup
(make it yourself in the morning—even better,
the day before)
Imperial Chicken Sandwich (page 23)
Butterscotch Bread Pudding   Beverage

On the Swedish side:

Fruit Soup
(Swedish specialty—and wonderfully good served
icy cold)
Sardines Göteborg (page 160)
Swedish Pancakes with Lingonberries   Beverage

It's never too hot to eat:

Vichyssoise
(don't forget a drift of chives on each serving)
Chutney-Lamb Sandwich (page 68)
Cantaloupe with Coffee Ice Cream   Beverage

Teen-ager's special:

Chili Bean Soup
(sprinkle with grated Cheddar before serving)
Party Patties (page 100)
Baked Apples   Cupcakes   Beverage

After the football game:

Oyster Stew
(make it with part cream, buttery rich, and serve in
big bowls)
Little Porky Pizzas (page 104)
Lemon Meringue Pie   Beverage

The Gourmet Way

Superb Pea Soup

This is, surely, what the Mock Turtle meant when he
sang of "Soup of the Evening, Beautiful Soup!"

> 1 package frozen peas
> 1 cup chicken broth
> 1 large lettuce leaf
> 1 tablespoon minced onion
> Salt, white pepper
> 1 cardamom seed
> 1 cup heavy cream

Break up block of peas with a fork. (No, we've left
nothing out—you do not cook them.) Put peas, broth,
lettuce, onion, seasonings into blender; blend for 1
minute. Add cream, mix smooth. Serve cold—or, if
you must heat it, use a double boiler. Makes 4 servings.

Perfect partners . . . This superb soup and any
meat-, fish-, or cheese-based sandwich you like for a
wonderful supper. Add a beverage and a sweet-tart
dessert—perhaps lemon pie?

Eggs for Everybody

Almost everyone likes eggs, and almost everyone can eat them. They can be cooked in a number of ways and used alone, or combined—and they make splendid partners—with any number of other flavors. No wonder they're for everybody—they're a kind of all-weather, all-purpose, all-meal food!

Eggs Benedict

2 English muffins, split,
    toasted, and buttered
4 slices Virginia ham

4 eggs
Hollandaise Sauce (page 20)

Sauté ham slices lightly in butter. Poach eggs. Place slice of ham on each muffin half, top with a poached egg. Spoon warm Hollandaise Sauce over each egg. Makes 2 servings.
Or try it this way . . . Substitute well-drained, cooked, chopped spinach, seasoned with a little sautéed onion, for the ham—which makes the dish into Eggs Florentine.

Oahu Sandwich

16 slices white bread
1/2 cup drained crushed
    pineapple
1 3-ounce package cream
    cheese

1 cup chopped hard-
    cooked eggs
1/8 teaspoon salt
Dash of pepper

Blend pineapple with cream cheese; combine with eggs, salt and pepper. Spread on 8 slices of bread, top with remaining slices. Makes 8 sandwiches.

Bull's-Eye

4 slices bread
Butter
8 filleted anchovies
4 onion rings

4 egg yolks
2 teaspoons capers
Fresh watercress

Cut bread into rounds, and butter. Arrange the anchovy fillets around the edge of the bread, place a ring of onion inside, a raw yolk of egg in the middle, with capers sprinkled around it. Garnish with watercress. Makes 4 servings.

The Supreme Sandwich

Scrambled Eggs

Put these most-useful of treats together quickly from ingredients any refrigerator and emergency shelf can yield up (or should!) for brunch, for lunch, for late-evening snacking.

> 4 slices white bread, toasted and buttered
> 5 eggs
> 1/4 cup light cream
> Salt, white pepper
> 12 cooked asparagus spears
> 4 slices Münster cheese

Break eggs into a bowl; beat lightly, beat in cream, seasoning. Over medium heat, scramble the eggs in butter until they barely hold together. Place 3 asparagus spears on each slice of toast, heap scrambled eggs over the spears, and top each open sandwich with a slice of cheese. Bake briefly in a 350° F. oven until cheese has begun to melt.

Or try this . . . No asparagus? Substitute a slice of tomato, or spears of broccoli. If you prefer the nutty-sweet flavor, use Swiss cheese instead of Münster.

Asparagus-Egg Sandwiches

> 6 slices white bread
> 2 tablespoons soft butter
> 3 hard-cooked eggs, sliced
> 24 cooked green asparagus spears
> Salt and pepper to taste
> 3/4 cup tomato sauce
> 2 tablespoons slivered almonds

Toast bread and spread with butter. Arrange egg slices on buttered toast. Top with asparagus spears. Sprinkle with salt and pepper. Pour tomato sauce over asparagus spears. Scatter almonds on top. Place on a cookie sheet and broil until nuts are browned and sauce is hot, about 2 minutes. Serve immediately. Makes 6 sandwiches.

Or try it this way . . . Instead of tomato sauce and almonds, use thick white sauce topped with a golden layer of grated Cheddar cheese. Serve with sliced tomatoes, seasoned as you like.

Egg-Anchovy I

4 slices of bread	Dash of cayenne pepper
3 hard-cooked egg yolks	2 tablespoons grated
10 anchovies	Parmesan cheese
1 teaspoon curry powder	Butter or cream

Work to a smooth paste 3 hard-cooked egg yolks, 10 anchovies, curry powder, cayenne pepper, cheese, and enough butter or cream to make it spreadable. Spread on 2 slices of bread and top with remaining slices. Makes 2 sandwiches.

Imperial

8 slices white bread	2 hard-cooked eggs, minced
3 teaspoons caviar	Mayonnaise

Mix caviar with eggs and moisten with mayonnaise. Spread thinly on 4 slices bread; top with remaining slices.

Brunchwich

Bread	Eggs
Butter	Salt
Swiss or American cheese slices, natural or process, cut into strips	Pepper

For each serving, toast 1 bread slice on one side. Spread untoasted side with butter. Place, toasted side down, in shallow pan. Along edges of each bread slice, place strips of Swiss or American cheese, with corners touching to form a frame. Break egg into center of each. Sprinkle with salt, pepper. Bake 10 to 15 minutes at 400° F. or until firm.

Even better . . . Try the unexpected addition of French dressing when you serve this. Those who like it will love it.

Chesapeake Bay

24 slices whole-wheat bread	1 teaspoon celery salt
6 hard-cooked eggs, chopped	3 tablespoons mayonnaise
1 6 1/2-ounce can or 2/3 cup flaked crab meat	1 teaspoon lemon juice

Combine chopped eggs, crab meat, celery salt, mayonnaise, and lemon juice. Spread on 12 slices of bread, top with remaining slices.

The Gourmet Way
Homemade Mayonnaise

Making her own mayonnaise is something in which a cook can take quiet pride—and quiet will be sufficient, for nobody will mistake this for the from-the-store variety.

> 2 egg yolks
> 1/2 teaspoon dry mustard
> Salt, cayenne pepper
> 1 cup salad or olive oil
> 3 tablespoons lemon juice or white wine vinegar

Beat egg yolks in small bowl of electric beater, at medium speed, 4 minutes. Combine and add dry ingredients. Beat again. Add the oil drop by drop, beating constantly. When mayonnaise begins to thicken, add lemon juice or vinegar. Add remaining oil in a very thin stream, continuing to beat. Store in the refrigerator.

Take your choice . . . For a light dressing, use lemon juice and salad oil; for a richer, more definite flavor, vinegar and olive oil.

French-Toasted Eggwiches

8 slices white bread	1 1/2 tablespoons mayonnaise
1 egg	or cooked salad
1/3 cup milk	dressing
1/4 teaspoon salt	1/4 cup pickle relish.
4 hard-cooked eggs,	1/2 teaspoon salt
chopped	1/3 cup soft butter
1 1/2 teaspoons prepared	
mustard	

Beat egg; mix in milk, salt. Mix chopped eggs with mustard, mayonnaise, pickle relish, salt. Spread bread slices with half of butter. Make 4 covered sandwiches, with chopped-egg mixture as filling. Dip each sandwich into egg-milk mixture. Heat remaining butter in skillet. Sauté sandwiches about 5 minutes on each side, or until lightly browned.

Perfect partners . . . Crisp coleslaw, tomato wedges—and a fork. This is not finger-food except, perhaps, for the very young.

Long Boys

French bread
Butter
Scrambled eggs

Green onion tops, chopped
Bologna slices, grilled

Cut French bread in 6-inch-long sections. Split each section in half lengthwise. Spread cut slices with butter, toast lightly under broiler. Place hot scrambled eggs on half of the slices. Sprinkle with chopped green onion tops. Place grilled bologna slices on remaining bread. For each serving, use 1 scrambled-egg slice, 1 bologna slice. They may be eaten separately as open sandwiches or put together for heartier hero-type eating. *Good companion* . . . Ketchup, particularly for the youngsters.

Sharp Egg-Cheese Sandwich

8 slices white or whole-
wheat bread
1/2 cup chopped hard-cooked
eggs
1 cup grated process
American cheese

3 tablespoons mayonnaise
1/2 teaspoon vinegar
2 teaspoons grated onion
1/2 teaspoon prepared
mustard
1/8 teaspoon salt

Combine eggs, cheese, mayonnaise, vinegar, onion, mustard, and salt. Spread on 4 slices of bread, top with remaining slices.

Country Lunch

White or whole-wheat bread,
buttered

Sliced liverwurst
Hard-cooked eggs, sliced

Spread liverwurst on 1 slice of buttered bread. Cover other slice with sliced egg. Count on 1 egg for each sandwich; these are peasant-lunch rather than tea-party sandwiches.

Cress Eggs

Whole wheat bread, buttered
Hard-cooked eggs, sliced
Salt
Pepper

Olive oil
Vinegar
Watercress, minced

Marinate sliced eggs in salt, pepper, olive oil, and vinegar for at least 1/2 hour. Spread minced watercress on half of bread slices. Cover with drained egg slices. Top with remaining bread slices.

The Gourmet Way

Pennsylvania Dutch Red Beet Eggs

1 can sliced beets, with liquid
2 whole cloves
2 tablespoons sugar
1/2 cup vinegar
1/2 teaspoon celery seed
1 bay leaf
1 medium onion
6 hard-cooked eggs

Bring all ingredients except onion and eggs to a boil. Slice onion very thin and separate into rings. Pour beet mixture into a deep bowl. Remove bay leaf and cloves. Add onion, stir, add eggs, being sure they are completely submerged. Refrigerate at least 24 hours before serving—the longer the eggs stay in the pickle the deeper blush they'll develop.

Anchovy-Capers-Egg

6 slices cracked or whole
  wheat bread
2 anchovies
2 pieces of pickle
Sprig of parsley, chopped
2 tablespoons capers

1 teaspoon mustard
3 teaspoons olive oil
3 teaspoons vinegar
2 hard-cooked eggs, chopped
Salt
Paprika

Pound anchovies, pickle, parsley, capers, mustard, olive oil, and vinegar to a paste. Add eggs, finely chopped, and season with salt and paprika. Spread on 3 slices bread, top with remaining slices.

Merchant's Special

White bread, buttered
Fried egg

Grated Parmesan cheese
Chopped green onion

Place fried egg on buttered bread. Sprinkle grated Parmesan cheese and finely chopped green onion on top of egg. Cover with another slice of bread, or eat as an open sandwich.

Make Mine Deviled

Deviled eggs, in all their infinite variety, form a wonderful partnership with a sandwich of almost any kind—well, any kind except an egg sandwich, that is. A perfect, and perfectly beautiful, invention, the egg! Obviously it was meant to reach its ultimate destiny deviled—hard-cooked, its yolk mashed and combined with any number of savory delights and piled back into the halves of white. Here's deviled egg know-how to broaden a cook's repertoire.

All about eggs . . . They should always be refrigerated, preferably stored large end up. Hens providently lay their eggs complete with a protective coating, so don't make the mistake of washing them before putting them away in the refrigerator. All eggs nowadays come with their grade prominently stamped or printed on the carton. Most stores carry four grades: AA—freshest, best for table use; A—also good for table use; B—good for use in baked goods, fair for table; C—can be used for baking, preferably not for table, as the white and yolk are hard to separate. For hard-cooking, use Grade AA or Grade A—in the former, the yolk will be beautifully centered, in the latter probably a bit off-center.

How to hard-cook eggs . . . Cover eggs with water to a depth of an inch above the eggs. Bring quickly to a boil. Take the pan off the heat and cover it. Let the eggs stand in the hot water for 20 minutes. For a variation, just as good, see page 13. Cool immediately under running cold water—that keeps an unpleasant gray-green surface from forming on the yolks and helps make the shells easier to remove.

How to tell a hard-cooked from a raw egg . . . Spin it! Although raw and hard-cooked eggs, stored in the refrigerator, look exactly alike, a raw egg will hardly spin at all when laid on its side on a flat surface, while a hard-cooked one will do you a fine dervish dance.

Basic Deviled Eggs

6 hard-cooked eggs
1 tablespoon mayonnaise
(or more)
Salt
White pepper

Shell eggs and chill. Halve lengthwise. Remove yolks carefully. Press yolks through a sieve or mash with a fork in a medium-size bowl. Add mayonnaise to make a smooth, light paste. Season. Lightly mound yolk mixture into whites, being careful not to break the whites. Refrigerate until ready to use.

Perk-ups for Basic Deviled Eggs . . . Eggs prepared as above will be bland—just about right for the very young, too nothing-tasting for their elders. So, to the egg-mayonnaise mixture for 6 eggs, add one of the following: 1 1/2 teaspoons Worcestershire sauce . . . 2 teaspoons snipped chives . . . 1 teaspoon dried mustard . . . 1 tablespoon finely chopped dill pickle . . . 1 tablespoon finely chopped sweet pickle . . . 1/4 cup grated sharp Cheddar cheese . . . 1/4 cup shredded raw spinach . . . 1 tablespoon grated onion . . . 2 teaspoons finely chopped radish . . . 2 drops garlic juice . . . 1/4 teaspoon turmeric . . . curry powder to taste . . . 2 tablespoons of any finely chopped leftover vegetable, plus a dash of onion salt or garlic salt. Or let your imagination run away with you and combine any two or three or even four of the above. In all cases, you'll probably need a bit more mayonnaise to moisten properly—deviled-egg mixture should never be dry, for it will dry out a little while it's chilling in the refrigerator.

Butter-Deviled Eggs . . . Follow the recipe for Basic Deviled Eggs, but don't chill the cooked eggs before deviling them. Into the still-warm yolks, incorporate 1 or 2 tablespoons of whipped sweet butter instead of mayonnaise. You'll need more salt in these. Try any of the perk-ups above with these butter-deviled eggs, too.

Ham Devils . . . Add 1 can deviled ham, 1 tablespoon prepared mustard, 1/4 teaspoon Worcestershire sauce, 3 drops onion juice to yolk mixture of Basic Deviled Eggs. Increase mayonnaise sufficiently to moisten.

Tongue Devils . . . Substitute 1/4 cup ground tongue for the ham in Ham Devils.

Artichoke Devils . . . Cook 1 package frozen artichoke hearts according to package directions. Marinate in a combination of 1/4 cup wine vinegar, 1/4 cup olive oil, 1 teaspoon salt, 1/4 teaspoon freshly ground black pepper for at least 4 hours. Drain well. Make Butter-Deviled Eggs, adding 2 teaspoons lemon juice to the yolk mixture. Put half an artichoke half in each egg-white half and pile the yolk mixture high on top.

Braunschweiger Devils . . . Slice Braunschweiger 1/2 inch thick, then cut each slice into pie-shaped quarters. Make Basic Deviled Eggs, adding 1/4 teaspoon dry mustard to the yolk mixture. Pile into whites and bury a piece of Braunschweiger in each, rounded-side up and sticking out a little.

Mushoom Devils . . . Chop fine 6 whole mushrooms and the stems of 6 more, reserving the 6 caps. Sauté the chopped mushrooms in 2 tablespoons butter until cooked but not browned—about 5 minutes. Make Butter-Deviled Eggs, using the butter in which the mushrooms were sautéed as part of the butter for the yolk mixture. Fill whites. Sauté mushroom caps, rounded side down, in 1 tablespoon butter. Drain. Top each egg half with a mushroom cap. Sprinkle with paprika.

Chicken Devils . . . Make Basic Deviled Eggs, adding 1/2 cup minced chicken (or make it turkey, if you prefer), 4 drops onion juice, 1 teaspoon anchovy paste, 3 drops lemon juice to yolk mixture. Fill whites, and top each egg half with a rolled anchovy fillet—the caper-stuffed kind.

Seafood Devils . . . To the yolk mixture in Basic Deviled Eggs, add 1 teaspoon of lemon juice and any one of the following: 4 skinless and boneless sardines, mashed . . . 1/4 cup of minced lobster or crab meat . . . 1/4 cup of tiny Danish shrimp, halved—and by all means top each filled egg white with a whole shrimp bedded on a small sprig of parsley . . . 1/4 cup of flaked salmon or tuna. If you like curry, a little curry powder—to taste—gives wonderful flavor to any of these Seafood Devils.

Vitamin Devils . . . To the yolk mixture of Basic Deviled Eggs or Butter-Deviled Eggs, add finely chopped onion, green pepper, celery, grated carrot, snipped chives, snipped parsley—in any combination or proportion that suits your fancy, but make the total no more than 1/3 of a cup.

Breakfast Devils . . . Start with 6 hard-cooked eggs and, as in Butter-Deviled Eggs, do your deviling while the eggs are still hot—immediately after their cold-water bath. Sauté until crisp 3 slices of bacon. Drain and crumble. To the sieved or mashed egg yolks, add 1 tablespoon bacon fat and enough cream —sour or sweet—to make a moist mixture. Taste and season; you will need little or no salt if the bacon is salty. (There's no law which says that these good deviled eggs can't be served at meals other than breakfast.)

Danish Devils . . . To the yolks in Basic Deviled Eggs, add 2 tablespoons soft Danish blue cheese, 1 teaspoon of snipped chives, 1/2 teaspoon of dried rosemary.

Deviled Egg Dress-ups . . . For pretty, decorate halves of deviled eggs—let the seasoning you've incorporated be your guide—with one of the following: sprig of watercress . . . sprig of parsley . . . drift of paprika . . . sprinkling of chopped parsley or watercress . . . 3 or 4 drained capers . . . piece of water chestnut rolled in chopped parsley or in paprika . . . cooked, drained asparagus tip, seated in a dab of lemon-juiced mayonnaise . . . anchovy fillet, halved, the halves crossed . . . 2 thin strips of pimento, crossed . . . small triangle of green pepper, partially buried point down . . . a small wedge of any sharp cheese.

Egg-Anchovy II

18 slices bread, spread
    thinly with mayonnaise
6 hard-cooked eggs, sieved
    or chopped

1/3 cup mayonnaise
1 tablespoon anchovy paste

Mix together eggs, mayonnaise, and anchovy paste with fork.
Spread on 9 slices of bread, top with remaining slices. Makes
9 sandwiches.

Hash-'n'-Egg

6 hamburger buns, buttered
1 can corned-beef hash,
    chilled

2 hard-cooked eggs, sliced
Lettuce

For ease in slicing, open can at both ends with can opener,
press hash slightly with thumb to remove from can. Cut hash
into 6 slices, brown in skillet with small amount of butter.
Place on roll, garnish with egg slices and lettuce.

Egg-and-Olive I

10 slices white bread
3 hard-cooked eggs,
    chopped
1 tablespoon sliced
    stuffed olives
2 1/2 tablespoons mayonnaise

1/8 teaspoon salt
1/4 teaspoon onion salt
Dash of pepper
1/8 teaspoon dry mustard
1/4 teaspoon Worcestershire
    sauce

Combine chopped eggs, olives, mayonnaise, salt, onion salt,
pepper, mustard, and Worcestershire sauce. Spread on 5 slices
of bread and top with remaining slices.

Egg-and-Olive II

8 slices white or whole-
    wheat bread
1 3/4 cups chopped hard-
    cooked eggs
1 teaspoon sliced stuffed
    olives

1 tablespoon chopped
    green pepper
1/2 tablespoon salt
2 tablespoons mayonnaise
    or salad dressing

Combine eggs, olives, green pepper, salt, and mayonnaise.
Spread on 4 slices of bread and top with remaining slices.

Peppered Egg-Cheese Sandwich

14 slices white or whole-wheat bread
3/4 cup chopped hard-cooked egg
1/2 cup creamed cottage cheese
1 teaspoon minced onion
1 tablespoon chopped green pepper
1/4 teaspoon salt
1/8 teaspoon paprika
1/8 teaspoon celery seed
Dash of pepper

Combine chopped egg, cottage cheese, onion, chopped green pepper, salt, paprika, celery seed, and pepper. Spread on 7 slices of bread, top with remaining slices. Makes 7 sandwiches.
Take note: Try sneaking this one in on children who think all they're getting is a "plain old egg sandwich."

Mushroom-Egg Sandwich

20 slices white bread, spread thinly with mayonnaise
1 8-ounce can mushroom stems and pieces, well drained
1 cup chopped hard-cooked eggs
1/2 cup chopped celery
1 teaspoon chopped chives
1/2 teaspoon salt
1/8 teaspoon pepper
1/2 teaspoon grated lemon peel
1/4 teaspoon dry mustard
1/4 cup mayonnaise

Combine mushrooms, eggs, celery, chives, salt, pepper, lemon peel, dry mustard, and mayonnaise. Spread on 10 slices of bread, top with remaining slices.

Zesty Salad Sandwiches

8 slices white bread
2 tablespoons soft butter
1/4 teaspoon garlic powder
3/4 teaspoon hot pepper sauce
1/4 cup mayonnaise or salad dressing
4 hard-cooked eggs, chopped
1 tablespoon finely chopped onion
1/4 tablespoon salt
3/4 cup shredded lettuce

Cream butter and garlic powder together. Combine hot pepper sauce, mayonnaise, chopped eggs, onion, and salt. Spread garlic butter on one side of each slice of bread. Spread egg salad on 4 slices of bread. Sprinkle with shredded lettuce and top with remaining bread slices.
Perfect partners . . . Crisp, cold, crunchy slices of radish and cucumber, frills of watercress, strips of dill pickle.

Better Butters

To go back for a moment to those lovely storybook tea tables which I shared, in my growing-up years, through the pages of my reading: There never was one (a tea table, I mean) on which thin bread-and-butter sandwiches did not appear. With good reason. What's better, in what my Aunt Hazel used to call the loop of the afternoon (you know, the lowest part of it, when you and everything else seem to be hanging down), than two pieces of thin brown bread, spread with good butter, salted, put together, and cut into nice little sections, to go with a cup of steaming, reviving tea (or coffee)?

Savory Butters

To 1 stick (1/4 pound) softened butter, add 1 of the following and cream together thoroughly (mortar and pestle are the thing for this, if you have a set):

- 1/2 cup grated Cheddar and a pinch of dry mustard
- 4 tablespoons horseradish
- 2 tablespoons chutney
- 1/2 tablespoon curry powder
- 1/4 cup finely chopped parsley, mint or basil leaves, plus a few drops lemon juice
- 1/4 cup chopped thyme, tarragon, chives—use any or all together—plus a few drops onion juice
- 2 tablespoons ketchup or chili sauce, plus dash of Tabasco
- 2 tablespoons caraway or sesame seeds
- 1 tablespoon anchovy paste or 6 anchovy fillets pounded into paste, plus few drops lemon juice
- 1 teaspoon Worcestershire sauce
- 1 tablespoon dehydrated onion flakes
- 2 tablespoons grated Parmesan cheese
- 4 skinless, boneless sardines
- 2 tablespoons well-drained India relish
- 2 teaspoons lime juice

Keep in mind . . . Any one of these savory butters makes a delicious snack on rye bread—seeded or not, as your taste dictates—or on the small, salty Party Rye. For a kingly snack— and a quick one if you, as a clever housekeeper, make up the butters beforehand and keep them in the refrigerator—try soft-scrambled eggs on a slice of toast that has been spread with one of these butters. They make straight-to-a-man's-heart eating!

Sweet Butters

  2 tablespoons honey
1/3 cup pecans, walnuts, cashews, black walnuts, or fil-
    berts (if you have a blender, use it; otherwise get your
    nuts as finely ground as possible)
  1 teaspoon vanilla and 1 tablespoon sugar
  1 teaspoon cinnamon and 1 tablespoon sugar
1/2 teaspoon nutmeg and 1 tablespoon sugar
6-7 ripe strawberries and 1 tablespoon confectioners'
    sugar, plus a few drops lemon juice
 20 ripe raspberries and 1 tablespoon confectioners' sugar,
    plus few drops lemon juice

Keep in mind . . . For a very special sandwich indeed, try any
of these delicious sweet butters on Homemade Egg Bread
(page 80), although plain white will do. And experiment with
them on corn bread or corn-and-molasses bread for tea or snack
sandwiches that leave very little in the way of goodness to be
desired!

Truffle Butter

The important thing to know about truffles is that they have
to be warmed to release their full flavor. For example, 1 tablespoon truffles added to a sauce just before serving does nothing.
But when you're scrambling eggs, warm 1/4 teaspoon truffles
with the butter in the pan before you add the eggs, and see
what happens. And try this:

1 teaspoon truffle peelings
1/2 pound butter

Put truffles and butter into pan; melt butter over slow fire so
that it has time to absorb truffle flavor without browning. Pour
into small crock, chill, and use as you like.
Keep in mind . . . Truffle butter, spread on fresh, hot toast—
which once again warms, and so reactivates, the truffles for
fullest flavor—is the perfect foundation for a slice of homemade
pâté. If you don't have a good pâté recipe that you swear by,
try the one on page 76; you'll find it delicious.

Fruit Butter

1 stick (1/4 pound) butter   1 tablespoon grated lemon
1 tablespoon lemon juice   rind

Allow butter to come to room temperature, then cream

thoroughly with juice and rind. Store in refrigerator, well covered.

Or try this . . . Substitute orange juice for lemon juice, and 2 teaspoons orange rind for the lemon rind. Add a small pinch of nutmeg.

Keep in mind . . . These fruit butters will make something special out of something ordinary (example: use the lemon butter for a plain sliced chicken sandwich, the orange for a ham sandwich, and see what happens!). Or use them as the only filling between slices of raisin, nut, or date-nut bread.

Parsley-Plus Butter

1/2 cup butter, softened
1/2 teaspoon seasoned salt
1/2 teaspoon garlic salt
   or
  1 small clove garlic, crushed

1/2 teaspoon each chopped parsley, chopped chives
Pinch of basil

Cream all ingredients thoroughly. Pack into crock and store in refrigerator, tightly covered. Or roll into cylinder and refrigerate wrapped in foil or waxed paper. This butter can also be frozen to use as you need it.

Tuna Butter

1 6- or 7-ounce can drained tuna
2 tablespoons butter

1 tablespoon salad oil
Salt and pepper

Cream ingredients together until the paste is as smooth as foie gras. Chill well.

Keep in mind . . . This makes—try it, before you say you don't believe me—a fine foundation for an anchovy canapé. Or use Tuna Butter as the spread for bread when making an egg-and-anchovy sandwich, or even just a plain, simple scrambled-egg sandwich.

Brandy Butter

1 stick (1/4 pound) butter
2 teaspoons light brown sugar
Few drops lemon juice

Dash grated nutmeg
1 liqueur glassful brandy

Beat butter and brown sugar to a light cream. Flavor with lemon juice and nutmeg. Add brandy, mix well. Rum or sherry may be substituted.

Sandwich-by-the-Sea

Straight from the sea or straight from a can, fish takes willingly to embellishments, pairs happily with all sorts of flavors. If your fish is straight from the sea (or the freezer) treat it kindly—cook it gently and briefly, then find, in this section, a way brand new to you to serve it up as a scrumptious sandwich for lunch, for dinner, for company.

Take a Can of Tuna . . .

. . . And add 1/2 cup mayonnaise or salad dressing. Then make it special with one of these extra added attractions: 1/2 cup chopped celery . . . 1/4 cup chopped walnuts or pecans . . . 1/4 cup chopped water chestnuts plus a sprinkling of lemon juice . . . 1/2 cup chopped olives, green, ripe, or stuffed . . . 1 cup drained pineapple tidbits plus a dash of nutmeg (reduce mayonnaise to 3 tbs. for this variation) . . . 1 tbs. ketchup, 1/2 tsp. each lemon juice, Worcestershire sauce.

Almond-and-Anchovy

3 ounces butter	1/2 teaspoon parsley and
3 ounces blanched almonds	onion, minced
1 teaspoon anchovy paste	Cayenne pepper

Mix butter with crushed almonds. Add anchovy paste, finely minced parsley and onion, and a dash of cayenne pepper. Blend. Spread on your favorite bread.

Tuna Kiev

16 slices thin-sliced	4 teaspoons lemon juice
pumpernickel	1/2 teaspoon horseradish
3/4 cup tuna, flaked	6 tablespoons commercial
1/4 cup chopped celery	sour cream
2 tablespoons finely	
chopped onion	

Combine flaked tuna, celery, onion, lemon juice, horseradish, and sour cream. Spread on 8 slices bread, top with remaining slices. Makes 8 sandwiches.

Good companions . . . Dill-sprinkled cucumber slices, tiny whole sweet-sour beets, plenty of parsley.

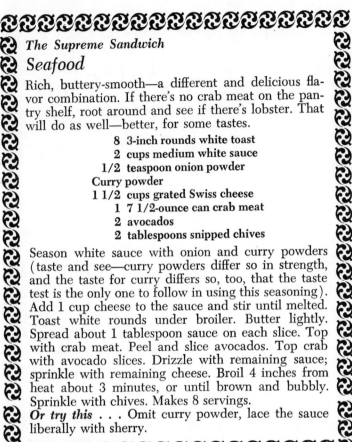

The Supreme Sandwich

Seafood

Rich, buttery-smooth—a different and delicious flavor combination. If there's no crab meat on the pantry shelf, root around and see if there's lobster. That will do as well—better, for some tastes.

8 3-inch rounds white toast
2 cups medium white sauce
1/2 teaspoon onion powder
Curry powder
1 1/2 cups grated Swiss cheese
1 7 1/2-ounce can crab meat
2 avocados
2 tablespoons snipped chives

Season white sauce with onion and curry powders (taste and see—curry powders differ so in strength, and the taste for curry differs so, too, that the taste test is the only one to follow in using this seasoning). Add 1 cup cheese to the sauce and stir until melted. Toast white rounds under broiler. Butter lightly. Spread about 1 tablespoon sauce on each slice. Top with crab meat. Peel and slice avocados. Top crab with avocado slices. Drizzle with remaining sauce; sprinkle with remaining cheese. Broil 4 inches from heat about 3 minutes, or until brown and bubbly. Sprinkle with chives. Makes 8 servings.
Or try this . . . Omit curry powder, lace the sauce liberally with sherry.

Cottage Tuna

8 slices pumpernickel
1 7-ounce can tuna, drained
2 heaping tablespoons cottage cheese
1/4 teaspoon chopped fresh basil
Mayonnaise thinned with fresh lemon juice

Combine drained tuna, cottage cheese, basil, and enough mayonnaise to make spreading consistency. Spread on half of bread slices, top with remaining slices. Makes 4 sandwiches.
Or try it this way . . . For dress-up serving, spread Cottage Tuna on thin whole-wheat bread. Decorate with radish roses and watercress "leaves."

Barbecued Fish-Stick Buns

5 frankfurter buns, sliced
2 tablespoons butter
1/4 cup onion, chopped
1 cup celery, chopped
7/8 cup (1 8-ounce can) tomato sauce
1/4 cup lemon juice
1/4 teaspoon thyme, if desired
1/4 teaspoon rosemary, if desired
1 package frozen fish sticks

Melt butter in a saucepan; add onion and celery. Sauté until tender. Add tomato sauce, lemon juice, thyme, and rosemary; simmer for 30 minutes. Heat fish sticks according to package directions. *To serve:* Place 2 fish sticks and 2 tablespoons sauce in each sliced bun. Makes 5 sandwiches.

Creamy Tuna Slices

4 thin slices pumpernickel or rye bread
1 can chunk-style tuna
1/4 cup commercial sour cream or mayonnaise
1 tablespoon horseradish
1/2 teaspoon salt
1/4 teaspoon pepper

Mix tuna with sour cream, horseradish, salt, pepper. Spread on bread slices. Makes 4 servings.
Good companions . . . Serve with hot tea or coffee, canned grapefruit sections for dessert.

Barbetuna Buns

4 sandwich buns, split and toasted
1 tablespoon butter
1 teaspoon garlic, finely minced
1/2 cup ketchup
2 tablespoons water
2 tablespoons stuffed olives, chopped
1 tablespoon lemon juice
1 teaspoon Worcestershire sauce
1/2 teaspoon dry mustard
1 cup tuna, drained and flaked

Melt butter in a skillet. Add garlic and sauté until brown. Add ketchup, water, olives, lemon juice, Worcestershire sauce, and mustard; simmer for 10 minutes. Add tuna; simmer for an additional 5 minutes until flavors are well blended. Place a portion of barbecued tuna mixture on each toasted bun half. Makes 4 servings.
Keep in mind . . . Next time you have to feed a crowd, Barbetuna Buns will do it with very little more trouble than it takes to feed four.

Hot Cheese-Tuna Sandwiches

6 slices bread
1/4 cup butter
1 teaspoon prepared
   mustard
1 tablespoon chopped onion
1/2 cup chopped celery
1 tablespoon chopped sweet
   pickle or sweet pickle
   relish

1/4 cup mayonnaise or salad
   dressing
1 6 1/2- or 7-ounce can
   tuna, drained, flaked
6 slices cheese
Paprika
Parsley sprigs

Cream butter and blend in mustard. Spread bread with mustard butter. Combine onion, celery, pickle, mayonnaise, and tuna. Spread bread with tuna mixture and cover with cheese. Sprinkle with paprika. Place sandwiches on a cookie sheet, 15 1/2 by 12 inches. Bake at 450° F. for 10 to 12 minutes or until cheese melts and bread toasts. Garnish with parsley. Makes 6 servings.
Even better . . . For heartier eating, use crusty French rolls instead of bread.

Tuna-Apple Surprise

12 slices whole or cracked
   wheat bread
1 7-ounce can tuna, flaked

2 tablespoons lemon juice
1/2 cup applesauce

Combine tuna, lemon juice, and applesauce. Spread on 6 slices bread, top with remaining slices. Makes 6 sandwiches.
Keep in mind . . . This filling is a good choice for sandwiches to make ahead and freeze.

Toasty Tuna de Luxe

8 thin slices light
   pumpernickel
2 tablespoons soft butter
1/2 cup flaked tuna
2 teaspoons lemon juice

1 teaspoon lemon rind
1/8 teaspoon salt
Few grains of pepper
1/4 cup sliced toasted
   almonds

Combine butter, tuna, lemon juice and rind, salt and pepper. Add almonds. Makes 4 hearty sandwiches.
Or try it this way . . . Substitute shredded, toasted Brazil nuts for the almonds, and spread the mixture thinly on bread to make open-faced sandwiches. Cut in triangles—what could be nicer for tea?

The Supreme Sandwich

Crab Meat

These, invented for unexpected company when the cupboard was nearly bare, have long since turned into old favorites at our house—add a green salad and you have the main part of a satisfying meal.

6 corn toaster muffins
3/4 pound crab meat
1/2 cup chopped celery
3-4 tablespoons mayonnaise
Curry powder to taste
Salt, pepper
1/2 cup potato-chip crumbs
6 slices Swiss cheese

Pick over crab meat, mix with celery. Season mayonnaise with curry powder to taste, mix with crab—you may need a bit more mayonnaise to hold the mixture together. Season with salt, pepper. Pile crab onto muffins, sprinkle with crumbs, top with a slice of cheese. Bake at 350° F. until heated through and cheese melts—10-15 minutes. Makes 6 servings.

Tunaburgers

6 toasted hamburger rolls
2 7-ounce cans tuna
1/2 cup chopped onion
1/4 cup tuna oil or other oil
1/3 cup tomato juice
2 eggs, beaten
3/4 cup dry bread crumbs
1/4 cup chopped parsley

1 teaspoon powdered
   mustard
1/2 teaspoon salt
1/3 cup mayonnaise or salad
   dressing
1 tablespoon chopped sweet
   pickle or drained
   pickle relish

Drain tuna, reserving oil. Flake tuna. Cook onion in oil until tender. Add tomato juice, eggs, 1/4 cup bread crumbs, parsley, mustard, salt, and tuna; mix well. Chill mixture. Shape into 6 cakes and roll in remaining crumbs. Fry in hot fat, at moderate heat, until brown on one side; turn carefully and brown the other side. Drain on absorbent paper. Combine mayonnaise and relish. Place burgers on bottom half of each roll. Top with approximately 1 tablespoon relish sauce and top half of roll. Makes 6 sandwiches.

Bridge Clubs

24 slices white bread
1 3-ounce package cream cheese
2 tablespoons chopped stuffed olives
2 tablespoons chopped nuts
1/2 cup cooked chopped shrimp
2 teaspoons minced onion
1 teaspoon lemon juice
2 tablespoons mayonnaise or salad dressing
3 tablespoons melted butter
1 teaspoon anchovy paste

With large (about 3 1/2-inch) cookie cutters, in the shapes of playing-card symbols, make 6 cutouts of each shape from as many slices of bread (24). Combine cream cheese, olives, and nuts. Spread 1 tablespoon of cream cheese mixture on 8 cutouts, using 2 of each symbol. Combine shrimp, onion, lemon juice, and mayonnaise. Spread 1 tablespoon of shrimp mixture on 8 similar cutouts. Place shrimp layers on matching cream cheese layers. Top with matching bread layers. Combine butter and anchovy paste. Brush anchovy butter on tops and sides of sandwiches. Place on a cookie sheet. Bake in a 450° F. oven for 5 minutes. Serve hot. Makes 8 sandwiches.

Or try it this way . . . For non-bridge occasions, use 16 slices white bread, 8 slices whole-wheat bread, cut in large rounds. Use the whole-wheat bread, spread with shrimp mixture, as the center deck of each triple-decker sandwich.

Tuna Skyscraper

1 package refrigerated biscuits
1 9 1/4-ounce can tuna
1/4 cup commercial sour cream
1/4 teaspoon Worcestershire sauce
1/4 teaspoon oregano
1/8 teaspoon garlic salt
Dash of pepper
1/3 cup chili sauce
5 slices large tomato
5 slices Bermuda onion
5 thick slices sharp Cheddar cheese
Watercress garnish

Drain and flake tuna. Mix with sour cream, Worcestershire sauce, oregano, garlic salt, and pepper; shape into 5 patties. On buttered baking sheet, roll biscuits into ten 3-inch circles. Spread 5 biscuits with chili sauce; top with tuna patties, tomato slices, and onion slices. Bake 10 to 15 minutes in 450° F. oven. Remove from oven and top sandwiches with plain, baked biscuits, then cheese slices. Bake an additional 3 to 5 minutes or just until cheese melts. Garnish with watercress. Makes 5 sandwiches.

The Supreme Sandwich
Oyster

These are a relative—not as close as kissing cousins —of Oysters Rockefeller, but they stand—deliciously —on their own merits.

          2 English muffins, split
          1 package frozen chopped spinach
          2 tablespoons butter
          2 tablespoons chopped onion
          2 teaspoons lemon juice
      Salt, pepper, nutmeg
         16 large oysters
          4 slices bacon, cut in half, partially cooked

Cook spinach according to package directions. Drain well. Melt butter in frying pan; cook onion in butter until softened, but not browned. Add spinach, lemon juice, salt, pepper, few grains of nutmeg. Toss. Divide over 4 toasted, buttered muffin halves. Place 4 oysters on each. Crisscross 2 strips bacon over each muffin half. Broil until bacon is crisp, the edges of the oysters curled. Serve at once. Makes 4 servings.

Tuna Hong Kong

          6 hamburger rolls
          2 6 1/2- or 7-ounce cans
             tuna
      1/2 cup chopped onion
          2 tablespoons tuna oil
      1/2 cup chopped celery
      1/2 cup chopped green pepper
          1 cup ketchup
          1 cup water
          2 tablespoons brown sugar
          2 tablespoons vinegar
          2 tablespoons Worcester-
             shire sauce
          1 teaspoon prepared
             mustard
      1/2 teaspoon salt
      Dash of pepper

Drain tuna, reserving oil. Break tuna into large pieces. Cook onion in oil until tender. Add remaining ingredients, except tuna and rolls. Simmer uncovered for 20 minutes, stirring occasionally. Add tuna and simmer 10 minutes longer, stirring occasionally. Split rolls and toast. Place approximately 1/2 cup tuna mixture on bottom half of roll. Cover with top half of roll. Makes 6 sandwiches.

Shrimp New Orleans

12 slices white bread,
   toasted and buttered
24 butterfly or fantail
   shrimp, French-fried
1/3 cup Tartar Sauce
   (page 151)

2 cups shredded sharp
   Cheddar cheese
12 thinly sliced green
   pepper rings
Tabasco sauce
4 tomatoes, quartered

On each of 4 slices of buttered toast, arrange 6 fried shrimp. Spread 4 more slices of toast with Tartar Sauce. Place on shrimp, sauce side down. On top of toast sprinkle shredded cheese, then pepper rings; add 2 dashes of Tabasco sauce per sandwich. Place under broiler until cheese melts. When cheese is bubbling, top with third slice of buttered toast. Fasten with toothpicks; cut in 4 sections. Garnish with ripe tomato quarters between sections. Serve at once. Makes 4 servings.

Keep in mind . . . Quick tartar sauce can be made by combining mayonnaise with India or sweet pickle relish in whatever proportions you like. Add a dash of horseradish for extra zest.

Shrimp-Olive Swirls

4 slices white bread
1/4 cup pimento cream cheese
1/4 teaspoon chili sauce

3 tablespoons cooked, finely
   chopped shrimp
1/4 teaspoon lemon juice
2 or 3 ripe olives

Combine pimento cream cheese, chili sauce, shrimp, and lemon juice. With a 1 1/2-inch cookie cutter, cut each slice of bread into 4 circles. Spread 1 teaspoon cheese mixture on each circle. Garnish top of each sandwich with slivers of ripe olives arranged in a swirl pattern. Makes 16 sandwiches.

Shrimp Salad Roll

6 frankfurter rolls
3/4 pound shrimp, cooked,
   cleaned
1/4 cup chopped green
   pepper
1/2 cup shredded lettuce
1 teaspoon grated onion

1/4 cup chopped celery
1/4 cup chopped cucumber
1/4 cup diced tomatoes
1/4 cup mayonnaise or salad
   dressing
2 tablespoons butter

Chop shrimp. Combine vegetables, mayonnaise, and shrimp. Mix thoroughly. Cut rolls almost through lengthwise. Spread with butter. Place about 1/2 cup salad on each roll. Makes 6 sandwiches.

Thousand Island Dressing

1 cup Homemade Mayonnaise (page 125)
1/4 cup chili sauce
1 tablespoon chopped parsley
2 tablespoons sweet pickle relish
2 tablespoons French dressing
2 tablespoons chopped green pepper
2 tablespoons chopped pimento
1/2 cup whipped cream

Mix first 7 ingredients well. Fold in whipped cream. Refrigerate until ready to serve.

Oyster Club Sandwich

18 slices buttered toast
12 slices bacon
1 pint oysters
1/2 cup flour
1/2 teaspoon salt
1/8 teaspoon pepper
12 lettuce leaves
12 slices tomatoes
1/2 cup mayonnaise

Fry bacon, and drain on absorbent paper. Drain oysters, roll in flour seasoned with salt and pepper. Brown on both sides in bacon fat. Cooking time about 5 minutes. Drain on absorbent paper. Divide oysters and bacon over 6 slices toast. Top with 6 more slices toast. Arrange lettuce, tomatoes, mayonnaise on this layer, top with remaining 6 slices toast. Fasten with toothpicks. Cut diagonally. Makes 6 sandwiches.

Tangy Salmon

4 French rolls
2/3 cup salmon, flaked
1/2 cup chopped cucumber
1 tablespoon chopped
green onion tops
1/4 teaspoon dill seeds
1/4 teaspoon salt
1/8 teaspoon pepper
Few drops of Tabasco
2 tablespoons prepared
sour cream

Combine salmon, cucumber, green onion tops, dill seeds, salt, pepper, Tabasco, and sour cream. Let stand for at least 1 hour to blend flavors. Drain off any excess liquid which may seep from the cucumber. Split rolls, spread with salmon mixture. Makes 4 sandwiches.

Hot Swiss Tuna

4 hamburger buns
1 6 1/2- or 7-ounce can
    tuna, drained, flaked
1/2 cup finely shredded Swiss
    cheese
1 cup chopped celery

1/4 teaspoon salt
Dash of pepper
1/4 cup mayonnaise
2 tablespoons ketchup
1 teaspoon lemon juice

Split hamburger buns. Combine tuna, Swiss cheese, celery, salt, pepper, mayonnaise, ketchup, and lemon juice and pile between bun halves. Wrap each sandwich in aluminum foil and refrigerate. To serve, heat in 350° F. oven for 15 minutes. Makes 4 sandwiches.

Curried Lobster Sandwiches

6 slices white bread
3/4 pound lobster meat,
    cooked
1/4 cup butter, melted
1 egg, beaten

1/4 cup milk
Dash of curry powder
1/4 teaspoon salt
Paprika

Chop lobster meat. Sauté in butter for 3 minutes. Combine egg, milk, and seasonings. Pour .over lobster meat and cook until thick, stirring constantly. Toast bread on one side. Spread lobster mixture on untoasted side of bread. Place on a broiler pan about 3 inches from heat. Broil for 2 to 4 minutes or until lightly browned. Sprinkle with paprika. Makes 6 servings.

Broiled Lobster Sandwiches

6 slices white bread
3/4 pound lobster meat,
    cooked
1/4 cup condensed mushroom
    soup

1/4 teaspoon Worcestershire
    sauce
Dash of pepper
1/4 teaspoon salt
1 hard-cooked egg, chopped

Chop lobster meat. Add soup and seasonings. Toast bread on one side. Spread lobster mixture on untoasted side of bread. Sprinkle with egg. Place on a broiler pan about 3 inches from heat. Broil for 2 to 4 minutes or until lightly browned. Makes 6 servings.

Or try it this way . . . Trim bread into rounds (or cut with large biscuit cutter) before spreading. Serve each round surrounded by circle of tiny minted peas.

Russian Dressing

> 1 cup Homemade Mayonnaise (page 125)
> 1/4 cup chili sauce
> 1/4 cup minced celery
> 1 tablespoon chopped parsley
> 2 tablespoons sweet pickle relish
> 1 teaspoon chopped chives
> 2 tablespoons French dressing
> 1 hard-cooked egg, minced

Mix all ingredients well. Refrigerate until ready to serve.

Golden Club

6 slices white bread, toasted	1/4 teaspoon salt
1 6 1/2-ounce can crab meat (1 cup)	6 thick slices tomato
	Seasoned salt
2 hard-cooked eggs, diced	Mayonnaise
1/4 cup French dressing	4 packaged process
1/4 cup sweet pickle relish	American cheese slices

Flake crab meat; mix with eggs, French dressing, pickle relish, and salt. Sprinkle both sides of tomato slices with seasoned salt. Spread toast slices with mayonnaise. Set 2 slices toast on wooden board or baking sheet. Cover with tomatoes. Top with 2 more slices spread with crab meat mixture, then with remaining 2 slices. Top each sandwich with 2 cheese slices; halve diagonally. Bake in 400° F. oven 7 to 10 minutes or until cheese is melted and sandwiches are golden brown. Makes 2 servings. *Good companions* . . . Bright red radishes and slices of pale green avocado.

Tuna-Chili Sandwich

6 slices white bread	1/8 teaspoon chili powder
1/3 cup tuna, drained and flaked	1/8 teaspoon oregano
	2 tablespoons tomato sauce
1 tablespoon chopped celery	

Combine tuna, celery, chili powder, oregano, and tomato sauce. Spread on 3 slices of bread, top with remaining slices.

Baked Tuna Ovals

1 package refrigerated pan-
   ready biscuits
1 can chunk-style tuna
   (1 cup)

1/2 cup diced natural sharp
   American cheese
3 tablespoons mayonnaise
1 tablespoon melted butter

Pat each biscuit into thin 3 1/2-inch by 4-inch oval. Arrange half of biscuits on greased cookie sheet. Mix tuna, cheese, mayonnaise. Spread on biscuits on cookie sheet. Top with remaining biscuits, pressing edges together. Brush tops with melted butter. Heat oven to 425° F. Let biscuits stand 15 to 20 minutes. Then bake about 15 to 20 minutes or until browned. Makes 5 sandwiches.

Brazilburgers

4 sandwich buns, split and
   toasted
1 tablespoon butter or
   margarine
1 tablespoon flour
1/2 cup milk

1 7-ounce can tuna, drained
1/4 cup diced celery
1/2 cup finely chopped Brazil
   nuts
1/4 teaspoon Worcestershire
   sauce

Melt butter in saucepan; remove from heat; stir in flour. Gradually stir in milk; cook over medium heat until sauce thickens; remove from heat. Add tuna, celery, nuts, Worcestershire sauce; blend well. Shape into 4 round patties. Place on foil-lined baking sheet. Bake 15 minutes at 350° F. Serve on toasted buns. Makes 4 servings.

Shrimp Tropicana

12 slices cracked wheat
   bread, buttered
1/2 pound shrimp, fresh or
   frozen, cooked, peeled,
   cleaned
        or
2 4 1/2- or 5-ounce cans
   shrimp, drained
1 cup creamed cottage
   cheese

1/2 cup drained crushed
   pineapple
1/3 cup mayonnaise or salad
   dressing
2 teaspoons lemon juice
1/2 teaspoon salt
6 lettuce leaves

Chop shrimp. Drain cottage cheese. Combine all ingredients except lettuce and bread. Chill. Spread 6 slices of bread with approximately 1/3 cup shrimp mixture. Cover with lettuce and remaining 6 slices of bread. Makes 6 sandwiches.

❀❀❀❀❀❀❀❀❀❀❀❀ ❀ ❀❀❀❀❀❀❀❀❀❀

The Gourmet Way

Avocado Dressing

2 tablespoons heavy cream
1 tablespoon lemon juice
1/2 teaspoon salt
1 teaspoon prepared mustard
6 drops hot pepper sauce
1 large avocado, peeled and well mashed

Combine all ingredients except avocado; beat well. Add the avocado pulp and beat again until dressing is perfectly smooth. Refrigerate until ready to use. *Perfect partners . . .* This Avocado Dressing and chicken, any seafood, tomatoes.

❀❀❀❀❀❀❀❀❀❀❀❀❀❀❀❀❀❀❀❀❀❀❀❀

Norwegian Delight

1 medium-size French loaf
Butter
1/2 cup peeled small shrimp
Mayonnaise
2 hard-cooked eggs, sliced

1 tomato, sliced
Parsley
4 slices boiled ham
4 slices cheese
4 radishes, finely chopped

Cut bread into 4 lengthwise slices. Butter. On the first, place shrimp garnished with mayonnaise, on the next, slices of hard-cooked egg and tomato sprinkled with parsley, on the next, rolls of boiled ham, and on the last, cheese and finely chopped radish. Cut each slice into 4 pieces, and make up 4 servings—each containing 1 slice of each variety.

Curried Shrimpwiches

6 slices of bread
3 4 1/2-ounce cans shrimp
1/4 cup butter, melted
1 egg, beaten

1/4 cup milk
1/4 teaspoon salt
Dash of curry powder
Paprika

Drain shrimp, rinse with cold water. Chop shrimp and sauté in butter for 3 minutes. Combine egg, milk, salt, and curry powder. Pour over shrimp and cook until thick, stirring constantly. Toast bread on one side. Spread shrimp mixture on untoasted side of bread. Place on a broiler pan about 3 inches from source of heat. Broil for 2 to 4 minutes or until lightly browned. Sprinkle with paprika. Makes 6 servings.

149

Shrimp Fantasies

12 sandwich buns, split and toasted	1 1/2 dozen slices hard-cooked eggs
1 tablespoon butter	3/8 cup shrimp cocktail sauce
6 small, flat lettuce leaves	1 1/2 dozen whole shrimp, cooked, cleaned, peeled
1 1/2 dozen pickle chips	

Butter top halves of toasted sandwich buns. Place a lettuce leaf on bottom halves of buns. For each sandwich: Arrange a ring of 3 pickle chips and 3 egg slices on each lettuce leaf, alternating them and overlapping edges. Spoon shrimp cocktail sauce into center of ring. Arrange 3 shrimp down across ˙center of ring. Serve open-face with top half of bun on the side. Makes 6 servings.

Even better . . . Bottled shrimp cocktail sauce will do if you're in a hurry, but a something-different sauce turns this into very special Sunday supper or midnight snack fare. Try: 1 cup chili sauce, 1 cup mayonnaise, 1/2 cup horseradish, 2 tablespoons vinegar, 3 tablespoons granulated sugar, 1/2 teaspoon bottled meat sauce. Mix well, season with 1/4 teaspoon each celery salt, garlic salt; 1/8 teaspoon coarsely ground black pepper; 1/2 teaspoon onion juice. Cap tightly and refrigerate before using, so that flavors may blend.

Shrimpfurters

6 heated frankfurter buns, sliced and buttered	1 1/2 teaspoons chopped chives
9 whole shrimp	1/8 teaspoon curry powder
1 cup bite-size pieces cooked shrimp	1/4 teaspoon salt
1/2 cup commercial sour cream	Pepper to taste
	6 lemon slices
1 1/2 teaspoons grated lemon rind	Stuffed olives, sliced
	Watercress

Cut whole shrimp in halves and reserve for garnish. Combine shrimp pieces, sour cream, lemon rind, chives, curry powder, salt and pepper. Fill each bun with 3 tablespoons of shrimp mixture. Insert 3 shrimp halves into the filling in each bun so they show through the open edge. Garnish with lemon swirl, sliced stuffed olives, and watercress. Makes 6 furters.

Take note: Filled buns may be securely wrapped in foil for storage, then heated over hot coals in the foil wrapping.

The Gourmet Way

Tartar Sauce

1 cup Homemade Mayonnaise (page 125)
1/4 cup chopped dill pickles
1/4 cup chopped stuffed olives
1 teaspoon chopped chives

Mix all ingredients well. Refrigerate until ready to serve.

Shrimp and Chutney Bites

6 to 8 small butter rolls, split, lightly toasted
1 cup cooked, diced shrimp
1/4 cup chopped chutney
1/4 cup ketchup

Mix together and spread on rolls. Makes 6 to 8 sandwiches, depending on how thickly you like the filling spread.
Keep in mind . . . These mouthful-size sandwiches go well on an informal buffet table.

Shrimp Dillies

8 thin slices dark pumpernickel
1 3-ounce package cream cheese
1/4 cup cooked chopped shrimp
1/4 cup diced cucumber
1/4 teaspoon dill seeds
1 teaspoon lemon juice

Soften cream cheese. Add shrimp, cucumber, dill seeds, and lemon juice. Spread on 4 slices of bread and top with remaining slices.

Roe Boats

4 slices rye bread, buttered
8 slices cod roe
2 tablespoons butter
Mayonnaise
4 slices lemon

Sauté cod roe slices in butter until both sides are lightly browned. Place 2 slices of roe on each bread slice. Garnish with mayonnaise and lemon. Makes 4 servings.
Or try it this way . . . Shad roe makes an elegant substitute; add scored, thin-sliced cucumber to the garnish.

151

Crab Imperial

12 slices white bread
1 6 1/2-ounce can crab
   meat, flaked
1/2 cup finely chopped
   celery
1/2 teaspoon chopped green
   onion tops or chives
1/8 teaspoon garlic salt
2 2/3 tablespoons commercial
   sour cream

3/4 teaspoon lemon juice
1/2 teaspoon prepared
   horseradish
2 tablespoons soft butter
6 lettuce leaves
1/2 13-ounce can tomato
   aspic
12 stuffed olives

Combine crab meat, celery, onion tops, garlic salt, sour cream, lemon juice, and horseradish. Spread 1/2 teaspoon butter over each bread slice. Place 6 of the bread slices on serving plates; top each with a lettuce leaf. Slice tomato aspic into 18 thin slices and arrange 3 slices on each lettuce leaf. Place 1/4 cup crab meat mixture in center of aspic slices. Garnish with 2 stuffed olives. Cut remaining bread slices in half diagonally, and place 2 triangles on each serving plate, 1 on either side of the open-face sandwich. Makes 6 servings.
Good companions . . . Deviled eggs, asparagus vinaigrette.

Halibut-Filled Rolls

6 large buttered rolls
2 cups flaked halibut
3/4 cup grated cheese
1/2 cup mayonnaise or salad
   dressing
2 tablespoons lemon juice

2 teaspoons Worcestershire
   sauce
1 teaspoon prepared
   mustard
3/4 teaspoon salt
Dash of pepper

Combine all ingredients except rolls. Fill rolls with fish mixture. Place on a baking sheet and heat in a 350° F. oven for 15 minutes or until heated through and cheese has melted. Makes 6 sandwiches.
Even better . . . Add 1/2 cup chopped celery and 1 teaspoon grated onion.

Smoked Surprise

4 slices bread, buttered
Scrambled egg

8 pieces smoked eel
Fresh watercress

On each piece of buttered bread place a strip of scrambled egg, with a piece of smoked eel on either side. Garnish with fresh watercress. Makes 4 servings.

The Gourmet Way

Green Goddess Dressing

This upgrades a simple shrimp sandwich into food for the—green, naturally—gods. Great on any seafood, or a wonderful raw vegetable dress-up.

   1 clove garlic, minced
1/2 teaspoon salt
1/2 teaspoon dry mustard
   1 teaspoon Worcestershire sauce
   2 tablespoons anchovy paste
   3 tablespoons wine vinegar
   3 tablespoons snipped chives
1/3 cup snipped parsley
1/3 cup snipped fresh spinach
   1 cup mayonnaise
1/2 cup sour cream
1/4 teaspoon white pepper

Several hours before serving, combine all ingredients. Mix well. Refrigerate until serving. Makes about 2 cups.

Hot Crab Sandwiches

12 slices white bread	3 tablespoons mayonnaise
1 pound crab meat	or salad dressing
1 tablespoon chopped	1 1/2 teaspoons salt
sweet pickle	Dash of pepper
1 tablespoon chopped	2 eggs, beaten
onion	1/2 cup milk
1 tablespoon chopped	1/4 teaspoon salt
celery	

Remove any shell or cartilage from crab meat. Combine pickle, onion, celery, mayonnaise, seasonings, and crab meat. Combine eggs, milk, and salt. Dip one side of each slice of bread in egg mixture. Place bread in a heavy frying pan which contains about 1/8 inch of fat, hot but not smoking. Fry at moderate heat until brown on one side. Drain on absorbent paper. Spread plain side of 6 slices of bread with crab mixture; cover with remaining 6 slices of bread, plain side down. Place on a well-greased cookie sheet, 15 1/2 by 12 inches. Heat in a 350° F. oven for 5 to 8 minutes or until heated through. Makes 6 servings.

Facts on Fish

All sorts of fresh- and salt-water fish—including their shell-covered cousins—can be the basis for delicious sandwich fillings, either the salad-type filling or used "as is" with a suitable sauce or garnish to bring out the flavor. There was a time when only people who lived close to the source of supply—the ocean, or a nearby lake or stream or "fishin' hole"— could enjoy fish. But now, between the twin miracles of rapid, refrigerated shipping methods and of freezing, fish is available to everyone, everywhere. Here are tips for cooks who want to make the best of a delicate, delectable food.

Cooking fish to use in sandwiches . . . Poaching is the simplest method for cooking fish to be used in sandwiches—either to be flaked for a salad-type sandwich filling or to be used as whole pieces and sauced or garnished. Poaching is cooking in shallow liquid that is kept below the boiling point. You *can* poach fish in salted water, but you'll end up with a much tastier finished product if you use a Court Bouillon—one made with, or without, wine.

Basic Court Bouillon

2 tablespoons butter
1 tablespoon grated carrot
1 tablespoon minced onion
1 tablespoon minced celery
1 tablespoon snipped parsley
1/2 bay leaf
1 teaspoon salt
1 tablespoon vinegar
   or lemon juice
1 1/2 quarts water

Choose a shallow pan that will accommodate your fish nicely, with the Court Bouillon just covering the top of the fish pieces. Melt the butter and sauté the vegetables in it briefly, but don't brown them. Add seasonings and vinegar or lemon juice. Add water and bring to just below the boiling point. Slip the fish into the water and simmer until the flesh flakes but holds together—about 15 minutes. Don't over-cook or the fish will be dry and lose flavor.

Basic Fish Fillet Sandwiches . . . Prepare a slice of toast, buttered, for each open-face sandwich. Trim a piece of fish fillet to fit, and place it on the buttered toast. Dress it with one of the following sauces.

Lemon Sauce . . . Melt 2 tablespoons butter. Stir in 2 tablespoons flour until smooth. Add 1 cup of Court Bouillon. Cook and stir about 5 minutes. Season to taste with salt, white pepper. Add 2 table-spoons lemon juice. Incorporate, little by little, 2 tablespoons butter.

Caper Sauce . . . Melt 1/4 pound butter. Add 1/2 cup snipped parsley, 2 tablespoons chopped capers, 1 teaspoon lemon juice, salt and pepper to taste. Serve at once.

Chili-Cream Sauce . . . Combine 1/2 cup sour cream, 1/2 cup chili sauce, 1 teaspoon lemon juice, salt to taste. Serve at once or refrigerate until needed.

Almond Sauce . . . Melt 2 tablespoons butter. Add 1/2 cup chopped blanched almonds; brown lightly. Add 2 tablespoons flour, stirring as you go. Blend well and stir in 1 cup light cream. Season to taste. Stir in 1 lightly beaten egg yolk. Do not boil. Serve at once.

Cold Cucumber Sauce . . . Peel, quarter, and seed 1 medium-size cucumber. Chop coarsely. Drain on paper towels. Fold the cucumber into 1 cup of heavy sour cream, along with 2 teaspoons lemon juice. Season to taste, and chill.

Garnishing fish sandwiches . . . Seafood has an affin-ity for lemon. If your sauce is not lemony, send your fish sandwiches to the table partnered by a wedge of lemon so that each diner may lemon-juice his own to taste . . . Or sauce your fish with a little lemon butter—melted butter with lemon juice stirred in—and garnish with one of the following: finely chopped hard-cooked egg white, with a drift of hard-cooked egg yolk, put through a fine sieve . . . a sprinkling of minced parsley or watercress . . . a sprinkling of finely chopped nuts—pecans, almonds, hazelnuts or, if you feel adventurous, pickled walnuts—or thin-sliced Brazil nuts . . . sprinkling of paprika.

Sardine and Egg

6 slices white bread
1/4 cup mashed sardines
1/3 cup hard-cooked, sieved
    egg yolk
1 tablespoon chopped
    sweet pickle

1 tablespoon mayonnaise or
    salad dressing
2 teaspoons olive oil
Dash of salt

Combine sardines, egg yolk, pickle, mayonnaise, olive oil, and salt. Spread on 3 slices bread, top with remaining slices. Makes 3 sandwiches.

Sardine-Cheese Buns

6 split hamburger buns
1/4 pound process American
    cheese, cubed
5 hard-cooked eggs,
    chopped
1/2 cup canned sardines,
    drained
1 tablespoon minced green
    pepper

2 tablespoons minced onion
3 tablespoons chopped
    stuffed olives
2 tablespoons pickle relish
1/2 cup mayonnaise
Soft butter

In advance: Combine cheese, eggs, sardines, green pepper, onion, olives, pickle relish, mayonnaise. Butter buns. Fill each split bun with cheese mixture; wrap in aluminum foil. Refrigerate. *About 25 minutes before serving:* Heat oven to 300° F. Bake buns in foil 15 minutes. Makes 6 servings.
Or try it another way . . .
TUNA-CHEESE: Use 3 eggs. Substitute 1 cup canned chunk-style tuna for sardines.
SALMON-CHEESE: Use 3 eggs. Substitute 1 cup flaked canned salmon for sardines.
CHICKEN- OR TURKEY-CHEESE: Use 3 eggs. Substitute 1 cup cut-up cooked or canned chicken or turkey for sardines.

French Salmon

14 slices rye bread, buttered
1 cup salmon, flaked
1/4 cup chopped green
    pepper
1 teaspoon minced onion

1 tablespoon French
    dressing
Few drops of Worcestershire
    sauce

Combine salmon, green pepper, onion, French dressing, and Worcestershire sauce. Spread on 7 slices bread, top with remaining slices. Makes 7 sandwiches.

The Supreme Sandwich

Anchovy (*Pissaladière*)

These are make-in-a-hurry treats. If it's cocktail time, quarter the muffin halves and you have a plate of deliciously different nibbles.

    4 English muffins, split, toasted, and buttered
    1 cup thinly sliced onion
    2 tablespoons olive oil
   12 fillets of anchovies, chopped
   12 black olives, chopped

Cook onion in olive oil until tender. Add anchovies and olives. Spread on English muffins. Serve hot. Makes 8 half-muffin servings.

Rolled Sardine Tea Sandwiches

24 slices fresh thin-sliced bread	Dash of black pepper
2 hard-cooked eggs, sieved	Mayonnaise
1 tablespoon lemon juice	Soft butter
1/4 teaspoon salt	3 4-ounce cans Maine sardines
Dash of cayenne	Watercress

Combine eggs, lemon juice, seasonings, and mayonnaise to moisten. Blend well. Remove crust from bread and roll lightly with rolling pin so bread will have less tendency to break. Butter each slice. Place a sardine across 1 end and spread it with 1 teaspoon egg mixture. Roll carefully and fasten with toothpicks. Cover sandwich rolls with a damp towel and chill thoroughly. *To serve:* Remove toothpicks, tuck in sprigs of watercress for crispness and garnish. Makes 24 sandwiches. **Good companions** . . . Hot tea with lemon, crispy-thin cookies make a satisfying snack meal out of these.

Swiss Sardines

4 slices white bread	1 4-ounce can Maine sardines
Butter	2 tablespoons prepared mustard
4 slices Swiss cheese	

Toast bread on both sides. Butter bread and cover each piece with slice of Swiss cheese. Broil until cheese turns golden. Drain sardines, roll in prepared mustard. Arrange sardines on grilled cheese. Grill for 2 minutes. Serve hot. Makes 4 servings.

Hot 'n' Crisp Sardine Sandwich

8 medium to thick slices rye bread or pumpernickel	2 tablespoons chopped parsley
2 4-ounce cans Maine sardines, drained	2 or more tablespoons freshly grated horseradish
1 cup mayonnaise	Salt and pepper to taste
1/4 cup coarsely shredded sweet onion	1 to 2 tablespoons lemon juice

Mash sardines and mix with mayonnaise, onion, and parsley. Add freshly grated horseradish—2 tablespoons for hot, 3 tablespoons for very hot, and 4 tablespoons for "Wow!" Season to taste with salt, pepper, and lemon juice. Spread on 4 slices bread, top with remaining slices. Makes 4 large sandwiches. *Or try this* . . . Add 1/4 cup finely chopped pecans to this sandwich filling.

Husky Sardine Hoagys

6 French bread buns	48 thin slices cucumber
Softened butter for spreading	3 3 3/4-ounce cans sardines
12 thin slices caraway cheese	

Cut buns in half horizontally. Spread thinly with butter. On each bottom half arrange 2 slices caraway cheese, 8 cucumber slices, 1/2 can sardines. Top with remaining bun halves. Makes 6 sandwiches.

Keep in mind . . . These should be made when they are to be eaten. Their flavor is not enhanced if they have to wait around. If you want to do some advance preparation, put together everything except the sardines. Add these at the last minute.

Crisp-and-Creamy Sardines

24 slices whole-wheat bread	2 tablespoons mayonnaise
2 3-ounce packages cream cheese	1 teaspoon Worcestershire sauce
2 cans Maine sardines in mustard sauce	1 small cucumber, scored and thinly sliced

Mash cream cheese and add sardines, mayonnaise, and Worcestershire sauce. Mix well. Spread on 12 slices of bread, top with thin slices of cucumber. Top with remaining bread. Makes 12 sandwiches.

Sardine Special

8 slices bread, buttered	2 teaspoons minced onion
1 4-ounce can Maine sardines	1 teaspoon lemon juice
1 3-ounce package cream cheese	1/2 teaspoon grated horseradish
3 tablespoons mayonnaise	Salt and pepper
2 tablespoons chopped radishes	1 cucumber, scored and thinly sliced
	Lettuce

Drain sardines. Mash cream cheese and mayonnaise until soft. Add radishes, onion, lemon juice, horseradish, and salt and pepper to taste. Blend well. Spread cheese mixture on 4 slices of buttered bread. Arrange sliced cucumbers on cheese, and top with sardines. Cover with lettuce and remaining bread slices. Makes 4 sandwiches.

South of the Border Buffet Sandwich

1 round home-style loaf (about 12 slices)	1/2 tablespoon grated orange rind
2 large ripe avocados, peeled	4 4-ounce cans Maine sardines, drained
1/4 teaspoon capers	1/2 teaspoon chili powder (or more to taste)
1 tablespoon minced onion	Salt and pepper to taste
2 tablespoons lemon juice	Pimento strips
3 tablespoons orange juice	Chili-Toasted Sesame Seeds
1/2 tablespoon grated lemon rind	

To prepare filling: Halve, peel, and pit avocados; mash to a cream with capers, onion, lemon and orange juice, grated rind, and 2 cans sardines. Season to taste with chili powder, salt and pepper. Chill mixture 1 hour or more to blend and ripen flavors. *To prepare sandwich loaf:* Discard very small end slices of loaf. Spread remaining 10 or 12 slices on one side with a generous amount of filling. Press spread slices together and reshape into loaf. *To serve:* Separate slices. Top each slice with whole sardines, strips of pimento, and sprinkle with Chili-Toasted Sesame Seeds. Makes 10 to 12 servings.

Chili-Toasted Sesame Seeds:

Cream 1 tablespoon butter with 1/2 teaspoon chili powder. Spread to cover bottom of shallow pan. Sprinkle 4 or 5 tablespoons sesame seeds over seasoned butter. Toast in 400° F. oven until seeds are golden. Spread on paper towels to drain.

Sardine Submarines

3 12-inch submarine rolls
3 3 3/4- or 4-ounce cans
   Maine sardines
6 lettuce leaves
2 tomatoes
1 onion
2 tablespoons butter

1 1/2 teaspoons prepared
   mustard
Salt
6 1-ounce slices cheese
1/3 cup mayonnaise or
   salad dressing

Drain sardines. Wash lettuce leaves. Wash and slice tomatoes crosswise into 12 slices. Peel onion and slice crosswise into thin slices. Separate into rings. Cream butter and blend in mustard. Cut rolls in half lengthwise. Spread bottom half with mustard butter. Cover with lettuce, tomato slices, and onion rings. Sprinkle with salt. Top with cheese and sardines. Spread top half of rolls with mayonnaise, place over sandwiches and secure with toothpicks. Cut in half crosswise. 6 servings.

Take note . . . Münster cheese gives a contrasting bland taste; sharp Cheddar adds authority.

Sardines Göteborg

4 slices pumpernickel bread
1 tablespoon butter
1 4-ounce can Maine sardines
   in mustard sauce

2 slices Cheddar cheese
1 small Bermuda onion, sliced

Spread butter on 2 slices of bread. Arrange sardines on buttered bread. Cover with cheese and onion rings. Top with remaining bread. Makes 2 hearty sandwiches.

Good companions . . . A platter of icy-crisp greens, including celery stalks, green pepper rings, slivered endive, thinly sliced fennel, parsley.

Lobsternut Specials

12 slices bread, buttered
1/2 pound lobster meat,
   cooked
1/4 cup chopped walnuts
1/4 cup chopped celery
1 tablespoon lemon juice

1/2 teaspoon salt
Dash of paprika
1/4 cup mayonnaise or salad
   dressing
Lettuce

Chop lobster meat. Add the next 6 ingredients. Spread 6 slices of bread with lobster mixture; cover with lettuce and remaining 6 slices of bread. Makes 6 sandwiches.

Crown Princess Martha's Special

4 slices white bread, buttered	Butter
1 pound fresh-boiled cod roe	1/2 cup thick Béchamel Dill Sauce
	1 cup shrimp, peeled

Cut cod roes into small pieces less than 1/2 inch thick. Sauté lightly in butter and divide immediately over the slices of buttered bread. Pour hot Béchamel Dill Sauce on top, and sprinkle with shrimp. Serve piping hot. Makes 4 servings.

Béchamel Dill Sauce

2 tablespoons butter
1 1/2 to 2 tablespoons flour
1/2 cup milk
1/2 cup meat stock or bouillon
Salt
Paprika
1 egg yolk
1/2 teaspoon dried dill
    or
1 teaspoon chopped fresh dill

Melt butter. Blend in flour; slowly stir in milk and meat stock. Stir constantly until sauce boils. Season. Beat a small amount of the sauce into the egg yolk, then add to the rest of the sauce. Stir constantly over low heat until sauce thickens. Do not allow to boil after yolk has been added. Stir in dill before removing from heat.

Barbecued Crabwiches

6 large buttered rolls, split	2 whole cloves
1/2 pound crab meat	2 teaspoons soy sauce
1/4 cup chopped onion	2 teaspoons Worcestershire sauce
1/2 cup chopped celery	
3 tablespoons butter or other fat, melted	1 chicken bouillon cube
1/4 teaspoon salt	1/2 cup tomato juice
Dash of pepper	2 tablespoons chopped parsley
2 whole bay leaves	

Remove any shell or cartilage from crab meat. Cook onion and celery in butter until tender. Add salt, pepper, bay leaves, cloves, sauces, bouillon cube, and tomato juice. Simmer for 5 minutes. Remove bay leaves and cloves. Add parsley and crab meat; heat. Serve on rolls. Makes 6 sandwiches.

Scallop Clubs

12 slices white bread, toasted	1/4 cup creamy blue-cheese
1 7-ounce package frozen	dressing
breaded French-fried	8 lettuce leaves
scallops	8 1/4-inch slices tomato
8 slices bacon	

Heat scallops according to package directions. Fry bacon until crisp; drain on absorbent paper. For each sandwich: Spread toast with blue-cheese dressing. On each of 4 slices toast, arrange a layer of scallops, 2 bacon slices. Top with 4 more slices toast, on which place lettuce leaves, tomato slices. Cover with remaining 4 slices toast. Fasten layers together with toothpicks. Cut diagonally into halves. Makes 4 sandwiches.

Keep in mind . . . Have everything ready so that scallops get to the table hot—makes all the difference with this sandwich.

Fried Fish Fillets

4 slices of bread, buttered	Parsley
4 crisply fried hot fish fillets	Remoulade Sauce
Fresh lemon	

Place the hot filleted fish on the buttered bread, and garnish with lemon and parsley. Serve with Remoulade Sauce. Makes 4 servings.

Remoulade Sauce

- 3 hard-cooked egg yolks
- 2 raw egg yolks
- 1 teaspoon dry mustard
- 1/4 teaspoon salt
- 1/8 teaspoon pepper
- 3/4 cup olive oil
- 3 tablespoons lemon juice or vinegar
- 1/4 cup commercial sour cream
- 1 tablespoon capers
- 1/2 teaspoon chopped anchovies
- 1/4 tablespoon each finely chopped tarragon, parsley, chives

Mash egg yolks. With wire whisk, beat in raw yolks, mustard, seasonings. Beat in by alternate dropfuls olive oil, lemon juice, turning the bowl as you beat. When the sauce has thickened, mix in remaining ingredients.

Scallop Broil

6 slices white bread	1 quart boiling water
1 pound scallops, fresh or frozen	12 slices bacon
2 tablespoons salt	6 slices cheese
	Paprika

Thaw frozen scallops. Remove any shell particles and wash. Place in boiling salted water. Cover and bring back to the boiling point. Simmer for 3 to 4 minutes, depending on size. Drain. Cut large scallops in half. Fry bacon until crisp; drain on absorbent paper. Reserve bacon drippings. Trim crusts from bread. Place 2 slices of bacon on each piece of bread. Cover with cheese. Place scallops on top of cheese. Brush with bacon drippings. Sprinkle with paprika. Place on a greased broiler pan about 3 inches from heat. Broil for 3 to 4 minutes or until lightly browned. Makes 6 servings.

Good companions . . . Sprinkle thick tomato slices with salt, pepper, oregano, dot with butter, and broil along with Scallop Broil. Just right for color and flavor.

Hot Fishwiches

6 finger rolls	3 tablespoons mayonnaise or salad dressing
1 egg, beaten	
1/2 teaspoon salt	1 tablespoon prepared mustard
Dash of pepper	
1 pound ocean perch fillets	6 slices tomato, cut in half
1/2 cup dry bread crumbs	1/4 teaspoon salt
2 tablespoons pickle relish	Dash of pepper
1/2 cup chopped onion	

Combine egg, salt, and pepper. Dip fish in egg and roll in crumbs. Fry at moderate heat in a heavy frying pan which contains about 1/8 inch of fat, turning carefully to brown both sides. Cooking time is about 10 minutes, depending on thickness of fish. Drain on absorbent paper. Cut rolls in half, and remove some of the soft inside center. Combine relish, onion, mayonnaise, and mustard; spread on rolls. Place fried fish on rolls, top with tomatoes, and sprinkle with salt and pepper. Replace tops. Wrap each sandwich in foil. Heat in a 350° F. oven for 10 to 12 minutes or until heated through. Serve hot. Makes 6 sandwiches.

Even better . . . Use herb-flavored packaged bread crumbs and one of the hotter mustards, like Dijon, to give these Fishwiches something special.

Lobster Pizzas

8 1 1/2-inch slices French
     bread
1/2 cup Rich Tomato Sauce
3/4 cup cooked, flaked lobster

4 1-ounce slices mozzarella
    cheese, each cut into 4
    equal-size squares

Place bread slices on a greased baking sheet. Spread with a tablespoon of Rich Tomato Sauce. Sprinkle 1 1/2 tablespoons of lobster over sauce. Cover with 2 overlapping cheese squares. Bake in a 350° F. oven until cheese is melted, or about 5 minutes. Makes 8 sandwiches.

Rich Tomato Sauce

1 clove garlic
2 tablespoons olive oil
1 17-ounce can peeled Italian plum tomatoes
1 can tomato paste
Salt
Pepper
Oregano
Bay leaf
1 tablespoon Burgundy

Mash garlic and brown in olive oil. Add tomatoes, tomato paste, seasonings. Stir well, partially cover. Simmer over low flame for 1/2 hour, stirring frequently. Add Burgundy, continue cooking 1/2 hour. Correct seasoning.

Crab-Slaw Roll

6 large rolls
1 pound crab meat
1/3 cup mayonnaise or
       salad dressing
1 1/2 tablespoons ketchup

1/2 teaspoon salt
3/4 cup chopped cabbage
1/4 cup grated carrots
2 tablespoons butter

Remove any shell or cartilage from crab meat. Combine mayonnaise, ketchup, and salt. Blend thoroughly. Combine cabbage, carrots, mayonnaise mixture, and crab meat. Cut rolls in half lengthwise. Spread with butter. Place about 1/2 cup crab slaw on each roll. Makes 6 sandwiches.

Keep in mind . . . Stuffed with vegetables and rich crab meat, Crab-Slaw Rolls need only a beverage to be a complete meal-in-the-hand.

Salad-Stuffed Rolls

4 white hard finger rolls
   or buns
3 tablespoons soft butter
2 hard-cooked eggs,
   chopped
2 tablespoons finely
   chopped celery

1/2 cup flaked salmon
1 teaspoon minced onion
1 tablespoon mayonnaise
1/2 teaspoon salt
1/8 teaspoon pepper

Cut rolls in half and hollow out bottom half. Spread with butter. Combine chopped eggs, celery, salmon, onion, mayonnaise, salt and pepper. Fill rolls with mixture and replace tops. Makes 4 rolls.
Perfect partner . . . Sliced, garden-fresh tomatoes, with oil-and-vinegar dressing and a liberal sprinkling of basil.

San Diego Crab

8 slices white bread
1 cup flaked crab meat
1 cup mashed avocado

Lemon juice and Tabasco to
   taste
Mayonnaise

Mix crab meat, avocado, lemon juice, Tabasco, mayonnaise. Spread on 4 slices bread. Top with remaining slices.
Even better . . . Use cream cheese in place of mayonnaise and spread this richer mixture on small butter or finger rolls.

Broiled Crab American

12 slices white bread
1 6 1/2- to 7 1/2-ounce can
   crab meat, drained
   and flaked (about 1
   cup)
2 teaspoons lemon juice
1/2 cup mayonnaise

3 tablespoons milk
1/8 teaspoon salt
Mayonnaise
2 tomatoes, sliced
6 slices American cheese
Sliced olives

Mix crab meat with lemon juice. Blend 1/2 cup mayonnaise, milk, and salt; add to crab mixture and toss lightly with fork until crab meat is coated. Arrange bread slices on broiler rack and broil 3 inches from heat until toasted on one side. Turn; spread untoasted sides with mayonnaise. Cover half the bread with tomato slices and then with crab mixture. Cover remaining bread with cheese slices. Broil until cheese is golden brown, about 5 minutes. Garnish with sliced olives and serve hot. Makes 4 to 6 servings.

Summer Pleaser

30 slices white bread
1 7 3/4-ounce can salmon,
   flaked
1/4 cup celery
1/2 cup sour cream

1/4 cup chopped cucumber
1/4 teaspoon salt
1 cup soft butter
4 medium-size tomatoes,
   thinly sliced

Combine salmon, celery, sour cream, cucumber, and salt. Butter bread. Spread 10 slices with salmon filling. Top with another bread slice and 2 tomato slices. Cover sandwiches with remaining bread slices. Secure with toothpicks. 10 sandwiches. *Good companions* . . . Serve with something crisp, such as julienne potato sticks. Start with jellied madrilène, finish with a fruit dessert—as pleasant a summer luncheon as anyone could want.

Pink Lobster

8 slices rye bread, toasted
Softened butter for spreading
1 cup diced lobster

1 cup diced celery
2 tablespoons ketchup
1/2 cup mayonnaise

Butter toast slices. Mix lobster, celery, ketchup, and mayonnaise; spread on 4 slices toast. Top with remaining slices. Makes 4 sandwiches.

Broccoli-Topped Crab Meat Sandwiches

6 slices white bread, toasted
1 10-ounce package frozen
   broccoli spears
1 7-ounce can crab meat,
   flaked
6 tablespoons butter,
   melted

1/2 teaspoon salt
1 teaspoon caraway seed
3/4 teaspoon dry mint,
   crushed, or chopped
   fresh mint

Cook broccoli spears according to directions on package; drain and cover until ready to use. Combine flaked crab meat, butter, salt, caraway seed, and mint; mix until ingredients are thoroughly blended. Heat just long enough to warm mixture thoroughly. Spread 1/4 cup mixture over each slice of toast. Arrange about 2 broccoli spears over the top of each sandwich in diagonal fashion. Garnish with a lemon slice and mint. Serve open-face immediately. Makes 6 servings.
Perfect partners . . . Thick slices of peeled tomato, lightly seasoned with salt and freshly ground black pepper.

Tropical Salmonburgers

6 sandwich buns, split, toasted	3 tablespoons pickle relish
	1 teaspoon salt
1 No. 2 can salmon, flaked	6 slices canned pineapple
1/4 cup lemon juice	1/3 cup grated process cheese

Combine flaked salmon, lemon juice, pickle relish, and salt. Arrange pineapple slices on greased baking sheet. Place 1/3 cup salmon mixture on each pineapple slice. Sprinkle about 1 tablespoon cheese over each salmonburger. Bake in a 400° F. oven for 5 minutes, or until cheese melts. Place a salmonburger between halves of toasted sandwich buns. Serve while hot. Makes 6 sandwiches.
Perfect partner . . . A crispy, tart-dressing mixed green salad.

Salmonburgers

6 hamburger rolls	2 eggs, beaten
1 1-pound can salmon	1/4 cup chopped parsley
1/2 cup chopped onion	1 teaspoon powdered mustard
1/4 cup butter or other fat, melted	1/2 teaspoon salt
1/3 cup salmon liquid	2 tablespoons butter
2/3 cup dry bread crumbs	Lemon wedges

Drain salmon, reserving liquid. Flake salmon. Cook onion in butter until tender. Add salmon liquid, 1/3 cup bread crumbs, eggs, parsley, mustard, salt, and salmon. Mix well. Shape into 6 cakes and roll in remaining crumbs. Place cakes in a heavy frying pan which contains about 1/8 inch of fat, hot but not smoking. Fry at moderate heat. When cakes are brown on one side, turn carefully and brown the other side. Cooking time approximately 5 to 8 minutes. Drain on absorbent paper. Cut rolls in half. Spread with butter. Place cakes in rolls. Serve with lemon wedges. Makes 6 sandwiches.

Minced Oyster

Thin-sliced bread	Paprika
12 oysters, minced	1/4 pint mayonnaise
Oyster liquor	Lemon slices
Lemon juice	

Gradually mix oysters, oyster liquor, a squirt of lemon juice, and paprika into mayonnaise. Spread on bread, cut into triangles, garnish with lemon slices.

Lobster Salad Boats

2 4-ounce loaves French
   bread
1 cup sour cream
1 tablespoon blue-cheese
   salad-dressing mix
2 cups diced celery
2 5 1/2-ounce cans lobster
   or 1 1/2 cups cooked
   lobster

1/2 cup finely diced green
   pepper
1 tablespoon grated onion
1 tablespoon lemon juice
1/2 cup softened butter
4 slices American cheese,
   cut in half

Combine sour cream and salad-dressing mix, blending well. Fold in celery, lobster, green pepper, onion, and lemon juice. Split loaves of bread but do not cut through. Spread with butter. Score top of each loaf into 3 or 4 portions. Fill loaves with salad mixture. Place cheese on filling, using 4 half slices for each loaf. Broil 6 to 8 inches from heat until cheese is .melted, or bake in a 350° F. oven 5 to 10 minutes. Cut into portions as marked. Makes 6 to 8 servings.

Shrimp on the Rocks

4 slices rye bread, buttered
2 cups cooked peeled shrimp

1 tablespoon lemon juice
2 tablespoons drained capers

Arrange shrimp pyramid-fashion on top of bread slices. Sprinkle with lemon juice, capers. Makes 4 open sandwiches.

Wonder Ways with Seafood Salad—

To 2 cups shrimp, crab, or lobster salad sandwich filling, add one of the following: 1/4 cup toasted sesame seeds . . . 1/4 cup slivered almonds . . . 1/3 cup chopped raw mushrooms . . . 1/2 cup diced artichoke hearts . . . 1/3 cup diced water chestnuts . . . 1/2 cup chopped walnuts . . . 1/3 cup chopped pistachio nuts . . . 1/3 cup pine nuts, whole . . . 1/3 cup snipped watercress . . . 1/3 cup snipped raw spinach . . . 1/4 cup snipped parsley . . . 1/2 cup diced celery . . . 1/4 cup diced green pepper . . . 2 tbs. diced pimento . . . 2 tbs. snipped chives . . . curry powder to taste . . . turmeric to taste . . . 2 tbs. chili sauce . . . 1/2 cup chopped cucumber . . . 3/4 cup cooked vegetable, such as peas, cut green beans, carrots, etc. . . . 1/2 cup diced tomato . . . 1/4 cup diced mustard pickle . . . 1/3 cup slivered Swiss cheese . . . 1 tbs. prepared horseradish . . . 1/2 cup diced, lemon-sprinkled avocado . . . 1 tbs. lemon juice . . . 1/2 cup diced fresh pineapple . . . 1/2 cup drained crushed canned pineapple . . . 3/4 cup halved seedless grapes .

Sea Tangle

8 sliced sandwich buns, toasted	2 tablespoons French dressing
1/2 cup or 1 4 1/2-ounce can shrimp, flaked	1/2 teaspoon seasoned salt
2/3 cup or 1 5-ounce can lobster, flaked	2 teaspoons lemon juice
1 cup or 1 7 1/2-ounce can crab meat, flaked	3 tablespoons soft butter
	8 lettuce leaves
1/4 cup chopped green pepper	8 cucumber slices
1/4 cup mayonnaise or salad dressing	Watercress sprigs
	8 lemon wedges

Combine shrimp, lobster, crab meat, green pepper, mayonnaise, French dressing, seasoned salt, and lemon juice. Butter bun halves. Place a lettuce leaf on bottom half of each bun. Spread a generous 1/4 cup of filling over lettuce leaf. Slit cucumber slices half way and place 1 slice, twisted corkscrew fashion, over filling. Serve open-face, with buttered bun top at side. Garnish with watercress and a lemon wedge. Makes 8 sandwiches.

Perfect partners . . . A calico coleslaw, with finely chopped red cabbage and green pepper, snipped parsley and grated carrot for zest and that pretty "calico" look.

Boiled Lobsters

2 live lobsters (1 pound each)
3 quarts boiling water
3 tablespoons salt
Melted butter

Plunge lobsters headfirst into boiling salted water. Cover and return to boiling point. Simmer for 20 minutes. Drain. Place lobster on its back. With a sharp knife cut in half lengthwise. Remove the stomach, which is just back of the head, and the intestinal vein, which runs from the stomach to the tip of the tail. Do not discard the green liver and coral roe; they are delicious. Crack claws. Serve with butter. Serves 2.

Take note: For recipes requiring cooked lobster meat, cool lobsters and remove meat. Two live lobsters, 1 pound each, yield approximately 1/2 pound cooked lobster meat.

Walnut Tunawich

12 slices white bread, buttered	1 tablespoon green pepper, finely chopped
1 7-ounce can tuna	1 tablespoon pimento, finely chopped
1/2 cup finely chopped walnuts	1/2 teaspoon salt
1/2 cup finely chopped sweet pickles	6 tablespoons mayonnaise

Flake tuna fish. Blend in remaining ingredients. Spread on 6 slices bread, top with remaining slices.

Salmon Verde

10 slices whole-wheat bread, buttered	3/4 cup cooked green peas
1 cup flaked salmon	2 tablespoons lemon juice
	1/4 teaspoon salt

Combine salmon, peas, lemon juice, and salt. Spread on 5 slices bread, top with remaining slices. Makes 5 sandwiches.

Sardine-Swiss Specials

12 slices rye bread, buttered	3 slices natural Swiss cheese
2 3 3/4-ounce cans sardines	1 large tomato

Arrange sardines on 6 slices of bread. Cut each slice of cheese in half; place over sardines. Cut tomato into 6 thin slices; place 1 on each cheese slice. Top with remaining bread. Makes 6 sandwiches.

Halibutwiches

12 slices white bread, buttered	1/2 cup mayonnaise or salad dressing
2 cups flaked halibut	1/2 teaspoon salt
1/4 cup sliced stuffed olives	Dash of pepper
1/2 cup chopped celery	1/2 teaspoon prepared mustard
1 teaspoon grated onion	
1 teaspoon Worcestershire sauce	

Combine all ingredients except bread. Chill. Spread 6 slices of bread with fish mixture; cover with remaining slices of bread. Makes 6 sandwiches.

Take note: Serve lemon wedges with these—the sharpness of a few drops of lemon juice on fish sandwich fillings sparks a tangy taste.

Merry-Maker Perch

6 slices toast, buttered
1 pound yellow perch
  fillets
1 quart water
1 1/2 teaspoons salt
2 tablespoons milk
3/4 cup mayonnaise or salad
  dressing

3 tablespoons chili sauce
1 teaspoon prepared
  mustard
2 drops Tabasco
1/4 teaspoon paprika
1/4 teaspoon celery salt
1/4 teaspoon lemon juice or
  vinegar

Skin fillets and place on a rack over boiling water; sprinkle with salt. Cover and steam until fish flakes easily when tested with a fork. Cool. Remove bones and flake fish. Combine fish and milk; mix well. Arrange toast on a cookie sheet. Cover each slice with fish mixture. Combine remaining ingredients. Cover fish with mayonnaise mixture. Bake in a 350° F. oven 12 to 15 minutes, or until lightly browned. Serves 6.

Curried Sardine Sandwiches

50 slices white, whole-
  wheat, or rye bread
1 1/2 dozen hard-cooked eggs,
  chopped
1 1/2 cups finely chopped
  celery
2 large cucumbers,
  chopped

1 1/2 tablespoons curry
  powder
1 1/2 tablespoons salt
1 cup mayonnaise
3 pounds tomatoes,
  thickly sliced
12 4-ounce cans Maine
  sardines, drained

Combine eggs, celery, cucumbers, curry powder, salt, mayonnaise. Spread on 50 slices bread. For each serving, place 3 slices of tomato and 6 sardines on 2 slices of egg-spread bread. Garnish with pickles, olives, and radishes. Makes 25 servings.

Tuna Cheesewiches

6 sandwich buns, split,
  buttered
1 7-ounce can tuna, flaked
1/2 cup chopped celery

2 tablespoons pickle relish,
  drained
1/4 cup mayonnaise
6 slices process cheese

Combine tuna, celery, pickle relish, mayonnaise. Spread 1/4 cup tuna mixture on bottom half of each bun and cover with a slice of cheese. Place both halves of the buns, cut sides up, on a cookie sheet. Bake in a 400° F. oven for 5 minutes, or toast under low broiler heat until bun tops are toasted and cheese is melted. Makes 6 sandwiches.

Shamrock Loaf

8 slices white bread
1 package lime gelatin
1 1/4 cups boiling water
1 cup mashed avocado
1 7-ounce can tuna, flaked
1 tablespoon chopped
   pimento
1 tablespoon lemon juice
1/4 cup chopped green
   pepper
1/8 teaspoon celery seed
1 tablespoon creamy
   French dressing
1/4 teaspoon seasoned salt
1/4 cup mayonnaise or salad
   dressing
3 tablespoons soft butter
1 hard-cooked egg, sliced
1 green pepper ring
1/2 3-ounce package cream
   cheese
1 tablespoon milk
3 drops green food
   coloring

Combine gelatin and water; let cool until slightly set; add mashed avocado, blending well with a rotary beater. Pour 1/2 cup of the gelatin mixture into oiled 1/2-quart loaf pan. Chill until firm. Combine tuna, pimento, lemon juice, green pepper, celery seed, French dressing, seasoned salt, and mayonnaise. Make 2 four-layer sandwiches, using soft butter on bread and 1/4 cup tuna filling in each layer. Trim off crusts and place sandwiches next to each other in the center of the loaf pan on top of gelatin layer. Pour remaining gelatin mixture around and over sandwiches. Refrigerate until firm. Unmold and garnish loaf with 3 slices of hard-cooked egg and a green pepper ring to represent a shamrock. Mix cream cheese with milk, green food coloring; pipe through a pastry tube to make an edge around bottom of loaf. Makes 6 to 8 servings.

Sticks on a Bun

6 rolls, toasted and buttered
12 frozen fish sticks
3/4 cup chili sauce
1 tablespoon lemon juice
1 tablespoon horseradish
1/2 teaspoon salt
6 slices (1 ounce each)
   cheese

Place frozen fish sticks in a single layer in a well-greased baking pan. Bake in a 400° F. oven for 15 to 20 minutes or until heated through and crisp. Combine chili sauce, lemon juice, horseradish, and salt. Place 2 fish sticks on bottom half of a toasted buttered roll. Cover with a slice of cheese. Place under broiler until cheese melts. Top with approximately 2 tablespoons chili mixture and top half of roll. 6 sandwiches.

Portions de Luxe

6 slices Vienna bread	2 tablespoons melted butter
6 frozen raw breaded fish portions	Garlic salt
Salt and pepper	12 tomato slices
1 package frozen French-fried onion rings	Salt and pepper
	De Luxe Dressing

Place frozen fish portions in a single layer in a frying basket. Fry in deep fat, 350° F., for 4 to 6 minutes or until brown. Drain on absorbent paper. Sprinkle with salt and pepper. Heat onion rings according to package directions. Toast bread. Brush with butter and sprinkle with garlic salt. Place a fish portion on each piece of toast. Top with 2 tomato slices and sprinkle with salt and pepper. Place onion rings on tomatoes. Top each open sandwich with approximately 3 tablespoons De Luxe Dressing. Makes 6 servings.

De Luxe Dressing

> 3/4 cup mayonnaise or salad dressing
> 1/4 cup ketchup
> 1 1/2 teaspoons lemon juice
> 1/2 teaspoon chili powder

Combine all ingredients and mix thoroughly. Chill.

Ocean Clubs

18 slices toast, buttered	Salt
2 cups Flaked Ocean Perch	Pepper
1 cup Tartar Sauce (page 151)	4 hard-cooked eggs, sliced
	6 lettuce leaves

Combine fish, half of Tartar Sauce, salt, and pepper. Spread 6 slices of toast with fish mixture. Place 6 toast slices over fish-spread slices and cover with egg slices, lettuce, and remaining sauce. Top with remaining toast. Fasten layers together with toothpicks. Cut into quarters. Makes 6 sandwiches.

Flaked Ocean Perch

> 1 pound ocean perch fillets
> 1 quart water
> 1 tablespoon salt

Skin fillets and place in boiling salted water. Cover and return to boiling point; simmer 10 minutes or until fish flakes easily.

173

Shrimp New England

12 slices bread
1/2 cup cooked chopped
  shrimp
1/2 cup grated process
  cheese

1 hard-cooked egg,
  chopped
1 1/2 tablespoons horseradish
1/4 cup mayonnaise

Combine shrimp, cheese, chopped egg, horseradish, and mayonnaise. Spread on 6 slices of bread and top with remaining slices.

Maine-and-California Sandwich

4 slices white bread
2 4-ounce cans Maine
  sardines
1/4 cup mayonnaise

1 avocado, sliced
1/4 cup lemon juice
1 medium onion, sliced

Drain sardines. Spread bread with mayonnaise. Dip avocado slices in lemon juice to prevent darkening and place on bread. Arrange sardines over avocado and top with onion rings. Makes 4 open-face sandwiches.

Perfect partners . . . Slice 1 lemon paper-thin and serve with this sandwich instead of the usual pickle garnish.

Tuna-Cheese Burgers

6 hamburger buns, split and
  toasted
2 cans chunk-style tuna
1/2 cup cooked salad dressing
1/2 cup dry bread crumbs
2 tablespoons minced onion
1/2 cup chopped dill pickles
1/2 teaspoon salt

1/4 teaspoon celery salt
1/4 teaspoon pepper
2 teaspoons lemon juice,
  fresh, frozen, or bottled
Soft butter
6 slices process American
  cheese
1/2 cup chili sauce

Several hours ahead: Mix tuna with salad dressing, 1/4 cup bread crumbs, onion, pickles, salts, pepper, lemon juice. Shape into 6 flat patties. Lightly coat patties with remaining bread crumbs. Place on cookie sheet. Refrigerate. *About 40 minutes before serving:* Heat oven to 400° F. Bake burgers 20 minutes, or until nicely browned, turning once. Butter buns. Place 1 burger on half of each bun; top with cheese slice. Bake 5 minutes longer, or until cheese is melted and golden. Spread other half of bun with chili sauce; put halves together. Makes 6 sandwiches.

Perch Salads

12 slices bread	1/2 teaspoon salt
2 cups Flaked Ocean Perch (page 173)	Dash of pepper
	2 tablespoons lemon juice
1 cup diced cucumber	1/4 cup mayonnaise or salad
2 tablespoons chopped pimento	dressing
1/4 cup chopped onion	Lettuce

Combine all ingredients, except lettuce and bread. Be careful not to break the fish into too-small pieces. Chill. Spread on 6 slices of bread, top with lettuce, cover with remaining bread. Makes 6 sandwiches.

Checkerboard Sandwiches

4 slices whole-wheat bread
4 slices white bread
3/4 cup pimento cream cheese
3/4 teaspoon chili sauce
1 cup cooked shrimp, finely chopped
3/4 teaspoon lemon juice
Softened butter for spreading

Combine cream cheese, chili sauce, shrimp, and lemon juice. Butter each slice of bread. Spread 1 1/2 tablespoons cheese-shrimp filling on all slices except 2 slices of whole-wheat bread, which will be used as top layer. Make 2 stacks of 3 slices each, alternating light and dark bread. Top each stack with the extra slice of whole-wheat bread, buttered side down. Press together gently. Cut off crusts and slice each stack into 6 equal-size portions, forming ribbon sandwiches. Put 4 alternating slices together to form a 4-row checkerboard pattern, using 1 1/2 tablespoons cheese-shrimp filling between each layer. This will make 3 sandwiches of 4 layers each. Wrap securely in waxed paper or foil and chill thoroughly. *To serve:* Cut each sandwich into 6 slices. Makes 18 sandwiches.

Keep in mind . . . Day-old bread is a must for these Checkerboards. So is a really sharp knife. Fuzzy edges spoil the pattern.

175

By the Dozens

For parties at which sandwiches will be served, you really have to think big. Hit or miss techniques that get you through four-at-a-time, or even eight-at-a-time, will get you no place when you're trying to figure for—let's say—fifty. If you get involved with that kind of crowd, you have to use production-line methods.

How to figure bread—For church suppers, my Aunt Hazel followed a rule of thumb that has worked for me—give or take a few mouthfuls—down through many years of crowd-feeding. If you are using sandwich loaves, multiply by 3 the number of people you are expecting to feed, then divide the total by 32. That's how many sandwich loaves you will need. If you are using regular baker's sliced loaves (approximately 1 pound each), divide by 6 the number expected to find out how many baker's loaves you will need. (Finger or party rolls can be counted on to disappear *at least* three to a customer. In numbers, and in the amount of filling required, these are a law unto themselves which you simply must figure out as you proceed.)

How to figure filling—Meat or cheese, thinly sliced: about three narrow slices per sandwich. Meat or cheese, thickly sliced: possibly two slices per sandwich. Spread-type fillings: quarter cup per sandwich.

How to prepare—Remember to buy all the breads you will need at least one day before you will be using them. Two days won't hurt, particularly if it's bread you plan to slice yourself. If you're going to slice bread extra-thin, buy it well in advance and freeze it. Use the sharpest knife you can lay hands on. To turn one slice of pre-sliced bread into two slices of tea-sandwich thinness, lay the frozen slice on a breadboard, steady it with the palm of one hand, and work your sharp knife through the center of it with a sawing motion, turning the slice as you saw so that you will be sure to keep the knife equidistant from top and bottom at all points.

If you don't have time to freeze your party breads, remember that all breads for sandwiches will benefit from spending a few hours in the refrigerator (well wrapped, of course, in foil or waxed paper).

Most fillings can be made a day ahead, except for particularly strongly flavored ones (such as those containing anchovy, sardine, lots of onion, etc.).

Do all your fancy cutting of garnishes at one time (shapes cut from jellied cranberry sauce or fruit jelly or aspic with tiny cookie cutters, slicing of pimento-stuffed olives, etc.) and refrigerate them on flat plates, with waxed paper or foil laid tightly over them to keep the cut surfaces from drying out. These can be done ahead of time also.

Take butter, cream cheese, and all combinations made with these two spreads out of the refrigerator about a half hour before using time. At room temperature they will spread much more easily.

How to assemble—Make all sandwiches of one kind at the same time.

Have enough space cleared to lay out all the bread you will need for a particular batch of sandwiches. If you can't manage that, try to do half at a time.

Most sandwiches call for some variety of spread on the bread before the filling is added. All salad-type sandwiches, or those containing fruit or raw vegetables, must be laid upon pre-spread bread or else the fillings will soak through. Whether your spread is butter, mayonnaise, or other, do all the spreading at the same time, bringing it thinly and evenly to the outer edges of each slice. A little practice, and you can do this in four strokes of a spatula per slice.

Line up, ready to hand, all the ingredients you will need for the batch you're working on. Have the parsley snipped, the nuts chopped, whatever you're using ready to be joined with its sandwich-mates. Don't forget seasonings.

Making twenty sandwiches? Pre-cut yourself twenty squares of waxed paper or foil of the right size to wrap an individual sandwich, or here's a timesaving trick for storing platters of sandwiches made ahead for parties. Cover a tray with waxed paper or foil. Arrange a layer of unwrapped sandwiches on this, top with another sheet of waxed paper or foil. You can stack three or four layers in this manner, being sure to top the final layer with your waxed paper or foil. Then cover the whole thing with a dish towel which has been dipped into cold water and well wrung out—in other words, it's only slightly damp. Refrigerated at once, your sandwiches will keep perfectly for as long as twenty-four hours.

The Wonderful Danish Idea

Danish smørrebrød—the open-face sandwich that is sheer poetry for both eye and palate—is Denmark's national dish. If you're dining on smørrebrød (And why not? The Danes often do!), you'll want three or four or even five of these sandwiches for each main-course serving. The Danish way is to have great platters of them, one holding meat and egg and sausage sandwiches, another varieties of fish, another many kinds of cheeses. They rest, in all their splendor, on a big buffet table, and it is quite impossible not to go back to the table again and again and yet one more time. Of course sandwiches, particularly highly flavored ones, are thirst-making. Foamy Danish beer is just right for these, or a glass of icy aquavit. Finish up with Danish pastry and plenty of coffee.

What makes the Danish smørrebrød different from just any old open-face sandwich is—one might say—the basic concept. If you think of the bread slice on which a Danish sandwich is composed as a plate, rather than a bread slice, you'll more or less have the idea. Danish smørrebrød isn't sandwich so much as it is a meal-on-bread.

Most smørrebrød combinations go best on bread of substance, like big slices of dark pumpernickel or rye. Some of the more delicate can be put together tastily on white bread, however. Use your own judgment and experiment, too, with the following combinations—and don't omit a thin buttering of the bread before you do anything else to it.

Smoked Salmon-Scrambled Egg . . . Place slices of fresh smoked salmon on bread to totally cover it. Add a ribbon of cold scrambled eggs diagonally across. Garnish with finely chopped chives.

Salami-Raw Egg . . . Cover bread with many thin slices of salami sausage. Place a thick onion ring in the center, and slip into it a raw egg yolk.

Samso Cheese . . . Cover buttered bread with thick slices of Samso cheese. Garnish with sliced fresh cucumber.

Salami-Onion . . . Cover bread with lettuce, then with slice of salami and onion rings.

Pâté de Foie-Cucumber . . . Spread pâté on buttered bread, top with tomato and cucumber slices.

Deviled Ham-Olive . . . Spread buttered bread with deviled ham, top with 4 or more pitted, unsliced olives.

Danish Brie . . . Cover buttered bread with 3 or 4 thick slices Danish Brie.

Shrimp . . . Cover buttered bread completely with layer of ice-cold cooked shrimp. Garnish with paper-thin lemon slice.

Danish Blue . . . Cover buttered bread with thin, overlapping slices of Danish blue cheese.

Danish Blue Plus . . . Spread buttered bread thickly with softened Danish blue cheese. Hollow out the cheese in the center, slip into the well a raw egg yolk.

Danish Caviar . . . Be careful—this is different. Center a slice of buttered bread *on* a large lettuce leaf. Spread the bread with Danish caviar; top with chopped egg white, thin lemon slice, and sprigs of parsley.

Danish Ham . . . Cover buttered bread with a few slices of Danish ham, a layer of Italian Salad, a sprinkle of snipped watercress. (*Italian Salad:* cooked peas and cooked, tiny carrot cubes, bound together with mayonnaise.)

Boiled Ham . . . Center bread on large lettuce leaf. Top with sliced boiled ham. Decorate with sliced peaches (canned or fresh) and glacé cherry.

Ham and Egg . . . Cover bread completely with thin-sliced ham. Fry an egg slowly in butter just until the white is set. Slide it, sizzling hot, on the ham; garnish with watercress, tomato slice, and serve warm.

Ham and Asparagus . . . Center bread on large lettuce leaf. Cover with sliced boiled ham. Place asparagus spears diagonally across ham, top with continuous strip of tomato peel.

Ham and Cheese . . . Place lettuce leaf on bread. Top with 1 large slice of ham, 1 large slice of cheese. Add tomato slices, watercress.

Ham and Scrambled Egg . . . Cover bread with sliced ham. Place scrambled egg on one-half of bread, sliced tomatoes on other half. Garnish with watercress sprigs.

Ham and Egg Plus . . . Place lettuce leaf on buttered bread. Top with slice of boiled ham. Add layer of scrambled eggs liberally sprinkled with chopped chives.

Canadian Bacon-Tomato . . . On buttered bread, combine slices of Canadian bacon, tomato, and sprigs of watercress.

Zesty Canadian Bacon . . . Cover buttered bread with lettuce leaf, then with sliced Canadian-style bacon. Decorate with strip of shredded horseradish diagonally across bacon; top with strip of tomato peel, sprig of parsley.

Braunschweiger . . . Cover buttered bread with lettuce leaf, then with 2 slices of Braunschweiger. Garnish with 1/2 ounce julienne Swiss cheese, 2 half slices of crisp bacon, sliced olives.

Cocktail Sausage . . . Place layer of cocktail sausages on buttered bread. Diagonally across them, place strip of crisp bacon. Top with sautéed mushroom caps, speared with toothpicks.

179

Danish Idea

Cocktail Eggs I . . . Place bread on large lettuce leaf. Cover with cocktail sausages. Decorate with strip of scrambled eggs, top with parsley sprigs.

Cocktail Eggs II . . . Place lettuce leaf on bread. Halve a hard-cooked egg lengthwise; place it face down on center of leaf, top with cocktail sausage speared with toothpick.

Beef Béarnaise . . . Cover buttered bread with slices of cold roast beef. Garnish with Béarnaise Sauce (page 182).

Boiled Beef . . . On buttered bread place slices of boiled breast of beef. Place chopped pickle at one end, shredded horseradish at other. Center with slice of tomato.

Beef-Egg . . . Cover buttered bread with slices of cold roast beef. Sauté a sliced onion in butter until light brown; spread over the beef. Top with a fried egg.

Danish Tartar . . . Cover buttered bread with a layer of raw ground beef. Top with an onion ring, into the center of which slip a hard-cooked egg yolk. Garnish with capers and chopped raw onion.

Smoked Eel . . . Cut the eel in pieces about the size of the bread slice. Skin and bone the eel slices; place on bread. Top with scrambled eggs, chive-sprinkled.

Tomato and Egg . . . On one-half of a slice of buttered bread place slices of hard-cooked egg. On the other half place tomato slices. Garnish with onion rings, watercress.

Hans Andersen . . . Cover buttered bread with slices of liver paste. Top with crisscrossed slices of crisp bacon. Garnish with tomato slices, grated horseradish, a strip of jellied consommé.

Liver Pâté . . . Cover buttered bread with a thick slice of good liver pâté. Top with thin slices of fried bacon. Sauté sliced mushrooms in butter, season with salt and pepper, and heap generously atop the bacon.

Lobster Salad . . . Mix small pieces of cold lobster and cooked or canned (well drained) asparagus with mayonnaise. On buttered bread, place large lettuce leaf, and spread lobster mixture on this. Garnish with extra asparagus tips.

Anchovies and Eggs . . . Slice 2 hard-cooked eggs and put them together again (wire egg-slicer is best for this) on a buttered slice of bread. Cover the eggs with anchovies and sliced tomatoes. Garnish with watercress.

The recipes that follow are to be served in exactly the same way as those that precede, but they require a somewhat more complicated preparation.

Fillet of Fish

Brown or white bread,
  buttered
Fillet of fish (flounder or
  sole), fried

Thin slices of lemon
Remoulade Sauce (see page
  162)

Butter the bread. Immediately before serving, lay the freshly
fried fish fillet on the bread. Garnish with 2 lemon slices, a
dab of Remoulade Sauce.

Nightcap

4 slices rye bread, buttered
4 thick slices liver paste

4 slivers Bouillon Aspic
4 thin slices corned beef

Spread bread with liver paste. Top with aspic and thin slices
of corned beef.

Bouillon Aspic—a good thing to have on hand even for
daytime eating

> 3/4 tablespoon gelatin
> 3/4 cup cold bouillon (canned will do)
> 1/4 cup boiling bouillon
>   2 tablespoons vinegar
> Salt, white pepper
> Paprika
> Celery salt

Soften gelatin in 1/4 cup cold bouillon, then add mixture to
boiling bouillon until gelatin dissolves. Add other ingredients.
Pour into lightly oiled mold, chill until firm enough to slice.

Roast Neck of Pork, Danish

Roast neck of pork
Prunes

Apples
Red cabbage

To prepare pork: Sprinkle the neck of pork with salt and pepper, place on rack in a cold oven. Roast at 250° F. until
browned and done; this takes about 6 hours. During first hour,
pour 2 cups boiling water into roasting pan under rack. *To
prepare apples:* Peel apples (1 for each sandwich), slice in
thick rings, stew until tender in sugared water to cover. *To
prepare prunes:* Place prunes (4 for each sandwich) in deep
dish and pour boiling water over them to cover. Allow them
to steep for the 6 hours the meat is roasting; they should become large, plump, and juicy. *To prepare cabbage:* Shred or
finely chop. *To assemble sandwich:* Allow the pork to cool to

lukewarm. Carve thick slices, arrange on buttered brown bread, and garnish with apples, prunes, and cabbage.

Danish Chicken

Chicken, braised or grilled   **Cucumber Salad**
Red currant jelly

Cut chicken into 4 or 6 suitably sized pieces, remove bones and place on buttered bread. Garnish with red currant jelly and Cucumber Salad.
Cucumber Salad . . . Parboil 1 cup water with 2 cups vinegar, salt, pepper, 2 tablespoons granulated sugar. Cool. Wash a large, firm cucumber (do not peel) and cut or shred into thin slices. Lay cucumber slices in deep dish; pour cooled brine over. Allow to steep for 2 to 4 hours.

Cold Roast Pork

Roast pork, sliced   **Cucumber Salad (see above)**
Raw beets, sliced

Cover a slice of buttered bread with thick slices of roast pork. Arrange a layer of sliced beets around the edge. Fill the center with Cucumber Salad.

Roast Veal

Roast joint of veal   **Cucumber Salad (see above)**
Red currant jelly

For this sandwich, roast a tender joint of veal. Carve in thin slices. Lay slices, overlapping, to completely cover thin slice of buttered bread. Garnish with big spoonful of red currant jelly, and add fresh Cucumber Salad around the edge.

Béarnaise Sauce

    1 shallot, chopped
    1 teaspoon dried tarragon
1/4 cup tarragon vinegar
    2 egg yolks
1/2 cup butter, melted

Cook shallot, dried tarragon, and vinegar until reduced to 1/4 of original amount. Cool. Add egg yolks, place pan over hot water. Whip with a fork until thickened. Remove from heat, add butter gradually, whipping until sauce is desired thickness. Makes about 1/2 cup.

Great Greens

When it comes to the greens that go into sandwiches, you simply must develop an open mind. Everything that's green—and full of crispness and vitamins—isn't iceberg lettuce! Sometimes it isn't lettuce at all. As a matter of fact, it doesn't even have to be green. What you're trying to do is add a fresh-tasting extra something to a bread-and-filling combination that, however tasty, can perhaps use an extra crunch or tang.

How about a layer of radishes sliced so thin you can see the filling through them?

How about two or three slices of peeled tomato? And don't forget the salt!

It's thinking for yourself, like that, that makes the difference between sandwiches people merely eat and enjoy, and sandwiches they eat, enjoy, and talk about for weeks afterward. Here are some greens and non-greens to start your thinking:

Iceberg lettuce . . . I didn't mean for you to forget about it. It's far too all-around useful, for it cuts and shreds well, and mixes well with all sorts of strong-flavored fillings. Just don't use it *all* the time.

Bibb lettuce . . . tiny head, deep green leaves, tender and succulent.

Boston lettuce . . . this too is tiny, with fragile, very tender pale leaves and a buttery texture. Use Boston with crunchy, high-flavored fillings.

Leaf lettuce . . . big, raggedy heads with medium to deep green ruffly leaves, and a taste that varies because it is home-grown. Get it at a farmer's roadside stand if you don't grow your own.

Romaine lettuce . . . elegant, long, crisp, somewhat boat-shaped leaves, which make excellent containers for garnishes (olives, chopped eggs, tiny shrimp).

Escarole . . . like a shorter-leaved, curly-edged romaine, with stronger taste.

Chicory . . . dark green, very frilled edges, with strong to bitter taste.

Green cabbage . . . the more tender leaves can be used whole, like lettuce, in sandwiches. Or shred finely as for slaw, sprinkle over filling.

Chinese cabbage . . . a combination taste halfway between cabbage and celery; the long, mild-flavored, frilly yellow-green leaves can be shredded or chopped to use over any filling with a sturdy flavor.

Watercress . . . pungent deep green leaves can be chopped or snipped.

Parsley . . . use same as watercress.

Belgian endive . . . celery-crisp, bitterish taste; slice in thin rounds.

Celery . . . crisp as endive but milder in flavor; chop or thin-slice.

Carrot . . . ever think of a layer of shredded carrot to top filling? Adds crispness, taste—and lovely color.

Cucumber . . . thin slices, crisped in salted ice water for a nice change of pace.

Onions . . . sliced *very* thin, and only for aggressive onion-fanciers, but how lucky they are! Try the Italian or Bermuda types for milder flavor.

Mushrooms . . . a layer of thin-sliced, raw mushroom caps (no stems) gives rich chewiness to crisp fillings.

Spinach . . . young leaves of raw spinach, washed and dried very well, can be finely chopped or snipped and sprinkled over filling. You'd be surprised!

Now, for the really exotic pathfinder, here are a few other experiments in taste: *dandelion greens, mustard greens, nasturtium leaves, kale, turnip greens.* Washed, dried, very finely chopped or snipped, these very special kinds of greens will really make your sandwiches memorable.

So do you have to reach for the iceberg lettuce every single time?

Something to Celebrate

Entertaining—and being entertained—are part of the social currency of any community. Here are two truths I state with neither hedging nor blushing: sandwich-type refreshments are the easiest to prepare, and they *can* be the most delicious, elegant kind as well. If you have any doubts, read on.

Watercress and Caviar Filling

Watercress, finely chopped
Butter

Caviar
Lemon juice

Mix butter with finely chopped watercress and spread on bread. Cover with caviar and sprinkle with lemon juice.

Heart Sandwiches

36 slices white bread
1/3 cup soft butter
3 3-ounce packages cream cheese

1/2 cup prepared sour cream
Currant jelly

Dried Beef Filling

2/3 cup chopped dried beef
2 teaspoons horseradish
1/4 cup chopped celery
1/4 cup mayonnaise or salad dressing

Pimento Chicken Filling

2/3 cup chopped cooked chicken
2 tablespoons chopped pimento
1 teaspoon lemon juice
Dash of nutmeg
2 tablespoons mayonnaise or salad dressing

With a cookie cutter, cut a heart shape from each bread slice. Butter the heart shapes. Combine dried beef, horseradish, celery, and mayonnaise. Spread beef filling on 12 of the buttered hearts. Combine chicken, pimento, lemon juice, nutmeg, and mayonnaise and spread on 12 of the buttered hearts. *To form sandwiches:* Place chicken layer on top of dried beef layer and top with an unspread heart shape. Combine cream cheese and sour cream and beat until smooth. Spread cheese mixture on tops and sides of sandwiches. Decorate with currant jelly. Makes 12 sandwiches.

Holiday Breakfast

4 slices white bread
1 egg, beaten
2 tablespoons milk
2 tablespoons butter

1 cup applesauce
1 teaspoon cinnamon
1 pound sausage links,
    cooked

Blend egg and milk. Dip bread into mixture and brown on both sides in butter. Heat applesauce and cinnamon in saucepan. Serve hot sausage links on French toast topped with warm applesauce. Makes 4 sandwiches.

Walnut and Watercress Filling

Watercress, chopped
Walnuts, chopped

Salt
Mayonnaise

Combine ingredients, spread on bread.

Vegetable Harlequin

12 slices whole-wheat bread
1/2 cup soft butter
3/4 cup grated raw carrot
1/4 cup chopped celery
  2 teaspoons minced onion
1/4 cup cooked peas

1/2 teaspoon salt
1 teaspoon prepared
    mustard
1/2 teaspoon Worcestershire
    sauce

Combine butter, carrot, celery, onion, peas, salt, mustard, and Worcestershire sauce. Spread on 6 slices bread, top with remaining slices.

Salad Bun

10 hamburger buns, split
1 cup chopped tomato
1 cup chopped celery

1 cup chopped olives
1 teaspoon grated onion
Salad dressing

Combine ingredients and moisten with salad dressing. Spread between bun halves. Makes 5 sandwiches.

Deviled-Egg Sailboats

8 butter-type crackers, spread
    with mayonnaise

2 1-ounce slices process cheese
8 deviled-egg halves

Cut each cheese slice diagonally in half twice to form 4 triangles or "sails" from each slice. Place a cheese triangle, pointed edge up, across top of each egg. Place each egg on a cracker. Serve cold. Makes 8 sailboats.

The Supreme Sandwich
Mushrooms

If you like mushrooms, if you like sour cream—well, your mouth will water, reading this, as mine does writing it down.

12 slices dark rye bread
1/4 pound butter
1 pound fresh mushrooms, sliced
1 large fresh dill pickle
Salt and pepper
1 teaspoon dried dill seed
Paprika
Onion powder
Sour cream

Melt half of butter in skillet. Add mushrooms. Cover and cook 10 minutes over medium heat. Remove cover. Continue to cook until mushroom juice is evaporated. Add remaining butter and cook until mushrooms are rich brown, about 20 minutes. Meanwhile, toast bread lightly. With a large cookie cutter, cut circles from 6 slices of toast. Cut pickle into 6 chunks. When mushrooms are ready, season with salt, pepper, and dill seed, sprinkle liberally with paprika and onion powder. Add about 1/2 cup sour cream. Stir over low heat until warmed through, adding more cream if necessary—use just enough to hold mushrooms together. Do not boil. Divide mushroom mixture over 6 slices of toast. Top with toast circles, held in place by a toothpick on which a chunk of pickle is impaled.

Celery-Seed Breadsticks

3 slices (5/8 inch thick) white bread
1 1/2 tablespoons melted butter

2 teaspoons celery seed

Trim crusts off bread slices. Brush both sides of bread slices with butter. Cut each slice into 6 equal-size strips. Roll strips in celery seed. Place on a cookie sheet and toast in a 350° F. oven for 15 minutes. Makes 18 breadsticks.

187

Tropicals

6 slices brown bread
1 tablespoon mayonnaise
    or salad dressing
1/4 cup cottage cheese

1 tablespoon well-drained
    crushed pineapple
1 tablespoon chopped dates
1 teaspoon finely chopped
    crystallized ginger

Combine mayonnaise with cottage cheese. Add pineapple, dates, and ginger. Spread on 3 slices bread, top with remaining slices.

Tomato and Anchovy

6 anchovies
1/2 pound tomatoes, skinned

Cayenne pepper
2 tablespoons cream

Pound anchovies with tomatoes, season with cayenne pepper, and add thick cream.

Pineapple-Slaw

10 slices bread
1 cup finely chopped
    cabbage
1/4 cup drained, crushed
    pineapple

1/8 teaspoon salt
3 tablespoons mayonnaise
    or salad dressing

Combine cabbage, pineapple, salt, and mayonnaise. Spread on 5 slices bread, top with remaining slices.

Rich Mushroom Sandwich

16 slices white bread
2 cups cooked ground meat
    (chicken, lamb, beef,
    veal, or ham)

1 can cream of mushroom
    soup
French Toast Mixture

Combine meat with soup and spread between slices of bread. Dip sandwiches in French Toast Mixture and brown on both sides in melted butter. Makes 8 hearty sandwiches.
French Toast Mixture: Combine 4 eggs, beaten, 1 3/4 to 2 cups milk, salt, and pepper.

Walnut and Olive Filling

12 slices of bread
1/2 cup stuffed olives, ground
1/2 cup walnuts, chopped

1 tablespoon mayonnaise
Butter

Combine ingredients and spread on bread. 6 sandwiches.

188

The Gourmet Way

Sautéed Bread

Almost any filling that makes a good canapé when served on toast makes a much better one served on Sautéed Bread. Simply cut the bread into whatever shapes you prefer—medium-size circles are simplest, and fillings do not tend to drip from them as they do from some of the fancier odd shapes. Sauté the bread in a little hot butter until it reaches the shade of golden brown that suits your taste.

Edam-Eggplant Spread

Crackers or pumpernickel
  rounds
1 large eggplant
2 tablespoons salad or
  olive oil
3 tablespoons grated onion

1 tablespoon dry parsley
  flakes
1/2 cup chili sauce
1 2-pound imported Edam
  cheese

Place eggplant in a large saucepan. Cover with boiling water. Place lid on pan. Simmer over low heat about 30 minutes or until tender. Cool, peel, and chop fine. Place oil in skillet. Add eggplant and onion. Sauté until thickened. Stir in parsley flakes and 1/4 cup chili sauce. Cool. Cut small slice from the top of the cheese. Hollow the center of the cheese leaving about 1/8 inch cheese to form a shell. Grate cheese. Combine eggplant mixture, grated cheese, and the other 1/4 cup chili sauce. Spoon into cheese shell. Refill as needed. Serve with crackers or pumpernickel rounds.

Cran-Banana

8 slices white bread
Butter
Jellied cranberry sauce,
  crushed

2 bananas, sliced
Brown sugar
Cinnamon

Place slices of bread under broiler and toast on one side. Butter the other side. Spread with crushed jellied cranberry sauce. Cover with sliced bananas. Sprinkle with brown sugar and a dash of cinnamon. Broil slowly until bananas are light brown and the cranberry sauce is bubbly. A surprise dessert for children's parties or for lunch.

Party Zoo

12 slices whole-wheat bread
12 slices white bread
Hawaiian Chicken Sandwich
   Filling

Ham-Peanut Sandwich Filling

Prepare both sandwich fillings (see below). With animal-shaped cutters, cut all the wheat bread into one shape and all the white bread into another shape. Spread about 2 tablespoons chicken filling on half the wheat bread, top with matching wheat shape. Spread 2 tablespoons ham filling on half the white bread, top with matching white shape. 12 sandwiches.

Hawaiian Chicken Sandwich Filling

1/3 cup flaked boned chicken
2 tablespoons chopped pecans or almonds
1/4 cup drained, crushed pineapple
1 tablespoon chopped celery
1 1/2 tablespoons mayonnaise or salad dressing

Combine chicken, pecans, pineapple, celery, and mayonnaise. Makes 3/4 cup.

Ham-Peanut Sandwich Filling

1/3 cup finely chopped cooked ham
1/3 cup finely chopped salted peanuts
1/4 cup finely chopped dill pickle
3 tablespoons mayonnaise or salad dressing

Combine ham, peanuts, dill pickle, and mayonnaise. Makes 3/4 cup.

Crab Canapés

12 slices of white bread
1 pound crab meat
3 tablespoons mayonnaise
1 tablespoon prepared
   mustard
1/4 teaspoon salt

Dash of pepper
1 tablespoon lemon juice
1/4 cup grated Parmesan
   cheese
2 tablespoons dry bread
   crumbs

Remove any shell or cartilage from crab meat. Combine mayonnaise, seasonings, lemon juice, and crab meat. Toast bread, remove crusts. Spread crab mixture on each slice of toast. Combine cheese and crumbs, sprinkle over top of each slice of toast. Cut each slice into 6 pieces. Place on a broiler pan about 3 inches from source of heat. Broil for 2 to 3 minutes or until brown. Makes approximately 72 canapés.

The Gourmet Way

French Salad

This is a wonderful way to accomplish two things at once: you'll put together a delicious, easy-to-make company-keeper for a sandwich—and you'll get the refrigerator cleaned out at the same time. Any combination of vegetables works fine—peas, potatoes, carrots, lima beans, corn, green or wax beans, cauliflower; whatever's begging to be used up.

1/2 cup of each of 3 cold, cooked vegetables	2 tablespoons minced onion
	1 tablespoon capers
1/2 cup diced celery	Mayonnaise

Mix all ingredients together, using just enough mayonnaise to bind. Serve in lettuce cups; makes 4 servings.

Avocado-Pineapple Leaves

16 slices whole-wheat bread	2 tablespoons mayonnaise
1 medium avocado, mashed	or salad dressing
1/4 cup drained, crushed pineapple	16 tiny pieces of green pepper
2 teaspoons lemon juice	

Combine mashed avocado, pineapple, lemon juice, and mayonnaise. Make a paper leaf-shaped pattern and cut 2 leaves from each slice of bread. Spread each leaf with 1 1/2 teaspoons avocado-pineapple mixture. Mark leaf veins on top of sandwiches with the blunt end of a toothpick. Insert a small piece of green pepper for the stem end of each leaf. 32 sandwiches.

Cucumber Sandwich Fillings

Mix chopped cucumber with one of the following:

1. mayonnaise or salad dressing
2. minced onion and mayonnaise or salad dressing
3. chopped nuts and mayonnaise or salad dressing
4. shredded almonds, chopped green pepper, and mayonnaise
5. chopped pickled onions
6. diced fresh or canned pineapple and mayonnaise

Do-It-Yourself Sandwich

One of the simplest—and it can be one of the most satisfactory—ways to feed a crowd is to set out a bountiful buffet table equipped with sandwich makings of several descriptions, plus all the trimmings, and invite your guests to fall to.

Arrange the sandwiches' component parts separately, in your prettiest plates and platters and bowls. You'll need butter and mayonnaise for spreading. Provide side dishes, too, for variety. Potato salad, oniony good—have you ever tried turmeric to season the dressing?—is a fine accompaniment. So is coleslaw—calico slaw is both tasty and more appealing to the eye. If it's a big, hungry crowd, have both. You'll want plenty of pickles and relishes, plus a pot of mustard and another of ketchup and, if there's roast beef—and there ought to be—a third pot, filled with freshly made horseradish sauce. And a platter of sliced tomatoes, of course.

Breads: A near-black pumpernickel, a good rye—seeded or not, as you like—and some crusty white rolls. That threesome covers most favorites for man-size sandwiches. Add a Cheddar cheese bread if you'd like a fourth variety.

Meats: Rare—very rare—roast beef is a must. Sliced turkey, both white meat and dark. Good ham—baked, not boiled—with some real ham flavor to it. Those three are bare necessities. Better the three with the addition of a spicy sausage, such as Lebanon bologna, and a really first-class Braunschweiger. Hot corned beef, the best you can buy, cooked at home and carved to order at the table by the man of the house—who could ask for anything more? Unless, come to think of it, it might be a home-cooked tongue, also sliced to order!

Fish: Never forget fish—especially if it's Friday. And don't settle for a bowl of tuna salad sandwich filling slapped on the table as a concession. Get some good smoked whitefish. Have some herring. Open a couple of cans of the best sardines.

Cheese: You'll want nutty Swiss, creamy Cheddar, mild Münster, and one of the glorious noisy varieties, such as Roquefort or blue.

Nice extras: For exotic-minded sandwich makers, a dish of capers, another of anchovy fillets, another of marinated artichoke hearts. For good taste, a couple of the gourmet dressings you'll find in this book. For dedicated trenchermen, a plate of thin-sliced Spanish onions and, for good measure, a dish of snipped chives.

The Supreme Sandwich

Avocado

These are always, to me, the height of luxury. I invented them when I moved to California and found that there was an avocado tree in my backyard. This was at a time when, in my Middle West home town, avocados sold in their very brief season for one dollar each. The sandwich is gloriously rich, jam-packed with calories . . . and worth every one.

Take note: The omission of butter on the bread is not an oversight—there's no point in adding butter unless you have a serious underweight problem.

> 6 slices white bread
> 1 3-ounce package cream cheese
> 1 avocado
> 3 teaspoons light cream
> 1 tablespoon lemon juice
> Salt
> Mayonnaise
> Freshly ground black pepper

Let cream cheese soften to room temperature. Mash it and salt it lightly. Peel avocado; mash pulp with the cream and season it with lemon juice, salt to taste. Spread 3 slices of bread with cream cheese, then with avocado. Spread the avocado with a thin layer of mayonnaise. Sprinkle the cream cheese liberally with pepper. Mate each avocado-spread slice with a cream-cheese slice. Makes 3 sandwiches. Cut them in thirds and trim the crusts—the only saving grace is that these are so rich you can't eat many of them!

Salmon-Avocado Canapés

Crackers
1 7 3/4-ounce can salmon
1 avocado
1 tablespoon olive or
    salad oil

1 clove garlic, finely
    chopped
1 1/2 teaspoons grated onion
1/2 teaspoon salt
4 drops of Tabasco

Drain and flake salmon. Peel avocado, remove seed, mash. Combine all ingredients. Toss lightly. Serve on crackers. Makes about 1 pint of spread.

✳✳✳✳✳✳✳✳✳✳✳✳✳✳✳✳✳✳✳✳✳✳✳✳✳✳

The Basic Way with
Soufflé Sandwiches

Soufflé sandwiches are puffed-high delicacies, a pleasure to behold and even more of a pleasure to eat. Almost anything that flavor-partners well with cheese can form the base for a soufflé sandwich. **Try this one first:**

Asparagus Soufflé Sandwich

> 6 slices white bread
> 2 tablespoons soft butter
> 18 spears cooked asparagus
> 3 eggs, separated
> Salt and pepper
> 1/8 teaspoon paprika
> 1/2 teaspoon Worcestershire sauce
> 1/2 teaspoon prepared mustard
> 3/4 cup grated sharp cheese

Spread bread with butter. Lay 3 asparagus spears on each slice of bread. Add 1/2 teaspoon salt to egg whites, and beat until stiff. To egg yolks add dash pepper, paprika, Worcestershire, and mustard; beat until light. Add cheese. Fold yolk mixture into egg whites. Top each sandwich with about 1/3 cup of this soufflé mixture. Place on greased baking sheet and bake at 350° F. for 15 minutes, or until puffed and brown. Makes 6 sandwiches.

Now experiment with: Thick slices of tomato . . . lemon-sprinkled broccoli . . . thin-sliced ham . . . crispy bacon with tomato . . . chive-sprinkled cauliflower . . . sliced chicken dressed with capers . . . sliced lobster tails.

✳✳✳✳✳✳✳✳✳✳✳✳✳✳✳✳✳✳✳✳✳✳✳✳✳✳

Swiss Dip

Crackers and Melba toast
Swiss cheese, grated fine
Sour cream
Olives, onions, pimentos, chopped
Salt and pepper to taste
Paprika

Add Swiss cheese to sour cream. Add finely chopped olives, onions, pimentos. Salt and pepper to taste. Spread on crackers and Melba toast. Dust with paprika.

The Supreme Sandwich

Chicken Salad Mollet

These are company-coming wonders—frankly fancy to bring to the table, absolutely delicious in the eating. Start with a cup of clear soup, serve asparagus vinaigrette with the salad, crown the meal with cold coffee soufflé.

> 6 slices white bread, toasted
> 6 Eggs Mollet
> 1/2 teaspoon dry mustard
> 1 teaspoon lemon juice
> Salt, white pepper
> 1 cup mayonnaise
> 2 cups diced cooked chicken
> 1/2 cup diced celery
> Watercress
> 3 slices cooked tongue, slivered
> 6 ripe olives, slivered

To make Eggs Mollet: Bring water to simmering in a saucepan. Lower eggs in gently, simmer 5 minutes. Run cold water over the eggs until cooled. Gently—*very* gently—break the shells and, just as gently, peel the eggs. *To make salad:* Stir mustard, lemon juice, salt and pepper into mayonnaise. Combine with chicken, celery. *To make sandwiches:* Place several sprigs of watercress on each slice of lightly buttered toast. Divide salad among the slices. Place an egg on each mound of salad. Sprinkle tongue and olives over salad and egg.

Edam Cheese-Pimento Spread

Crackers or Sautéed Bread
  (page 189)
2 pounds of imported
  Edam cheese

1/4 cup sweet pickle relish
2 tablespoons chopped
  pimento
3/4 cup mayonnaise

Cut the Edam cheese in half. Hollow the center of each half leaving about 1/8 inch cheese to form a shell. Grate the cheese. Combine cheese with remaining ingredients. (Add a little more mayonnaise if needed to obtain spreading consistency.) Refill shells. Serve with crackers or Sautéed Bread.

Glazed Caviar Canapés

24 slices small party rye
    bread, buttered
1/8 teaspoon sweet basil
  1 cup water
  1 3-ounce package lemon
    flavor gelatin
1/2 teaspoon salt

1 tablespoon lemon juice
1 cup dry Sauterne
1 6-ounce package cream
    cheese, whipped
1 4-ounce jar black caviar
1 4-ounce can pimento,
    drained

Simmer the sweet basil in water for about 3 minutes. Strain. Then dissolve gelatin and salt in the hot liquid. Add lemon juice and wine. Chill until slightly thickened. Meanwhile, place rye bread on a rack set on a tray. Spread with whipped cream cheese. Cover cream cheese with caviar. Cut pimento into small squares, or diamond, heart, or bell shapes and place a piece in the center of each canapé. Spoon slightly thickened gelatin mixture over canapés, allowing about 2 tablespoons mixture for each. Chill until firm. If necessary, cover each canapé with more gelatin mixture and chill again. (If gelatin mixture becomes too firm for glazing canapés, set bowl in a pan of hot water.) Makes 24 canapés.

The Supreme Sandwich

Olive Pâté

If you're serving this for the first time, you'll have to be fleet on your feet to get the cook's share—Olive Pâté disappears in no time.

Thin, lightly buttered white toast
  1 cup pitted black olives
  3 tablespoons butter
1/2 teaspoon powdered thyme or rosemary
  1 crumbled bay leaf
  1 teaspoon finely minced onion
1/2 garlic clove minced
Dash of cayenne pepper

Chop the olives finely or cream as a mush. Mix with butter and seasoning herbs. Chill and serve on toast slices cut in half.

Hors d'Oeuvres with Lemon-Herb Glaze

1 2/3 cups water
 1/8 teaspoon peppercorns
 1/2 bay leaf
 1/2 teaspoon dried dill
 1 3-ounce package lemon-
    flavor gelatin

1/2 teaspoon salt
Dash of cayenne
 3 tablespoons vinegar
12 to 14 open-faced hors
    d'oeuvres (see
    below)

Combine water, peppercorns, bay leaf, and dried dill in a saucepan. Cover and simmer for about 10 minutes. Strain. Dissolve gelatin and salt in the hot liquid. Add cayenne and vinegar. Chill until slightly thickened. Place open-faced hors d'oeuvres on a rack and pour the slightly thickened glaze over the filling, allowing about 2 tablespoons glaze for each hors d'oeuvre. Chill until glaze is firm. Makes about 1 3/4 cups glaze, or enough for 12 to 14 hors d'oeuvres.

Suggested hors d'oeuvres combinations:

1. Turkey pâté or paste and chopped egg on fingers or triangles of whole-wheat bread.
2. Sliced egg and shrimp, garnished with caviar or sliced olive on buttered salty rye bread—half slices or whole.
3. Sliced ham, asparagus spears, and chopped ripe olives on buttered fingers or triangles of pumpernickel.
4. Horseradish and chili sauce topped with tiny shrimp on salty rye.
5. Cream cheese and sliced smoked salmon on pumpernickel.

Hot Tuna-Mushroom Canapés

32 round crackers
 1 6 1/2- or 7-ounce can
    tuna
1/2 cup condensed mushroom
    soup
 1 tablespoon finely chopped
    pimento

 1 tablespoon finely chopped
    green pepper
1/4 teaspoon salt
Dash of paprika
1/2 cup grated cheese

Drain tuna. Flake. Add soup, pimento, green pepper, and seasonings; blend into a paste. Spread on crackers. Sprinkle with cheese. Place on a baking sheet. Broil about 3 inches from source of heat for 5 minutes or until cheese browns. Makes 32 canapés.

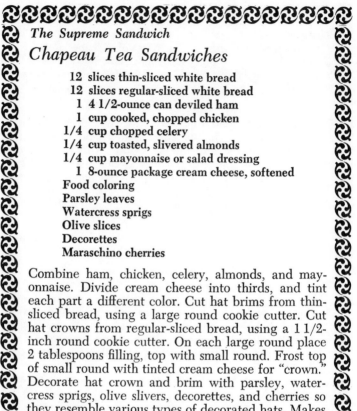

The Supreme Sandwich

Chapeau Tea Sandwiches

12 slices thin-sliced white bread
12 slices regular-sliced white bread
1 4 1/2-ounce can deviled ham
1 cup cooked, chopped chicken
1/4 cup chopped celery
1/4 cup toasted, slivered almonds
1/4 cup mayonnaise or salad dressing
1 8-ounce package cream cheese, softened
Food coloring
Parsley leaves
Watercress sprigs
Olive slices
Decorettes
Maraschino cherries

Combine ham, chicken, celery, almonds, and mayonnaise. Divide cream cheese into thirds, and tint each part a different color. Cut hat brims from thin-sliced bread, using a large round cookie cutter. Cut hat crowns from regular-sliced bread, using a 1 1/2-inch round cookie cutter. On each large round place 2 tablespoons filling, top with small round. Frost top of small round with tinted cream cheese for "crown." Decorate hat crown and brim with parsley, watercress sprigs, olive slivers, decorettes, and cherries so they resemble various types of decorated hats. Makes 12 sandwiches.

Ham Stars

4 slices white bread	1 tablespoon mayonnaise
1/4 cup ground ham	1 tablespoon caviar
3/4 teaspoon minced onion	16 pieces chopped green
1 tablespoon chopped green pepper	pepper

Combine ham, onion, green pepper, and mayonnaise. Cut each slice of bread into four 1 1/2-inch stars with a cookie cutter. Spread 1 teaspoon ham mixture over each star. Garnish points of star with a bit of caviar. Place a tiny piece of green pepper in center of each star. Makes 16 stars.

Mushroom-Pecan-Cheese Bits

12 slices of bread
Soft butter
1 10-ounce can condensed
    cream of mushroom
    soup

1 cup chopped pecans
1/4 cup cut-up drained
    canned pimento
Imported Edam or Gouda
    cheese

Toast the bread and trim off crusts; cool. Spread slices with butter and cut each slice into 4 squares. Combine the soup, pecans, and pimento. Spread soup mixture thickly on toast squares. Center each with a 1/3-inch cube of cheese. Arrange on cookie sheet or broiler rack. Bake in 450° F. oven or broil until heated through. Serve piping hot. Makes 48 appetizers.

Pacific Sardine and Egg Canapés

Crackers, toast, or bread
1 15-ounce can Pacific
    sardines
12 stuffed olives
1 cup grated egg yolk

1 cup mayonnaise
2 tablespoons lemon juice
Dash Worcestershire sauce
Paprika

Drain sardines; flake. Cut olives into sixths crosswise. Combine egg yolk, mayonnaise, lemon juice, Worcestershire sauce, and sardines. Blend into a paste. Spread on crackers. Garnish with a slice of olive and sprinkle with paprika. Makes approximately 72 canapés.

Tuna-Cranberry Snacks

Crackers, toast, or bread
2 7-ounce cans tuna
1/2 cup mayonnaise
1 cup chopped celery
2 tablespoons chopped
    sweet pickle
2 tablespoons chopped
    onion

2 hard-cooked eggs,
    chopped
1/2 teaspoon salt
Dash of pepper
3 1-pound cans jellied cran-
    berry sauce, chilled

Drain tuna. Flake. Combine all ingredients except crackers and cranberry sauce. Spread crackers with tuna salad. Open one end of can of jellied cranberry sauce. Punch hole in other end to let in air. Mold will slide out. Cut molds into slices about 1/8 inch thick. Using a star cookie cutter, cut out a cranberry star from each slice. Place a star on top of tuna salad. Makes approximately 60 snacks.

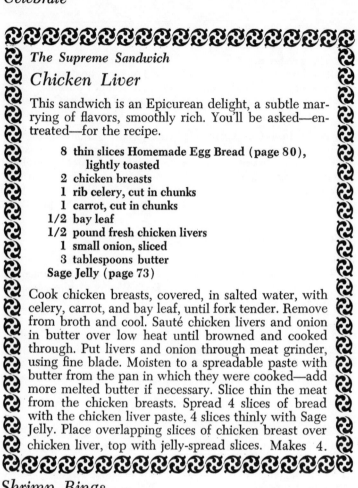

The Supreme Sandwich

Chicken Liver

This sandwich is an Epicurean delight, a subtle marrying of flavors, smoothly rich. You'll be asked—entreated—for the recipe.

    8 thin slices Homemade Egg Bread (page 80),
        lightly toasted
    2 chicken breasts
    1 rib celery, cut in chunks
    1 carrot, cut in chunks
    1/2 bay leaf
    1/2 pound fresh chicken livers
    1 small onion, sliced
    3 tablespoons butter
    Sage Jelly (page 73)

Cook chicken breasts, covered, in salted water, with celery, carrot, and bay leaf, until fork tender. Remove from broth and cool. Sauté chicken livers and onion in butter over low heat until browned and cooked through. Put livers and onion through meat grinder, using fine blade. Moisten to a spreadable paste with butter from the pan in which they were cooked—add more melted butter if necessary. Slice thin the meat from the chicken breasts. Spread 4 slices of bread with the chicken liver paste, 4 slices thinly with Sage Jelly. Place overlapping slices of chicken breast over chicken liver, top with jelly-spread slices. Makes 4.

Shrimp Rings

    4 French finger rolls
    1/2 cup cooked, finely
        chopped shrimp
    1/4 cup finely chopped
        celery

    3 tablespoons mayonnaise
        or salad dressing
    2 teaspoons lemon juice

Hollow out French rolls from end to end with an apple-corer. Combine shrimp, celery, mayonnaise, and lemon juice. Stuff 3 tablespoons shrimp filling into each roll. Wrap rolls in waxed paper and chill in refrigerator. *To serve:* Cut each roll across into 12 slices. Makes 48 rings.

Tangy Seafood Canapés

32 toast points
1 cup canned crab meat, lobster meat, or shrimp, flaked
3 tablespoons mayonnaise or salad dressing

1 tablespoon finely chopped celery
1/2 cup butter
3 tablespoons horseradish
Chopped parsley

Drain canned fish; remove any shell or cartilage, flake. Combine mayonnaise, celery, and fish; blend into a paste. Combine butter and horseradish. Spread horseradish butter on toast points. Top with fish mixture. Sprinkle with parsley. Makes 32 canapés.

Pineapple Sunbursts

8 slices whole-wheat bread
1 3-ounce package cream cheese
1/4 cup crushed pineapple, drained
3 tablespoons chopped ripe olives

32 slices green Maraschino cherry
6 black olives, cut into slivers

Combine cream cheese, pineapple, and chopped olives. Cut each slice of bread into 4 circles with a cookie cutter. Spread each circle with 1 teaspoon pineapple-olive mixture. Place a slice of green cherry in the center of each sandwich. Arrange ripe olive slivers so that they radiate from cherry to form a sunburst design. Makes 32 sunbursts.

Pinwheel Sausage Appetizers

8 slices white bread
1 3-ounce package cream cheese
2 tablespoons cream

1 tablespoon frozen orange juice concentrate
1/3 cup chopped pecans
1 package sausage

Blend cream cheese, cream, and orange juice concentrate. Add nuts and mix thoroughly. Cut crusts from bread and flatten each slice with a rolling pin. Spread with a thin layer of cheese mixture. Trim sausage to size of bread, but 1/2 inch shorter in length. Place in center of bread slices. Roll up bread and sausage jelly-roll fashion. Cover with a damp towel and chill. Slice rolls into 5 pieces and pierce each with a toothpick to serve. Makes 40 appetizers.

Wonderful Swedish Idea

With a big assist from Sweden, where food—and ways of serving it—are so delightful, here we have a useful, all-weather, all-purpose invention: the Expandable Snack. Start with airy Swedish pancakes, silver-dollar size. Add assorted fillings, a bit of dress-up for extra good taste, and serve. Where does the Expandable Snack idea come in? If you're serving them with drinks, serve each guest two—or three at the most. If it's the end of the evening, be generous; let each plate hold six, seven, even eight.

Swedish Pancakes

1 1/4 cups sifted all-purpose flour	3 cups milk
1/2 teaspoon salt	1/4 cup melted butter
3 eggs	Salad oil

Sift flour with salt into medium bowl. With rotary beater, beat in eggs, milk, and butter until smooth. Heat griddle until a drop of water will sizzle and roll off. Brush lightly with oil. Just before using, stir batter. Make each pancake with 1 scant tablespoon batter. When surface of cake bubbles, turn and brown on other side.

To assemble snacks: Place as many pancakes as you wish on each plate. Top each with a spoonful or neat slice of filling, then with a dollop of sour cream. Decorate as you like—a few chives here, a sliver of pickle or a slice of olive there, 3 or 4 capers, a tiny chili pepper—whatever fancy dictates.

Fillings: On each assorted plate, try for variety—a bland, a hot, a soft, a chewy filling. Here are some suggestions . . . caviar, chopped hard-cooked egg, chopped onion . . . grated Gruyère cheese with a few slivers of onion . . . a slice of Potted Meat (page 111) . . . a thin slice each of Swiss cheese, Westphalian ham . . . Pâté Maison (page 76) . . . smoked salmon, plus a few capers . . . Olive Pâté (page 196) . . . Wilted Cucumbers (see below) . . . any well-flavored salad-type sandwich filling . . . 1 large shrimp or 3 small ones, plus Green Goddess Dressing (page 153).

Wilted Cucumbers: Into a bowl, thin-slice 2 small, unpeeled cucumbers. Combine 1/2 cup vinegar, salt, pepper, 1 teaspoon dried dill seed. Pour over cucumbers. Refrigerate several hours, stirring now and then. Drain, dry on paper towels.

Sandwich Pie

1 round loaf bread, 8- or
9-inch diameter,
unsliced
1/2 cup butter
1 3-ounce package cream
cheese
1 cup grated sharp Cheddar
cheese
Horseradish

1 7-ounce package bologna
1 7-ounce package salami
1 cucumber, sliced
1 package liver cheese
Mustard
8 slices American cheese
Radish roses
Parsley sprigs
Watercress sprigs

Cream butter, cream cheese, and Cheddar cheese together, using electric mixer. Cut bread crosswise into 4 round slices. Spread each slice with creamed mixture. Cut each slice into 6 wedges. Arrange these combinations on alternate wedges: horseradish, bologna, and salami; cucumber slices and liver cheese; mustard and American cheese. Re-form into 4 rounds on 4 separate plates, garnish with radish roses, parsley and watercress sprigs.

Lobster-Cheese Delights

48 small rounds Sautéed
Bread (page 189)
1/2 pound cooked lobster
meat
1 tablespoon grated cheese

2 tablespoons butter
1 egg yolk, beaten
1 teaspoon lemon juice
Paprika

Grind lobster meat. Cream the cheese and butter; add egg yolk, lemon juice, and lobster meat. Shape by pressing into a teaspoon, and place on a well-greased baking sheet. Sprinkle with paprika. Bake in a 400° F. oven for 5 minutes. Serve hot on small rounds. Makes approximately 48 hors d'oeuvres.

Sardine Canapés

16 slices sandwich bread
3 3 3/4-ounce cans Maine
sardines
1 2-ounce jar pimentos

1/2 cup butter
2 tablespoons prepared
mustard

Drain sardines and pimentos. Cut pimentos into 96 narrow strips. Soften butter. Add mustard and mix well. Spread bread with mustard-butter. Remove crusts. Cut each slice of bread into thirds. Place a sardine on each piece of bread. Garnish with 2 strips of pimento. Makes approximately 48 canapés.

Antipasto Sandwiches

6 brown-and-serve club or
   French rolls
2 tablespoons soft butter
6 stuffed olives, sliced
6 Italian pickled green
   peppers, chopped

3 green onions, sliced
2 dozen slices small salami,
   1/8 inch thick
6 anchovy fillets
6 slices mozzarella cheese, 1
   by 3 by 1/8 inch

Cut each roll in half horizontally, and spread each roll with 1 teaspoon butter. Combine sliced olives, chopped pickled peppers, and sliced onions. For each sandwich: Place 4 slices salami, 1 1/2 teaspoons olive mixture, 1 anchovy, and 1 slice of cheese between halves of each roll. Place rolls on a greased baking sheet. Bake in a 400° F. oven for 12 minutes. Makes 6 sandwiches.

Deviled Ham-Leyden Cheese Spread

Crackers or pumpernickel
   rounds
1 3/4 cups grated Leyden
   cheese
  1/2 cup (4 1/2-ounce can)
   deviled ham

1/4 cup mayonnaise
  2 tablespoons snipped
   parsley
  1 tablespoon grated onion
Parsley sprigs

Combine cheese, deviled ham, mayonnaise, seasonings. Mix well. Spread on your favorite crackers or pumpernickel rounds. Garnish each canapé with a tiny parsley sprig.
Take note: This is a delectable mixture with just enough "bite" to whet the appetite.

Edam-Corned Beef Spread

Rye or pumpernickel rounds
1 2-pound imported Edam
   cheese
1 12-ounce can corned beef

1/2 cup mayonnaise
1/4 cup sweet pickle relish
  2 tablespoons horseradish

Cut Edam cheese in half. Hollow half of cheese, leaving about 1/8-inch cheese to form a shell. Grate cheese. Mince corned beef. Add mayonnaise, relish, horseradish. Mix well. Fold in cheese. Spoon about 1/3 of mixture into shell. Refill as needed. Serve with small rye or pumpernickel rounds. Repeat for second half of Edam cheese, if desired.

****

The Basic Way with

Party Sandwiches

Pretty snacks for a tea-type party or a reception. The trick is not to rely on looks alone, but to make the fillings tasty and different.

Ribbon Sandwiches: Put 3 or more slices of at least 2 kinds of bread together with well-seasoned, soft fillings—a different filling for each layer. Wrap the sandwiches tightly in a damp cloth, refrigerate under a light weight. Shortly before serving, trim crusts and cut each sandwich into finger-length slices.

Pinwheel Sandwiches: Cut lengthwise slices from a loaf of unsliced bread. Spread with creamed butter and any well-seasoned soft filling. Roll each slice like a jelly roll. Wrap snugly in a dry towel, then in a slightly damp one. Refrigerate. When ready to serve, cut in thin slices.

Rolled Sandwiches: Trim the crusts from slices of very fresh bread. Spread with soft filling or with one of the seasoned butters. Roll as they are, or around a center: a finger of baked ham—use your imagination. Fasten with toothpicks. Refrigerate. When ready to serve, remove toothpicks. If the sandwiches don't have a solid center, tuck a sprig of parsley or watercress into each end.

Sandwich Loaves: Cut lengthwise slices from a loaf of unsliced bread. Stack the slices and trim off the crusts evenly, so that you'll have a neat loaf all around. Spread slices with soft butter and/or filling, using well-seasoned, different fillings for each layer, ending up with an unspread slice on top. Wrap and refrigerate. An hour before serving, soften cream cheese, salt lightly and season if you wish with onion powder, depending on the flavors of the fillings you've used. Frost the sandwich, à la cake, with the cream cheese. Decorate the top of the loaf as your fancy dictates—carrot curls, chopped nuts, pimento, sliced olives; those will get your fancy moving in the right direction. Refrigerate again. When ready to serve, slice—in the presence of your guests, so they can see how attractive the loaf is—and serve on plates. And with forks—this isn't finger food.

****

Kaasbroodjes

8 slices bread, trimmed and
   halved
1 cup shredded Dutch cheese
1 hard-cooked egg, chopped
2 tablespoons sweet pickle,
   chopped

1 teaspoon grated onion
1 teaspoon Worcestershire
   sauce
2 tablespoons mayonnaise
Salt to taste

Combine all ingredients except bread. Mix well. Spread bread
with the cheese mixture and place on broiler rack. Broil about
6 inches away from heat until heated through and golden on
top, about 3 to 5 minutes.

Wonder Ways When Unexpected Company Comes—

Stretch (and improve the taste, too) these salad sandwich
fillings as follows: any mild-flavor fish salad with skinless and
boneless sardines . . . veal salad with chopped Vienna sausages or ham or hard-cooked egg plus chives or diced pineapple or halved grapes or mandarin orange sections or lemon-
sprinkled avocado . . . pork salad with halved, pitted Tokay
grapes or cut-up grapefruit or orange sections or 2 large, mild,
fresh dill pickles diced or coarsely chopped nuts of any kind or
hard-cooked egg plus shallots or diced water chestnuts or
cooked green beans, wax beans, peas, carrots, or raw cabbage,
Chinese cabbage, cauliflower, mushrooms, or drained sauerkraut plus caraway seeds . . . tuna salad with Swiss cheese or
Cheddar cheese or hard-cooked egg plus onion or raw mushrooms or drained cottage cheese plus chives or water chestnuts
or diced fruit of almost any kind or cooked vegetables or raw
vegetables of almost any kind. Or make up an unexpectedly
delightful sandwich filling of cooked eggplant plus a small jar
of black caviar or eggs scrambled with red caviar or with
crumbled bacon, diced onion, green pepper, and mushrooms.

Pretty Party Loaves

Here are make-aheads, suitable for almost any kind of party, that are sure to earn you an enviable reputation as a hostess. Some of these you can build—and that's the right word—early in the day. Some can be made at the last minute, from component parts put together earlier and waiting in the refrigerator. But all of them can be served with a flourish—they're beautiful!

Creamy Party Loaf

1 loaf day-old unsliced
   white bread
Ham Salad
1/2 recipe Egg Salad
Chicken-Nut
  2 tablespoons hot water
1/2 5-ounce jar blue cheese
  spread

4 3-ounce packages soft
  cream cheese
1/3 to 1/2 cup light cream
  6 thin tomato slices
Dill-pickle slivers

To prepare ahead: Make Ham Salad, Egg Salad, and Chicken-Nut for fillings. Refrigerate. This can be done the day before. Make fourth filling by blending hot water with blue cheese spread until smooth and creamy. For "frosting," blend cream cheese with enough cream to make it spread easily. *To assemble:* With sharp knife, trim crusts from top, bottom, and sides of bread loaf. Lay loaf on side; slice lengthwise into 5 even slices, about 1/2 inch thick. (You may use a ruler as a guide to keep slicing straight.) Spread bottom slice with blue cheese spread. Spread second slice with half of Chicken-Nut Filling; top this with tomato slices, then with rest of chicken filling; place on cheese layer. Spread third slice with Egg Salad; place on chicken layer. (When arranging bread slices on top of each other, be careful not to press them together too firmly lest mixtures ooze.) Spread fourth slice with Ham Salad; place on egg layer. Top all with last bread slice, with rounded side up. With hands, gently shape loaf so all sides are even. Remove any oozing bits. With spatula, frost top and sides with cream cheese mixture. Refrigerate loaf several hours so it will cut easily. *To serve:* Garnish top of loaf with dill pickle. Fork makes eating easier. Makes ten 1-inch-thick servings.
For a crowd: When serving 12 or more, make 2 Creamy Party Loaves, using 1 loaf each white and whole-wheat bread. Make up 1 party loaf with 2 white slices alternated with 3 whole-wheat slices, the other with 3 white slices alternated with 2 whole-wheat slices.

Ham Salad

1/2 cup ground ham, cooked or canned
2 tablespoons minced green pepper
1 teaspoon prepared mustard
2 tablespoons mayonnaise
1 tablespoon minced onion

Several hours ahead: Mix together all ingredients. Refrigerate. Makes about 3/4 cup.

Egg Salad

6 hard-cooked eggs, chopped
1/4 cup finely chopped ripe olives
2 teaspoons salt
1/4 teaspoon pepper
2 teaspoons prepared mustard
1/2 cup mayonnaise or cooked salad dressing

Several hours ahead: Mix together all ingredients. Refrigerate. Makes 2 cups filling.

Chicken-Nut

2 cups minced chicken, cooked or canned
1/2 cup minced celery
1 cup finely chopped pecans
1/3 cup mayonnaise or cooked salad dressing
1/2 teaspoon seasoned salt
1/4 teaspoon pepper

Several hours ahead: Mix together all ingredients. Refrigerate. Makes about 3 1/2 cups of filling.

Buffet Cheese Loaf

1 long slim loaf of French
    bread
Soft butter
Celery, sesame, or caraway
    seeds (optional)

Imported Edam or Gouda
    cheese

Cut the loaf of French bread, almost through to the bottom, into diagonal slices about 1 inch apart. Spread 1 side of each slice of bread with soft butter and sprinkle with celery, sesame, or caraway seeds. Cut cheese (either Edam or Gouda) into slices and slip a slice into each slash in the bread; place on a baking sheet. Bake in a 350° F. oven, until heated through—about 10 minutes.

Salmon-Chive Loaves

12 bread slices	Egg Salad
1 6-ounce package chive	8 tomato slices
cream cheese, softened	Lettuce
2 tablespoons milk	2 tablespoons snipped
Soft butter	parsley
Salmon Salad	4 thinly sliced radishes

Several hours ahead: Mix cheese with milk until fluffy. Spread bread with butter. Spread 4 slices bread with Salmon Salad, cover with 4 slices spread on top side with Egg Salad. Place 2 tomato slices and lettuce on Egg Salad, cover with remaining 4 slices bread. Spread top slice of each sandwich with chive cheese mixture. Refrigerate until well chilled. *To serve:* Garnish with parsley, radishes; cut each loaf in half. Fork makes eating easier. Makes 4 servings.

Salmon Salad

    1 1-pound can salmon (2 cups)
    1 tablespoon fresh, frozen, or canned lemon juice
    1 cup minced celery
    1/2 cup mayonnaise or cooked salad dressing
    3/4 teaspoon salt

Several hours ahead: Drain salmon; then flake. Mix with rest of ingredients. Refrigerate. Makes 3 cups filling.

Egg Salad: See recipe for Creamy Party Loaf.

Ham and Cheese Loaf

10 slices white bread	1 cup pickle relish
1/4 cup soft butter	1/4 cup prepared mustard
2 cups coarsely ground	1 tablespoon snipped
cooked ham	parsley
1 1/4 cups grated process	
American cheese	

Several hours ahead: Butter bread. Mix ham with 1 cup grated cheese, pickle relish, mustard. Spread 9 bread slices with filling. On aluminum foil, put bread slices back together in loaf form, with tenth slice at end. Sprinkle top of loaf with 1/4 cup grated cheese. Bring foil up around sides of loaf; wrap. Refrigerate. *About 1 hour before serving:* Heat oven to 425° F. Bake loaf, in foil, 25 minutes, uncovering it last 10 minutes to crisp. *To serve:* Transfer loaf to serving plate, and fold down sides of foil; garnish with parsley. With fork and pie server, serve 2 slices per guest. Makes 5 servings.

Austrian Sandwich Torte

2 loaves day-old unsliced
    white bread
Butter
Egg Filling
    3 tablespoons chopped
      parsley
Pâté Filling
Caviar Filling

Cream Cheese Frosting
1/2 cup finely chopped,
    salted, toasted almonds
    (optional)
Anchovy fillets
    2 unpeeled radishes, finely
      chopped
Parsley

Cut bread into 8 thin lengthwise slices; remove crusts. Spread 6 slices thinly with butter, leaving 2 slices plain for top layer of each torte. For each torte: Cover 1 slice bread with half the Egg Filling, then sprinkle half the chopped parsley completely over egg mixture. Top with second bread slice; spread with half the Pâté Filling. Top with third slice; cover with half the Caviar Filling and top with fourth (plain) bread slice. Chill thoroughly. Spread top and sides of chilled tortes with Cream Cheese Frosting. Press almonds on sides. Decorate top with rolled anchovy fillets and a sprinkling of chopped radishes. Serve garnished with parsley. Makes about 6 servings.

Egg Filling

4 hard-cooked eggs, finely chopped
1/4 cup butter.
2 white onions, finely chopped
2 tablespoons chopped olives
1/4 cup mayonnaise
Salt, Pepper

Combine eggs, butter, onion, chives, mayonnaise, salt and pepper in small bowl.

Pâté Filling

2 4 1/2-ounce cans liver pâté
4 tablespoons mayonnaise

Blend in small bowl.

Caviar Filling

1 6-ounce jar red caviar
1 8-ounce package cream cheese, softened

Blend in small bowl.

Cream Cheese Frosting

2 8-ounce packages cream cheese, softened
1 tablespoon anchovy paste

Blend in small bowl.

Lemon Gelatin Loaf

8 slices white bread	2 tablespoons evaporated
2 packages lemon gelatin	milk
2 2/3 cups boiling water	Olive-Nut Filling
1 3-ounce package cream	Chicken Filling
cheese, softened	Avocado Filling

Dissolve gelatin in the boiling water. Cool. Soften cream cheese with milk. Prepare the 3 fillings by combining the ingredients for each. Make 2 four-layer sandwiches, using 1 filling for each layer. Trim off crusts. When gelatin mixture begins to thicken, blend in cheese mixture. Pour 1 cup of partially thickened gelatin mixture into a 1 1/2-quart loaf pan. Place sandwiches, side by side, in the center of the loaf pan on top of gelatin layer. Refrigerate until gelatin layer is firm. Pour remaining partially thickened gelatin mixture around and over top of sandwiches. Chill until firm. *To serve:* Unmold by running spatula around edge of gelatin. Turn out onto platter. Slice crosswise. Makes 6 servings.

Olive-Nut Filling

Combine 1/4 cup finely chopped nuts, 1/4 cup finely chopped stuffed olives, 2 tablespoons mayonnaise or salad dressing.

Chicken Filling

Combine 1/3 cup minced cooked chicken, 2 tablespoons finely chopped green pepper, 2 tablespoons mayonnaise or salad dressing.

Avocado Filling

Combine 1/4 cup mashed avocado, 2 tablespoons cream cheese, 1/4 teaspoon lemon juice.

Cheese-and-Bacon Loaf

1 loaf bread	1 tablespoon poppy seeds
1/2 cup butter	1/2 pound sliced process
1/4 cup minced onion	Swiss cheese
1/4 cup prepared mustard	3 slices bacon, chopped

Remove crusts from loaf of bread. Mix softened butter with onion, mustard, and poppy seeds. Spread each slice of bread with part of butter mixture and top with slice of cheese. As you go along, press slices together in buttered loaf pan to form bread loaf. Spread top with any remaining butter mixture or softened butter. Sprinkle with chopped bacon. Bake at 350° F. for 15 minutes or until cheese is melted and loaf is browned. Pull apart to make 6 to 8 servings.

Frosted Tuna Loaf

1 1 pound loaf unsliced
   white bread
1 6 1/2-ounce or 7-ounce
   can tuna
1/3 cup mayonnaise or salad
   dressing
1/2 cup butter
   3 tablespoons mayonnaise
   or salad dressing
   2 tomatoes, peeled and
   sliced

1 5-ounce jar pimento
   cheese spread
2 tablespoons milk
1/4 teaspoon salt
1 8-ounce package cream
   cheese
Sliced stuffed olives
Tomato wedges
Parsley sprigs

Drain tuna. Flake. Add mayonnaise, blend. Remove crusts from bread. Cut bread lengthwise into 4 even slices. Spread all inside slices with butter. Spread tuna mixture on the top of the first slice. Cover with the second slice, spread with mayonnaise, and top with a layer of tomatoes. Cover with the third slice and spread with pimento cheese spread. Cover with the top slice. Combine milk, salt, and cream cheese. Whip until light and fluffy. Spread over the entire loaf. Chill for at least 2 hours. Garnish with olives, tomatoes, and parsley. Makes about 6 servings.

Tuna Ribbon Loaf

1 2-pound loaf sandwich
   bread, unsliced
6 tablespoons soft butter
6 slices boiled ham
1 1/4 cups Tuna-Cheese
   Filling
6 large slices tomato, 1/4
   inch thick

1 8-ounce package cream
   cheese
1 1/2 tablespoons lemon juice
1/4 cup milk
1/2 cup chopped pecans
1 canned pimento
12 sprigs parsley
Carrot curls

Remove crusts from unsliced loaf of bread and cut lengthwise into 4 equal slices. Spread each bread slice with butter. Arrange 2 layers of sliced boiled ham between first and second slices of bread; Tuna-Cheese Filling between second and third slices of bread; sliced tomatoes between third and fourth slices. Press loaf firmly together. Wrap in waxed paper and refrigerate until just before serving time. Frost top and sides of loaf with cream cheese softened with lemon juice and milk. Sprinkle chopped pecans on sides of loaf. Garnish top with heart cut out of pimento and parsley sprigs. Arrange carrot curls and parsley along sides of platter. Cut into 12 slices when serving.

Tuna-Cheese Filling

1/3 cup grated process cheese
1 hard-cooked egg, chopped
1/2 cup flaked tuna or salmon
1 tablespoon chopped green pepper
1 tablespoon chopped onion
1 tablespoon chopped stuffed olives
3 tablespoons mayonnaise or salad dressing

Combine cheese, chopped egg, tuna, green pepper, onion, olives, and mayonnaise. Makes 1 1/4 cups.

Cranberry-Avocado Loaf

1 2-pound loaf sandwich bread, unsliced
1/2 cup soft butter
6 large slices cooked chicken
7 slices canned jellied cranberry sauce
3/4 cup Avocado-Cream Cheese Filling

6 slices tomato
6 slices cooked bacon
2 pints creamed cottage cheese
2 tablespoons chopped chives or finely chopped green onion tops

Remove crusts from unsliced loaf of bread and cut lengthwise into 5 equal slices. Spread each bread slice with butter. Place each of the 4 fillings on a buttered bread slice and stack in the following order: sliced chicken, sliced jellied cranberry sauce, Avocado-Cream Cheese Filling, and finally, sliced tomatoes and cooked bacon. Finish with fifth slice of bread, placing buttered side on filling. Press loaf firmly together. Wrap in waxed paper and chill for an hour. Mash cottage cheese with a fork and force it through a sieve. Add chives. Spread top and sides of loaf with cottage cheese-chive mixture. Refrigerate until serving time. *To serve:* Cut crosswise into 12 to 14 portions.

Avocado-Cream Cheese Filling

1/3 cup mashed avocado
1 3-ounce package cream cheese
1 teaspoon lemon juice
Dash of Worcestershire sauce
1 tablespoon finely chopped onion
1/8 teaspoon salt

Blend avocado into cream cheese. Add lemon juice, Worcestershire sauce, onion, and salt. Makes 3/4 cup, or filling for 4 sandwiches.

Barbecued Ham Roll

8 frankfurter rolls	1/4 teaspoon salt
4 cups coarsely ground cooked ham	1/4 teaspoon ground cloves
	1 1/2 cups fresh bread crumbs
1/4 cup brown sugar, packed	1/2 cup milk
	1 egg, slightly beaten
1/4 teaspoon dry mustard	Smoky Barbecue Sauce

Mix ham with brown sugar, mustard, salt, cloves. Toss bread crumbs lightly with milk, egg. Add to ham mixture. Mix well. On cookie sheet, shape mixture to fit frankfurter rolls, allowing about 1/3 cup mixture for each roll. Freeze. When ham rolls are frozen, remove from cookie sheet; freezer-wrap. *To serve:* Start heating oven to 350° F. Unwrap frozen ham rolls; place in shallow pan. Bake 15 to 20 minutes, basting with Smoky Barbecue Sauce. Serve on frankfurter rolls, heated in oven last 5 minutes of baking time. Ideal with pineapple coleslaw or sauerkraut. Makes 8 servings.

Smoky Barbecue Sauce

- 1/4 cup vinegar
- 1/2 cup water
- 2 tablespoons sugar
- 1 tablespoon prepared mustard
- 1/2 teaspoon pepper
- 1 1/2 teaspoons salt
- 1/4 teaspoon cayenne pepper
- 1 thick lemon slice
- 1 sliced onion
- 1/4 cup butter
- 1/2 cup ketchup
- 2 tablespoons Worcestershire sauce
- 1 1/2 teaspoons liquid or powdered smoke (optional)

In saucepan, mix vinegar, water, sugar, mustard, pepper, salt, cayenne, lemon, onion, butter. Simmer uncovered 20 minutes. Add ketchup, Worcestershire, smoke; bring to boil.

Tongue-in-Cheese Roll

1 8-inch loaf French bread	3-4 tablespoons chopped pickles
1/2 cup diced tongue	
1/2 cup diced ham	6 anchovy fillets, mashed
1/2 cup diced cheese	Butter

Scoop out French loaf, fill with mixture of all other ingredients, using butter as needed to bind. Wrap loaf in foil, chill several hours. Slice to serve. Makes about 6 servings.

Individual Cheese Dream Loaves

18 slices white bread
3/4 cup grated process
    American cheese
1 tablespoon caraway seeds

1/2 cup soft butter
3 tablespoons prepared
    mustard
1/3 cup minced onion

Combine cheese and caraway seeds. Blend butter with mustard and add onion. Remove crusts from bread. Make 6 three-deck sandwiches, using the cheese mixture as filling. Cut sandwiches in half crosswise. Spread top and sides of each individual loaf with a thin coating of butter mixture. Place on a baking sheet. Bake in a 375° F. oven until lightly browned, about 12 to 15 minutes. Makes 6 servings of 2 loaves each.

Hot Sandwich Loaf

1 2-pound loaf sandwich
    bread, unsliced
6 tablespoons soft butter
6 slices boiled ham
Turkey-Cheese Filling
6 large slices tomato

Snappy Cheese Filling
  2 egg whites
1/4 cup mayonnaise or salad
    dressing
Dash of salt

Remove crusts from unsliced loaf of bread; cut loaf lengthwise into 4 equal-size slices. Butter slices. Place 2 layers of sliced boiled ham between first and second bread slices; spread Turkey-Cheese Filling and sliced tomatoes between second and third slices; Snappy Cheese Filling between third and fourth slices. Press loaf firmly together. Wrap in waxed paper and refrigerate until serving time. *To serve:* Beat egg whites until stiff; fold in mayonnaise and salt. Unwrap sandwich loaf and place on a cookie sheet. Spread top and sides of loaf with whipped topping. Brown in a 450° F. oven for 10 minutes. Serve hot and cut crosswise into 12 to 14 portions.

Turkey-Cheese Filling

1/3 cup chopped turkey
3 tablespoons cream cheese
1 tablespoon milk
Dash of salt
1/4 teaspoon minced onion
1 1/2 teaspoons chopped pimento

Combine ingredients.

Snappy Cheese Filling

1 cup (1/4 pound) grated sharp cheese, firmly packed
1/4 cup chopped stuffed or ripe olives
2 tablespoons canned deviled ham
1 tablespoon prepared mustard
3 tablespoons mayonnaise or salad dressing

Combine ingredients.

Wedding Loaf

1 1 1/2-pound loaf sandwich bread, unsliced	Salt, pepper
	Chicken-Celery Filling
Ham-Pickle Filling	1 1/2 pounds creamed cottage cheese
1/2 cup sharp cheese spread	2 teaspoons lemon juice
Vinegar-Butter Filling	1/8 teaspoon paprika
1 small cucumber, unpeeled, sliced into 1/8-inch rings	1/2 teaspoon silver shot

Remove crusts from unsliced loaf of bread; cut loaf lengthwise into 5 equal slices. Spread Ham-Pickle Filling between first and second bread slices; sharp cheese spread between second and third bread slices; 2 tablespoons Vinegar-Butter Filling and sliced cucumbers sprinkled with salt and pepper between third and fourth slices; 2 tablespoons Vinegar-Butter and Chicken-Celery Filling between fourth and fifth bread slices. Press loaf firmly together. Wrap in waxed paper and refrigerate until serving time. *To serve:* Beat cottage cheese until smooth; add lemon juice and paprika, continuing to whip until blended. Spread top and sides of loaf with cottage-cheese topping. Sprinkle silver shot over top. Chill until served. Cut into 10 portions.

Ham-Pickle Filling

Combine 1/3 cup ground cooked ham, 2 tablespoons pickle relish, 1 tablespoon mayonnaise or salad dressing.

Vinegar-Butter Filling

Combine 2 teaspoons vinegar, 1/4 cup soft butter.

Chicken-Celery Filling

Combine 1/2 cup chopped cooked chicken, 2 tablespoons chopped celery, 1/4 teaspoon minced onion, 1/4 teaspoon salt, 1/16 teaspoon pepper.

216

Top of the Mountain

White bread
Raisin bread
Butter
Chopped hard-cooked egg
Mayonnaise
Chopped ripe olives
Peanut butter

Ketchup
Canned jellied cranberry sauce
Canned pineapple slices,
  drained
Shrimp salad
Curry cream cheese
Radishes

For each sandwich, cut thinly sliced white bread into 4-inch, 2-inch, and 1-inch round. Cut raisin bread into 3-inch and 1 1/2-inch round. Spread rounds with butter. Next: Spread 4-inch round with mixture of chopped hard-cooked egg, mayonnaise, and chopped ripe olives; top 3-inch round with peanut butter mixed with ketchup; top 2-inch round first with slice of canned jellied cranberry sauce, then with drained canned pineapple slice; top 1 1/2-inch round with shrimp salad; top 1-inch round with curry cream cheese and radish rose. Place rounds on top of one another to form mountain. Eat layer by layer with fork.

Harlequin Loaf

1 2-pound loaf sandwich
     bread, unsliced
1/2 cup soft butter
Roquefort-Cucumber Filling
Beef-Egg Filling
Tuna-Celery Filling
1/2 13-ounce can tomato
     aspic

Pineapple-Cheese Topping
5 long stems of chives or
     green onions
6 to 8 radishes
1 carrot
10 sprigs watercress

Remove crusts from unsliced loaf of bread; cut loaf lengthwise into 5 equal slices. Butter slices. Spread Roquefort-Cucumber Filling between first and second bread slices; spread Beef-Egg Filling between second and third bread slices; spread Tuna-Celery Filling between third and fourth bread slices; slice tomato aspic into thin (1/4-inch) slices and arrange them between fourth and fifth bread slices. Press loaf firmly together. Wrap in waxed paper and refrigerate until serving time. *To serve:* Unwrap sandwich loaf. Spread top and sides of loaf with Pineapple-Cheese Topping. Garnish top of loaf by arranging long stems of chives or green onions in a continuous curved line, ending with corner diagonal to the one where it was begun. Make petals out of red portion of radishes and carrots, using a corer-vegetable peeler. Use about 15 radish petals to make each of 3 flowers, placing them about 3 inches from each end of chive stem, and in center of loaf. Use carrot petals to make 2 more flowers, placing them evenly between radish flowers. Arrange watercress beside each flower for leaves. Serve cold and cut crosswise into 12 to 14 portions.

Roquefort-Cucumber Filling

> 3 tablespoons chopped cucumber
> 1 1/2 teaspoons chopped green onions
> 1 1/2 tablespoons chopped pimento
> 1 3-ounce package cream cheese
> 1 1/2 tablespoons crumbled Roquefort cheese
> 1 tablespoon milk

Combine ingredients.

Beef-Egg Filling

> 1 cup chopped dried beef
> 1/2 cup chopped hard-cooked egg
> 3 tablespoons mayonnaise or salad dressing

Combine ingredients.

Tuna-Celery Filling

> 1 7-ounce can tuna
> 3 tablespoons chopped celery
> 2 tablespoons pickle relish
> 1/4 cup mayonnaise or salad dressing

Combine ingredients.

Pineapple-Cheese Topping

> 1 5-ounce jar pineapple cheese spread
> 8 ounces prepared sour cream
> 1/4 teaspoon seasoned salt
> 1/8 teaspoon Tabasco
> 1/4 teaspoon nutmeg

Combine ingredients.

Party Biscuit Loaves

1 can Southern-style
   biscuits
Fillings (see below)
  4 3-ounce packages cream
    cheese
1/4 cup light cream or milk

Food coloring (optional)
Parsley sprigs
Pimento
Sliced stuffed olives
Hard-cooked egg yolk, sieved

Bake biscuits according to directions on container. When cool, slice each biscuit into 4 thin slices crosswise. For each loaf: Spread 3 of the biscuit slices with about 1 tablespoon of a desired filling. Stack together; cover with top biscuit slice. Let cream cheese stand at room temperature until softened. Beat cheese until smooth and fluffy. Add cream or milk; beat until blended. If desired, tint cheese pale pink, green, or yellow. Frost sides and top of each loaf with cream-cheese mixture. Decorate with parsley, pimento, sliced olives, or sieved hard-cooked egg yolk.

General directions for fillings: Let cheese stand at room temperature until softened. Beat until smooth and fluffy. Stir in flavoring ingredients.

Mushroom-Cheese (Makes about 3/4 cup)

> 1 5-ounce jar process cheese spread
> 2 tablespoons mayonnaise
> 2 tablespoons chopped white mushrooms

Mayonnaise-Cheese (Makes about 1/2 cup)

> 1 5-ounce jar process cheese spread
> 2 tablespoons mayonnaise

Egg-Caper-Chive Cheese (Makes about 2/3 cup)

> 1 6-ounce bar chive-cheese spread
> 1 hard-cooked egg, chopped
> 2 teaspoons capers

Herb-Cheese (Makes about 1/2 cup)

> 1 5-ounce jar process cheese spread
> 1 teaspoon celery seed
> 1/2 teaspoon lemon juice
> 1/8 teaspoon rubbed sage
> 1/8 teaspoon powdered thyme

Caraway-Relish Cheese (Makes about 1/2 cup)

> 1 5-ounce jar relish-cheese spread
> 1 tablespoon capers
> 1 teaspoon caraway seeds

Curried Pineapple-Cheese (Makes about 1/2 cup)

> 1 5-ounce container Neufchâtel cheese spread with
>   pineapple
> 1 teaspoon curry powder

India Relish-Cheese 'n' Bacon (Makes about 2/3 cup)

1 5-ounce jar cheese 'n' bacon process cheese spread
2 tablespoons India relish

Mint and Blue Cheese (Makes about 1/2 cup)

1 5-ounce jar blue process cheese spread
2 teaspoons minced mint leaves, dried or fresh,
  marinated in 1 tablespoon brandy for 20 minutes

Pickle and Olive-Pimento Cheese. (Makes about 3/4 cup)

1 5-ounce jar process cheese spread with olives and pimento
3 tablespoons candied sweet pickle relish

Oregano and Pimento Cheese (Makes about 1/2 cup)

1 5-ounce jar process cheese spread with pimento
1 teaspoon crushed oregano

Deviled Ham-Smoky Cheese (Makes about 1/2 cup)

1 5-ounce jar process cheese spread with added smoked flavor
1 2 1/4-ounce can deviled ham

Liverwurst-Blue Cheese (Makes about 3/4 cup)

1 5-ounce jar blue process cheese spread
1/4 pound liverwurst, mashed

Seven-Layer Loaf

1 loaf day-old white bread, unsliced
Mayonnaise or cooked salad dressing
1 6-ounce package pimento-cheese spread, soft
1 can tuna, chunk-style (1 cup)
Mayonnaise
6 thin tomato slices
Salt
Pepper
3 hard-cooked eggs, chopped
Mayonnaise
2 3-ounce cans deviled ham
Chunky peanut butter

Several hours ahead: Cut 1 loaf day-old unsliced white bread, crust and all, lengthwise into 7 layers. Spread each layer with cooked salad dressing or mayonnaise. Working from bottom up, fill each layer with one of following: soft pimento-cheese spread; tuna mixed with mayonnaise; tomato slices sprinkled with salt, pepper; 3 finely chopped hard-cooked eggs mixed with mayonnaise; deviled ham; chunky peanut butter. Top with crust, pressing down firmly. Refrigerate. *At serving time:* Slice into 3/4-inch-thick portions. Serve with fork for easier eating. Makes about 10 servings.

Toasted Tuna French Loaf

1 8-ounce loaf French bread
1 6 1/2- or 7-ounce can
    tuna
1/4 cup butter
1 teaspoon prepared
    mustard

1 tablespoon grated onion
1 cup grated cheese
2 tablespoons chopped
    sweet pickle or sweet
    pickle relish

Drain tuna. Flake. Cream butter and blend in 1 teaspoon mustard. Cut bread in half lengthwise and remove a small amount of the center. Spread bread with mustard butter. Combine remaining ingredients with tuna. Fill bread with the tuna mixture. Cut loaf into 12 slices, keep together in loaf form, and wrap in aluminum foil. Bake in a 450° F. oven for 30 minutes. Makes 4 servings.

Luncheon Loaf

1 9-inch round loaf rye,
    white or whole-wheat
    bread, unsliced
6 tablespoons butter
4 hard-cooked eggs,
    chopped fine
1/4 teaspoon salt
1/4 cup mayonnaise
1 4 1/2-ounce can deviled
    ham
2 tablespoons chopped
    sweet pickle
2 tablespoons mayonnaise

1/8 pound sharp cheese,
    softened
2 tablespoons mayonnaise
2 tablespoons mayonnaise
4 lettuce leaves
2 medium-sized tomatoes,
    sliced
2 8-ounce packages cream
    cheese, softened
Paprika
Parsley
Stuffed olives

Trim crusts from bread; slice bread into 6 layers. Butter each layer, top and bottom. Combine eggs, salt, 1/4 cup mayonnaise; mix thoroughly. Combine deviled ham, pickles, 2 tablespoons mayonnaise; mix well. Blend sharp cheese, 2 tablespoons mayonnaise. Spread layers with the following: No. 1 —half of egg mixture; No. 2—deviled-ham mixture; No. 3— sharp cheese mixture; No. 4—Spread layer with 1 tablespoon mayonnaise; line with lettuce leaves; spread with 1 tablespoon mayonnaise; place tomato slices on top; No. 5—half of egg mixture. Frost complete loaf with softened cream cheese; cut loaf in wedges; garnish with paprika, parsley, sliced stuffed olives. Makes 12 servings.

Sandwich + Salad = Supper

A cook's "Shall we eat lightly tonight?" will likely as not come down to sandwiches-and-salad on the table. But such a meal needn't be unimportant—unless looked at from the point of view of a Diamond Jim Brady-type appetite. To be sure, both sandwich and salad can be snack-type, if you really want a light meal. But if you're hungrier than that, either the sandwich or the salad—or both—can be as hearty as you wish. Besides, there's always dessert to consider (there is, at least, if I'm to have anything to do with this meal), and these can help maintain balance.

One type of sandwich that goes particularly well with salads is the finger sandwich. If you think they're a bit on the dainty side, just make twice as many. And keep in mind that much of the preparation for salads can be dealt with in advance. This can also be true—with proper planning—of many of the sandwiches and desserts. Which means that sandwich-and-salad night can be easy-on-the-cook night without starving the customers!

Lovely for the ladies:

Perfect Chicken Salad
(half breasts of chicken, dressed with capers, Homemade
Mayonnaise (page 125)—that's all)
Ham-Asparagus Roll-ups (page 31)
Hot Fruit Compote   Beverage

When there are men to feed:

Caesar Salad
(by now this is a classic—and a great favorite with
women, too)
Rich Mushroom Sandwich (page 188)
Peach Pie à la Mode   Beverage

Friday's fish day:

Shrimp Salad
(fold in cubes of Münster cheese for a chewy surprise)
Asparagus-Egg Sandwich (page 123)
Banbury Tarts   Beverage

Set up a table under the trees:

Tomato Aspic
(add chopped celery, cucumber, onion for looks and flavor)
Saucy Pork Buns (page 83)
Coffee-Chocolate Ice Cream Sodas

Janie's invited her gang over:

Special Marinated Tomatoes
(thick-sliced beefsteaks, oil-and-vinegar dressed, sprinkled
with basil)
Barbetuna Buns (page 139)
Three-Layer Devil's Food Cake   Beverage

Let's go Dutch:

Pennsylvania Dutch Wilted Lettuce
(like nothing else in this world—see this section for
how-to)
Super Supper Sandwich(page 103)
Apple Crumb Pie   Beverage

First chilly fall night:

Hot Vegetable Salad
(carrots, limas, broccoli, hard-cooked egg—and heated
Italian dressing)
Big Wheel Sandwich (page 89)
Gingerbread with Applesauce   Beverage

After the bridge game:

Antipasto Salad
(mixed greens, julienne salami, hard-cooked egg, cubes
of provolone)
Anchovy Butter Sandwiches (page 57)
Platter of Fresh Fruit   Beverage

Mother and kids, home alone:

Candlestick Salad
(pineapple slice, upright half banana, Maraschino cherry
"flame")
Hobgoblin Hamburgers (page 92)
Lemon Sugar Cookies   Beverage

Lunch-Box Super

8 slices bread	2 tablespoons chopped green
6 tablespoons peanut butter	pepper
1 6 1/2- or 7-ounce can tuna	4 tablespoons chopped celery
fish	

Combine peanut butter, tuna fish, green pepper, and celery. Mix well. Spread on 4 slices bread, top with remaining slices. Makes 4 sandwiches.

Rosy Peanut Sandwich

8 slices bread, buttered	1/2 cup jellied cranberry
1/2 cup peanut butter	sauce, crushed

Spread 4 slices of bread with peanut butter, remaining 4 slices with crushed jellied cranberry sauce. Sandwich together. Makes 4 sandwiches.

Peanut Butter Special

12 slices white bread	2 tablespoons milk
1/3 cup peanut butter	3 tablespoons pickle relish
1 3-ounce package cream	2 tablespoons chopped
cheese, softened	stuffed olives

Combine peanut butter, cream cheese, and milk until well blended. Add pickle relish, olives. Spread on 6 slices bread, top with remaining slices. Makes 6 sandwiches.

Peanut Carrots

8 slices raisin bread	1/2 cup grated carrot
3/4 cup peanut butter	

Spread 4 slices bread with peanut butter, then with layer of grated carrot. Top with remaining slices. Makes 4 sandwiches. *Perfect partners* . . . Hot cocoa in wintertime, banana milk shakes in warm weather.

Nuts 'n' Dates

8 slices white or whole-	1/4 cup mayonnaise or salad
wheat bread	dressing
1/2 cup chopped, pitted dates	1/4 teaspoon salt
1/2 cup peanut butter	

Combine dates, peanut butter, mayonnaise, and salt. Spread on 4 slices bread, top with remaining slices. Makes 4 sandwiches.

226

Peanut-Bacon Savories

12 slices bread
1/2 cup peanut butter
1/2 cup chili sauce

1/2 cup chopped crisp bacon
1/4 cup soft butter

Mix peanut butter with chili sauce, bacon, and butter. Spread on 6 slices bread, top with remaining slices. 6 sandwiches.
Keep in mind . . . For those who can do without chili sauce, plain peanut butter and bacon is a time-tested combination.

Ham-Peanut Stars

9 slices white bread
1/3 cup peanut butter
1 3-ounce can deviled ham
1/4 cup mayonnaise or salad dressing

3 tablespoons chopped dill pickles
1 teaspoon chopped green pepper

Cut each slice of bread into 4 small stars with a 1 1/2-inch cookie cutter. Combine peanut butter, deviled ham, mayonnaise, pickles. Place 1 teaspoon of the mixture in the center of each star. Garnish with bit of chopped green pepper. Makes 36 small sandwiches.

Crunchy Peanut Spread

8 slices bread
12 tablespoons peanut butter
4 teaspoons chopped onion
4 teaspoons chopped green pepper

4 teaspoons chopped cucumber

Combine peanut butter, onion, green pepper, and cucumber. Mix until well blended. Spread on 4 slices bread, top with remaining slices. Makes 4 sandwiches.

Cheesy Peanut Grill

8 slices bread
12 tablespoons peanut butter
4 slices process American cheese

4 slices tomato
Butter

Spread peanut butter on 4 slices of bread. Top with slice of cheese, tomato, and remaining slices of bread. Spread butter on outside of bread. Grill in hot skillet until golden brown on both sides. Serve hot. Makes 4 sandwiches.

The Supreme Sandwich

Peanut Butter

4 slices whole-wheat bread, toasted
4 thin brown-and-serve smoked pork chops
1 cup chunk-style peanut butter
2 large cooking apples
2 tablespoons sugar
1 teaspoon mace

Brown pork chops on both sides according to package directions. Spread peanut butter on toast. Place 1 chop on each slice of toast. Cut off ends of apples, core; cut each apple into 2 thick slices. Sauté apples briefly in butter in pork chop pan. Put 1 apple slice on each chop. Mix sugar and mace, sprinkle over apples. Brown under broiler. Makes 4 open-face dinnertime sandwiches.

Peanut Slaw Buns

8 hamburger buns, split
1 cup finely chopped cabbage
1/2 cup chopped salted peanuts
1/4 cup Creamy Slaw Dressing
2 tablespoons chopped olives
1/2 teaspoon minced onion
1/2 cup chopped dried beef

Combine all ingredients except buns. Spread between bun halves. Makes 8 hearty sandwiches.

Creamy Slaw Dressing

1 cup sour cream, 1 teaspoon sugar, 1 tablespoon prepared mustard, 1 teaspoon onion powder, 1 teaspoon paprika, salt, white pepper to taste. Mix all seasonings with about 1 tablespoon of the sour cream, then mix into remaining sour cream. *Even better* . . . If your family likes horseradish (mine doesn't), add 1 tablespoon drained prepared horseradish to the dressing.

Honey-Peanut Sandwich

6 slices bread
1 3-ounce package cream cheese
2 tablespoons honey
2 tablespoons chopped salted peanuts

Blend cream cheese and honey. Add peanuts. Spread on 3 slices bread, top with remaining slices. Makes 3 sandwiches.

Peanut Butter Plus

8 slices bread	Mayonnaise
6 ounces potted ham	Chopped sweet pickles
3 ounces peanut butter	

Mix ham and peanut butter; moisten with mayonnaise. Add chopped sweet pickles. Spread on 4 slices bread, top with remaining slices. Makes 4 sandwiches.
Even better . . . Deviled ham makes a more grown-up combination.

Cottage Cheese Crunch

8 slices bread	1/4 cup chopped dill pickles
1/2 cup cottage cheese	1/8 teaspoon Worcestershire
1/4 cup chopped salted peanuts	sauce

Combine cottage cheese, peanuts, dill pickles, and Worcestershire sauce. Spread on 4 slices bread, top with remaining slices. Makes 4 sandwiches.

Pickled Peanuts and Cheese

10 slices bread	1/4 cup sweet pickle relish
1/2 cup pimento cheese spread	1 tablespoon minced onion
1/3 cup chopped salted peanuts	1/4 teaspoon Worcestershire sauce

Combine cheese spread, peanuts, pickle relish, onion, and Worcestershire sauce. Spread on 5 slices bread, top with remaining slices. Makes 5 sandwiches.

Make Now, Enjoy Later

How many lunch-box sandwiches are you responsible for each weekday morning? Even if it's only one, why bother? You can reach into your freezer, or the freezing section of your refrigerator, and simply pick out what you need—if you've been smart enough to make up a batch ahead of time, and freeze-till-needed. And if you're planning a party, you can freeze sandwiches ahead for that, too—even open-face sandwiches, if you mind the few dos and don'ts and wrap them properly. One week is fair keeping time, but you can keep sandwiches in your freezer two or even three weeks. Withdrawn from the refrigerator entirely, sandwiches will thaw in about two hours. Open-face types thaw more quickly. Try to figure on having them ready to serve just about when you're going to need them, because they don't take to standing around too well after they're thawed. Do not remove their protective wrappings until you are almost ready to serve them.

Do . . . Spread bread thinly with butter or margarine, to keep fillings from soaking through. Use any meat, sliced or chopped; cheese, fish, peanut butter, chicken and turkey, chopped hard-cooked egg. Wrap well in foil, parchment, or special freezer paper. Put all of one kind in a box or a labeled pile, for easy withdrawal. Open-face party sandwiches can be placed on cardboard sheets before being wrapped. Loaf sandwiches, rolled and ribbon sandwiches, frosted squares are more easily stored uncut; leave a little extra time for slicing after they are thawed.

Do not . . . Spread bread with mayonnaise, salad dressing, or jelly. They tend to soak into the bread. They can, however, be used in the filling. Do not put lettuce, celery, carrots, tomatoes, parsley, or watercress in the filling or atop it before freezing. Add them when the sandwiches are thawed. For lunch-box meals, wrap a wedge of lettuce or tomato or whatever separately in waxed paper or foil (you ought to do this even when your lunch-box sandwich is not frozen, for lettuce that has been resting upon filling for several hours becomes a pretty sad and listless item). Don't use sliced hard-cooked egg; chopped (see above) freezes more satisfactorily.

Further note: Lunch-box sandwiches taken from the freezer in the morning will be defrosted and ready to eat just in time for lunch—it takes them a bit longer than it does for sandwiches removed from the freezer and waiting on the counter.

Sandwich Sweets

Nothing for dessert? Make a sweet sandwich. Neighbor drops in for a cup of coffee, looking more-than-coffee hungry? Same answer. Have in mind that splendid old-fashioned (but not old-fashioned in England, and I go along with them) custom, afternoon tea? Same answer. Try these sweet sandwiches to make any sandwich occasion delightful and different.

Peanut Honeys

8 slices nut or raisin bread   1/2 cup peanut butter
2-3 tablespoons honey

Spread 4 slices bread with honey, then with peanut butter. Dribble extra honey over peanut butter. Top with remaining bread slices. Cut into fingers or triangles, or into fancy shapes with large cookie cutters. Makes 4 full-size servings, 16 fingers or triangles, 4 large "shapes."
Keep in mind . . . That which is good as is, is often better French-toasted. See the Basic Way with French Toast Fancies (page 232) to find out how you can improve on Peanut Honeys.

Brapples

4 thin slices white bread,   3/4 cup brown sugar
    buttered   1/2 cup chopped walnuts
2 to 3 good-sized apples   Butter
Few drops lemon juice

Peel, core, and slice apples as for pie. Mix with lemon juice, brown sugar, walnuts. Arrange bread on cookie sheet, pile apple mixture on each slice. Dot well with butter. Broil slowly until sugar and butter run together. Makes 4 servings.
Keep in mind . . . Brapples are a wonderful wits'-end dessert, for the makings are almost always on hand. They can be dressed up after broiling with a finishing touch of whipped cream or maple syrup—or better still, for those who fancy sour cream, with a good spoonful of thick commercial sour cream sprinkled with brown sugar.

✳✳✳✳✳✳✳✳✳✳✳✳✳✳✳✳✳✳✳✳✳✳✳✳✳✳

The Basic Way with

French Toast Fancies

8 thin slices white bread
Strawberry preserves or jam
2 eggs, lightly beaten
3/4 cup milk
2 teaspoons sugar
Dash of salt
1/2 teaspoon vanilla
Powdered sugar

Spread strawberry preserves on 4 slices of bread, top with remaining slices, pressing well together. With sharp knife, cut each sandwich diagonally twice, making 4 triangles. Beat eggs lightly, add milk, sugar, salt, vanilla; mix well. Dip triangles into mixture so that all sides are coated. Sauté triangles on lightly greased griddle until golden brown on all sides. Drain on absorbent paper. Serve hot, sprinkled with powdered sugar. Makes 16 small sandwiches.

For extra-specials . . . Spread 4 slices bread thinly with softened cream cheese before spreading with jam; then continue as above.

Even better . . . If strawberry preserves aren't your favorite kind, then your favorite kind will make these Fancies even better. Try plum, raspberry, black currant, peach, apricot . . . take your pick. For a really walloping dessert, cut Fancies diagonally only once, omit the powdered sugar, serve instead with a dollop of sour cream on top, into the center of which put a bit of preserve to show what's inside.

And sometimes . . . A single slice of French toast can become a delightful open-face "sweet," when spread—for instance—with a blend of cream cheese and drained crushed pineapple. Sprinkle brown sugar—or crystallized ginger—over the top. Serve with knife and fork—you don't want to lose a crumb!

✳✳✳✳✳✳✳✳✳✳✳✳✳✳✳✳✳✳✳✳✳✳✳✳✳✳

Spicy Apple Fingers

4 slices thinly cut brown
   bread
2 tablespoons softened cream
   cheese
1 cup seeded raisins, chopped

1 large apple, peeled, cored,
   and chopped
2 tablespoons sugar
Powdered cinnamon
Few drops lemon juice

Spread bread very thinly with cream cheese. Mix together raisins, chopped apple, sugar, a dash of cinnamon, and a few drops lemon juice. Spread on 2 slices bread. Top with remaining slices. Cut each sandwich into 4 fingers. Makes 16 small sandwiches.

Sundae Sandwich

4 slices brown bread, buttered
2 to 3 bananas, thinly sliced
Lemon juice

Brown sugar
Chopped pecans

On each slice of buttered bread place a layer of thinly sliced banana. Sprinkle with lemon juice and brown sugar and a few finely chopped nuts. Cut each slice diagonally into triangles or into 4 fingers. Makes 16 dainty servings.

Jelly Cubes

1/2 loaf white bread, unsliced
   1 3-ounce package cream
      cheese

1 tablespoon milk
3 tablespoons fruit jelly or
   preserves

Trim crusts from half loaf of bread. Cut it into 1-inch-thick slices. Cut each slice into 1-inch squares. This will yield about 36 cubes of bread. With tweezers or a very small, sharp knife, hollow out part of the center of each cube. Mix cream cheese with milk until of spreadable consistency. Spread the mixture on the rim of each cube around the hollow center, or pipe it around with a pastry tube. In the hollow center, place 1/4 teaspoon jelly or preserves. Makes 36 teatime mouthfuls.

Orange-Peanut Butter

3/4 cup peanut butter
1/2 cup snipped light or dark
   raisins

1/2 cup orange juice

Several hours ahead: Mix together all ingredients. Refrigerate. Makes 1 1/4 cups.

✿✿✿✿✿✿✿✿✿✿✿✿✿✿✿✿✿✿✿✿✿✿✿✿

The Gourmet Way

Thousand Island for Fruit

1 cup Homemade Mayonnaise (page 125)
1/2 cup whipped cream
1/4 cup chopped cherries
1/4 cup chopped pineapple

Mix all ingredients well. Refrigerate until ready to serve.

✿✿✿✿✿✿✿✿✿✿✿✿✿✿✿✿✿✿✿✿✿✿✿✿

Raisin-Peanut Pinwheels

2 thin lengthwise slices
    white bread (cut from
    unsliced loaf)

6 tablespoons chopped
    seedless raisins
6 tablespoons orange juice
3/4 cup peanut butter

Combine raisins, orange juice, and peanut butter. Trim crusts from bread. Spread 1/2 cup raisin-peanut butter mixture on each slice of bread. Cut each slice in equal halves crosswise. Roll each half slice of bread as for jelly roll. Wrap each roll in waxed paper, twisting ends of paper. Place on a flat surface so that roll rests on last turn of bread. Chill. *To serve:* Unwrap and cut each roll into 6 slices. Makes 24 sandwiches.

Peanut Squash

5 slices white bread
1/3 cup peanut butter

10 slices banana
2 tablespoons orange juice

Cut each slice of bread into two 2-inch circles with a cookie cutter. Spread 1 1/2 teaspoons peanut butter on each circle. Dip banana slices into orange juice, then place 1 slice in center of each sandwich. Makes 10 servings.

Coconut Crunch

8 slices nut or orange-nut
    bread
3/4 cup cottage cheese,
    uncreamed variety

1/2 cup shredded coconut
Few drops almond extract
1/2 cup slivered toasted
    almonds

Mix cottage cheese, shredded coconut, and almond extract. Pile on 8 slices bread. Top each slice with sprinkling of toasted almonds. Makes 8 servings.

Cream Cheese Sweets

A package of cream cheese and your ingenuity—plus a few
little extras thrown in—can become a delicious dessert sandwich for a family meal. A few packages of cream cheese, and
you have the basis for a whole trayful of elegant tea or party
sandwiches. There are almost limitless possibilities, and nothing to keep you from inventing some of your own. In the
meantime, try these to start:

To a 3-ounce package of softened cream cheese, add . . .

1/4 cup chopped nuts, 1/4 cup chopped dates, 1/4 cup
    drained crushed pineapple
  3 tablespoons apricot jam, 2 tablespoons chopped
    pecans
  3 tablespoons plum jam, a few drops rum
  3 tablespoons strawberry preserves
  4 tablespoons orange or pineapple marmalade, 1/4 cup
    slivered almonds
1/4 cup drained crushed pineapple, 1 tablespoon finely
    chopped preserved ginger
1/2 cup mashed bananas, sprinkled with lemon juice, 1/2
    cup chopped pecans or walnuts, 1/2 cup drained
    crushed pineapple

Frosted Raspberry

8 thin slices nut bread
1 pint vanilla ice cream

1 12-ounce container frozen
    raspberries in syrup,
    defrosted

On each of 4 individual pie or dessert plates, put a slice of nut
bread. Spread with softened vanilla ice cream, cover with
raspberries and syrup. Top with remaining slices; repeat layers
of ice cream, raspberries, pour over remaining syrup. Serve at
once. Makes 4 servings.

Nuts and Dates

Dates, finely chopped
Nuts, finely chopped

Thick cream or mayonnaise

Combine ingredients. Spread on bread, or refrigerate until
ready to use.

Fruit Sweets

8 finger or tiny round party rolls	2 to 3 crisp apples, peeled, cored, and thinly sliced
1/2 small package cream cheese (about 1 1/2 ounces)	

Split the rolls, and spread both halves thinly with softened cream cheese. Lay a few slices of apple on bottom half of roll, cover with top half. Serve soon after making. Makes 8 sandwiches.

Or try it this way . . . Add a sprinkling of raisins over the apples . . . Use sliced bananas, sprinkled with lemon juice, instead of apples . . . Use sliced drained strawberries, sprinkled with powdered sugar, instead of apples . . . Use thinly spread apple jelly instead of cream cheese, or on top of cream cheese, before adding fruit. Luscious! . . . Throw caution to the winds and serve Fruit Sweets in a larger version, between extra-thin slices of white or nut bread. Be sure the cream cheese covers the whole area of the bread so that the fruit juices do not soak through, but spread the cheese thinly—it's the "butter" for these sandwiches, not a cream cheese mixture.

Floridians

12 slices raisin bread, buttered	1 tablespoon butter
3 oranges	1 cup boiling water
2 cups granulated sugar	3/4 cup chunky peanut butter

Put oranges, rind and all, through coarse blade of food chopper. Combine in medium saucepan with sugar, butter, and boiling water. Boil about 15 minutes, or until mixture is thick. Store in covered jar in refrigerator. (Makes about 3 cups filling.) *To serve:* Spread 6 slices raisin bread with peanut butter, then with 2 tablespoons of orange mixture. Top with remaining slices of bread.

Added thought . . . These freeze beautifully. And the left-over orange filling has a dozen uses. Try it with cream cheese for tea sandwiches, or stirred into whipped cream as quick frosting for angel food cake.

Let's Have a Picnic!

There are a number of schools of thought on the subject of picnics. Some people feel that a picnic should be a spur-of-the-moment business, in which everyone scurries around getting things together, Mom hard-cooks a few eggs, slaps delicatessen cold cuts between bread for sandwiches, adds a bag of potato chips, another of store-bought cookies, those bananas that are going to spoil if they aren't eaten today, and an afterthought can of ripe olives she won't be able to open because she's forgotten the can opener. (She'll forget the salt and pepper, too, so you might as well brace yourself.) Other schools plump for the elegant picnic—the cold roasted bird, the foie gras sandwich, the bottle of chilled-to-perfection dry white wine, the pear with a wedge of Camembert. My sentiments fall somewhere in between. I'm all for elegance and comfort and fine flavor—but I'm old-fashioned enough to believe that there really should be a law against picnics without sandwiches and hard-cooked eggs. Of course, the sandwiches must be carefully planned and as carefully executed, the hard-cooked eggs deliciously deviled. And I also subscribe to the theory that one of the best of picnics is the backyard gathering in which the sandwiches are made of meat hot from the barbecue spit. However you feel on the subject, here are picnic ideas to guide you.

The watchword: preparedness . . . To a certain extent, you can be ready to go on a picnic at a moment's notice—if you have equipment you keep solely for picnic purposes and store it where you can lay hands on it easily. Your picnic basket should be ample in size and should hold, always ready, large, heavy paper napkins and plates (the plastic-coated kind that don't die a soggy death halfway through the meal), a tablecloth (preferably not paper; they're so flimsy), stainless-steel cutlery (don't forget service spoons and forks), drinking cups and/or glasses, a bottle opener, a can opener, salt and pepper in containers that can be tightly closed, and sugar ditto.

Stored cheek-by-jowl with the basket should be a refrigerated container for perishables and bottled or canned beverages and a Thermos bottle and/or jug. Wide-mouthed Thermos containers are fine for hot foods. Of course, if you plan on real elegance, you can take along your grandmother's Haviland and the best crystal wineglasses—but those are for Full Meals in the Wilderness. We're talking about *picnics!* (But I do admit that a picnic hamper fitted with its own utensils is an outdoor luxury of which I heartily approve.)

Planning the menu . . . If you have children, and they are the kind who won't want anything but peanut-butter sandwiches and hamburgers at home, don't expect that they'll come all over gourmet and enjoy truffled partridge the minute they get away from home. Otherwise, though, the world's yours when it comes to putting together a picnic. Perhaps you *will* want a cold bird—there's little better than a perfectly roasted chicken or small, young turkey, moist and tender, or a duck, or even that partridge we just sniffed at. If such is your choice, take along finger sandwiches made on thin-sliced bread and spread with your favorite—or two or three—of the delectable butters you'll find beginning on page 134. A salad goes well, too. Clean, dry, and chill your greens well in advance and take them to your picnic in a plastic bag (however did we keep house without them?) in your refrigerated container. Make the dressing at home, too, and carry it in a screw-top jar, ready for a final shaking to mix before pouring it over the greens. (A little Roquefort cheese to crumble over that salad would do no harm, either.) Or, if you like the idea better, take along your salad as finger foods—sticks of carrot and cucumber, tender scallions, blushing radishes, see-through-thin circles of raw white turnip, blades of Belgian endive, whatever else suits your fancy. In this case, you'll have some members of the party voting for just plain salt, others wanting a dip of some sort to dunk the vegetables in. Once again, Roquefort is a good choice, mixed half-and-half with cream cheese and thinned to good dunking consistency with sour cream. As

.for me, I'll go along with the finger-food salad, add a variety of sandwiches, deviled eggs, julienne potato sticks for crunch, some good fruit, a few homemade cookies, and plenty of coffee—that's my idea of a picnic, which I *don't* want to resemble a dinner at home in any way, shape, or form!

Picnic in the backyard . . . Basic to backyard picnics are the inevitable hamburgers and hot dogs—inevitable but wonderful, because everyone likes them, they're easy to fix, and they're subject to so many variations nobody ever tires of them. But for a sandwich-change, meat roasted on a spit just can't be beaten—hot, juicy, freshly salted and peppered, or delightfully sauced.

Basic rotisserie roasting . . . Start your charcoal fire early, so that you'll have coals burning evenly for a low, steady heat, when you're ready to roast. (Or, rather, have a man start the fire—men feel that outdoor cooking is their province. As long as charcoal is messy and fires are sometimes difficult to start, let the men have the job.) . . . With a damp cloth, wipe the meat you've chosen for today's feast. Rub all surfaces with the cut side of a clove of garlic. Season with salt and pepper . . . Insert the spit rod carefully all the way through the center of the meat and out the other side. Stick the spit forks into each end and tighten the fastenings . . . Check the meat for balance by rotating the spit—if it isn't balanced properly it won't turn at all or only in jerks, like a wheel with a flat tire . . . If you're going to use a meat thermometer—and it's a good idea; even the best of cooks isn't blessed with X-ray vision—insert the thermometer into the thickest part of the meat, making sure that the business end doesn't touch bone, fat, or gristle . . . Arrange (speaking to the man of the house, now) charcoal briquettes at the back of the firebox. Knock off the gray ash . . . Place a drip pan—you can make a fine, throw away-able one from aluminum foil—in front of the coals . . . Now attach the spit and start the motor. Be sure the firebox is at its highest position until the meat is seared, or you'll lose those good juices and the meat will be dry . . . When meat is seared, lower the firebox 6 to 7 inches and continue cooking until thermometer tells you it's done.

Gilding the lily . . . Now that your meat is roasted, enjoy it. But if you want to point up the flavor, by all means sauce your meat with something special. Here are some suggestions:

Bourbon Barbecue Sauce for Beef . . . Combine 2 cups thick tomato sauce, 1/4 cup chopped chives, 1 teaspoon seasoned salt, 1/4 teaspoon pepper, 1/2 teaspoon celery salt, 1/4 cup bourbon, 1 4-ounce can chopped mushrooms with their liquid. Simmer over low heat for 15 minutes, and serve.

Hot Mint Sauce for Lamb . . . Combine 1/2 cup vinegar, 1 cup water, 1/4 cup chopped fresh mint leaves, and simmer until sauce is reduced by one-half. Strain. Add 1/4 cup lemon juice, 2 tablespoons sugar, 1/2 cup water, 1/4 teaspoon salt, and heat just to boiling. Add another 1/4 cup chopped fresh mint leaves, and serve immediately.

Orange Sauce for Veal . . . Melt 3 tablespoons butter. Stir in 1/4 cup flour. Cook, stirring, over low heat until lightly browned. Gradually blend in 1/3 cup chicken stock; cook, stirring, over low heat until thickened and smooth. Stir in 1 teaspoon salt, 1/4 teaspoon white pepper, 1 tablespoon grated orange rind, 2/3 cup orange juice, 2 tablespoons sherry. Heat through, but do not boil. Serve at once.

Cider Sauce for Pork . . . Melt 2 tablespoons butter. Blend in 1/2 cup flour, stir smooth. Gradually add 1 1/2 cups water, blend in and cook, stirring until thickened and smooth. Add 3/4 cup apple cider and 1/2 cup apple jelly. Bring to a boil and serve. A drop or two of red food coloring cheers this up.

Simple Sauce for Beef . . . Melt 3 tablespoons butter. Add 3 tablespoons lemon juice, 1/2 teaspoon dry mustard, 1 tablespoon Worcestershire sauce, salt and pepper to taste. Heat to bubbling and serve at once.

Raisin Sauce for Pork . . . In the top of a double boiler, combine 1/2 cup firmly packed brown sugar, 1 1/2 teaspoons dry mustard, 1 1/2 tablespoons flour. Add 1/4 cup cider vinegar, 1 3/4 cups water, 1/2 cup seedless raisins. Cook, stirring occasionally, over boiling water for 20 minutes. Serve hot.

Index

242

CHICKEN

J

JELLIES
Bouillon Aspic 181
Herb 73

M

MEAT

Beef

Barbecued Beef Sandwiches 68
Barbecued Steakettes 62
Beef-and-Onion 65

Beef Tartare 64

Cheese-and-Beef Sandwich 66, menu 119
Curry-Beef 67, menu 119
French-Roll Beef 68, menu 120

Italian Beef 62
Jumbo Steakwiches 65
Longshoreman's Special 67

Pot Roast of Beef, Supreme 63-64, menu 224
Potted Meat, Supreme 111

Roast Beef and Tomato 31
Roast Beef for Sandwiches 67

Steak Plus 66
Teriyaki Kabobs 66
Beef, Corned
Bermuda-Burgers 91
Big Wheel Sandwich 89, menu 223
Breakfast in a Bun 91
Coleslaw Corned Beef 88
Corned-Beef Doubles 90
Corned-Beef Fry 90
Corned Beefies 87

Corned Beef, Supreme 88
Dinty-Burgers 89
Double Decker Corned Beef 88
Dutch Special 31
Edam-Corned Beef Spread 204
Horseradish Corned Beef 90
Nightcap 181
Onion Corned Beef 91
Spicy Corned Beef 89
Waffled Sandwich Reuben 87

Beef, tongue

Brandied Tongueburgers 118
Cover Girls 118
Ginger Tonguewiches 118
Tongue-and-Eggs 116
Tongue and Swiss Cheese 31
Tongue Cranwiches 117
Tongue for Sandwiches, 117
Tongue-in-Cheese Roll 214
Tongue-on-Wheat 116
Tongue Salads 117
Variation on the Benedict Theme 116
Frankfurters
Bacon-Frankfurter Roll-ups 115
Barber Poles 114
Chili Hot Dogs 114
Frank Frizzles 115
Frankfurter Bake 113
Frankfurter-Cheese Rolls 114
Frankfurter Rockets 112
Frankfurter-Sauerkraut 110

251

Rotisserie Roasting, Basic 239

S